THE CASH BOOK
High Yields with Safety

THE Cash Book ™

HIGH YIELDS WITH SAFETY

1992-'93 Edition

High Yield, Low Risk Cash Investments

James U. Blanchard, III

New York Institute of Finance

New York London Toronto Sydney Tokyo Singapore

This publication is designed to provide accurate and
authoritative information in regard to the subject matter
covered. It is sold with the understanding that the publisher
is not engaged in rendering legal, accounting, or other
professional service. If legal advice or other expert
assistance is required, the services of a competent professional
person should be sought.

From a Declaration of Principles
Jointly Adopted by
a Committee of the American Bar Association
and a Committee of Publishers and Associations

Printed in the United States of America
10 9 8 7 6 5 4 3 2 1

ISBN 0-13-120544-7

 NEW YORK INSTITUTE OF FINANCE
Englewood Cliffs, NJ 07632

Simon & Schuster, A Paramount Communications Company

Foreword

Mark Skousen
Editor, *Forecasts & Strategies*

How can you become financially successful? There's one simple way—invest in free enterprise! It is free market capitalism that created the high standard of living that we enjoy in the United States and around the world. The more we invest in this financial system, the better. That means working hard, working smart, watching our costs in business and personal spending habits, and saving as much as we can.

The question facing every investor is: where should I put my hard-earned savings? The answer to that question depends on what kind of investor you are. Essentially, there are two kinds of investors—conservative investors and liberal speculators. Fortunately, there is room for both kinds of investors in the financial marketplace.

For speculators, there's the stock market, a direct way to participate in the ownership of a real business. There are many ways to speculate in the stock market—trading individual shares, stock options, and even financial futures. Sometimes it's easy to conclude that the stock market is a casino, and that stock certificates are just betting slips. But not so. You're actually investing in the capital structure of the world economy. The rewards can be tremendous, but your principal is also at risk. You can win big, but you can lose big too.

CASH IS KING FOR CONSERVATIVE INVESTORS

Conservative investors are afraid of risk. They have worked hard for their savings, and don't want to lose it by investing in a bad stock or investment. They don't want to lose their principal under any circumstances. They want safety and security. In short, they want "cash" investments, investments that earn a decent return and the principal is guaranteed. For the conservative investor, cash is king!

Often we think that investing in "cash" is dropping out of the market. You may be scared that the stock market is about to collapse and you want to get out and move to the sidelines. So you put your money into "cash" like Treasury bills

v

or money market funds. You won't make any money, but you won't lose any money either.

In reality, you're still invested in the market, but it's limited to short-term securities that have very little risk. Money market funds, for example, consist of short-term obligations (three months or less) of major corporations, banks, insurance companies and the federal government. Money funds are a safe, convenient way to participate in these short-term debt instruments.

There are other ways to invest conservatively in the global marketplace. You can invest in large banks and financial institutions through certificates of deposit (CDs). Foreign banks often issue international certificates of deposit (ICDs). This way you can take advantage of higher interest rates overseas, although you do have a currency risk. Some global income funds seek to limit the currency risk by currency hedging.

You can also achieve high interest income and security through top-rated insurance companies which offer annuities and cash-value insurance. This is another great way for the conservative investor to participate in an expanding economy.

In short, you don't have to put your money in banknotes and hide them under your bed. There are plenty of opportunities for conservative investors to earn income on their investments and still maintain safety.

I applaud Jim Blanchard and his staff for bringing together the best ways for conservative investors to earn the highest yields possible while still preserving their capital. Jim has done a great service to investors everywhere, whether they be conservative investors or speculators wanting to keep their powder dry while waiting for a money-making opportunity.

In closing, remember the words of Ben Franklin, *"There are three faithful friends—an old wife, an old dog, and ready money!"*

Preface

We have used as much due diligence a possible on all the organizations and companies we recommend in this edition of *The Cash Book*. However, we cannot emphasize enough that you should check out all aspects of the potential investment and the company offering it, BEFORE you commit any money.

While we have been careful to recommend only those organizations that we have some personal knowledge of, it is essential that you also check them out to see that you are comfortable with them.

In these volatile times, it is possible for an organization to be completely sound at the time this book goes to press, and then some time later, be less than sound because of a default.

Once you have made an investment, it is essential that you continually monitor all the financial institutions where you place your money, either personally or by using one of the rating services recommended in this book.

The facts and figures presented here are believed to have been accurate at press time. However, this publication contains an enormous amount of information. Errors can creep in and the markets change daily, so you should always check current rates and other information before taking action. We have provided complete contact information for all financial institutions in order to make this as simple as possible.

For your convenience, we have provided a "Resources" section at the end of each chapter listing contact information for people, organizations, and financial institutions mentioned in the text. The contact information is also listed in the appendix at the end of the book.

James U. Blanchard, III

Contents

1

Mapping Your Financial Success in the 1990s

The Decade of Conservative Compounding in High Yields with Limited Risk

---

"It is a profound mistake to think the horizon
is the boundary of the world."

Antoine Marin Lemierre

I n the first edition of *The Cash Book*™, we forewarned our readers of the pending pitfalls of investing in the 1990s—and the need for *high yields* and *safety*.

The fact that most investors were already seeing more and more of their hard-earned capital disappearing through low-yield investments was concern enough. But, we also warned of the increasing need for safety—not only in the type of investment, but also where you held your investment.

Unfortunately, our worst fears came true. As you will find throughout this book, yields on certain investments are shrinking. As the Fed attempts to jump-start our sluggish economy, interest rates have dropped to 30-year lows. And as these rates drop, investment in the more conservative instruments (such as CDs) will mean that you will lose even more of your capital. (In a moment, we will show you precisely why this is so.)

However, many of the higher-yielding instruments and the winners of 1991 are showing increased volatility and risk. Not only should you concern yourself about the investment itself, but you must carefully consider the stability of where you placed your hard-earned dollars. For instance, solid-as-a-rock annuities and pension programs may now be at risk, with the increase of insurance company failures.

In the following chapters, we will show you how to choose the right investment for the 1990s—and the appropriate and safest bank, brokerage, and insurance company as well.

DEVELOPING A PLAN

Making money in the 1990s will involve much more than simply picking the right investment and institution. To make money, you must know where you are headed. You must have a plan.

In preparation of your plan, you must first include an understanding of the principle of compounding. This may sound boring, but you'll find that compounding is the safest method for making money.

Your plan will also require discipline, persistence, intelligence, and time. You need discipline to consistently save, you need persistence to stick with the plan, and you need time to allow the power of compounding to work. Then, you need the intelligence to understand the rewards that compounding will bring you. (In Chapter 2, we will discuss the "Magic of Compounding.")

Furthermore, one of the secrets of making money is not to lose money. This may sound a little ridiculous, but it's true. Many investors lose thousands of dollars chasing the "sure thing," or the highest yields, while forgetting about the associated risks. Other investors follow this strategy: When the market "looks good," they buy; and when it "looks bad," they sell.

Now, does that sound more familiar? It should, because it happens to the best of us.

Recently, we saw a story that we felt best describes the nature of the U.S. investor.

Rich Man, Poor Man

In the investment world, wealthy investors have one major advantage over the little guy, the stock market amateur and the neophyte trader. The advantage that the wealthy investor possesses is that he doesn't need the markets.

The wealthy investor doesn't need the market because he already has all the income he needs. He has money coming in via bonds, T-bills, money market funds, real estate, and stocks. In other words, the wealthy investor never feels pressured to "make money" in the market.

The wealthy investor tends to be an expert on values. When bonds are cheap and bond yields are irresistibly high, he buys bonds. When stocks are on the bargain table and stock yields are attractive, he buys stocks. When real estate is a great value, he buys real estate. When great art or fine jewelry is on the "give-away table," he buys art or jewelry. In other words, the wealthy investor puts his money where the values are. And if there are no outstanding values, the wealthy investor waits. He can afford to wait. He has money coming in daily, weekly, and monthly. The wealthy investor doesn't need the market. He knows what he's looking for, and he doesn't mind waiting months or years for it.[1]

What About the Little Guy?

This fellow always feels pressured to "make money," to force the market "to do something for him." When the little guy isn't buying stocks at 3% or 2% yields, he's off to Vegas or Atlantic City trying to win at craps, or he's spending 10 bucks a week on lottery tickets, or he's "investing" in some crackpot real estate scheme with an outfit that his bowling buddy told him about (in strict confidence, of course). And because the little guy is trying to force the market "to do something for him," he's a constant, sure-fire loser. The little guy doesn't understand values, so he always overpays. He loves to gamble, so he always has the odds against him. He doesn't understand compounding, and he doesn't understand money. He's the typical American, and he's perpetually in debt.

The little guy is in hock up to his ears, and he's always sweating—sweating to make payments on his house, his refrigerator, his car or his lawn mower. He's impatient, and he constantly feels pressured. He tells himself he has to make money fast. And he dreams of those "big bucks." In the end, the little guy wastes his money in the market, he loses his money gambling, or he dribbles it away on senseless schemes. In short, this "money-nerd" spends his life dashing up the financial down escalator.

Now here's the sad part of it, the ironic part of it. If, from the beginning, the little guy had adopted a strict policy of never spending more than he made, and if he had taken that extra income and compounded it in safe, income-producing securities, in due time he'd have money coming in daily, weekly, and monthly just like the rich guy. In brief, the little guy would become a financial winner instead of a pathetic loser.[2]

---

[1]*Dow Theory Letters*, P.O. Box 1759, La Jolla, CA 92038; (619) 454-0481.

[2]Reprinted with permission. *Dow Theory Letters*, P.O. Box 1759, La Jolla, CA 92038; (619) 454-0481.

As you read *The Cash Book,* we hope you will remember this story. In the process of writing this book, we have tried to provide you with investment ideas that provide the *highest yields,* but with the *utmost safety.*

BEWARE OF THE DANGERS THAT LIE AHEAD

As the "Easy Eighties" have given way to the "Nervous Nineties," caution should be the order of the day.

That does not mean throwing your money haphazardly into Treasury bills, money market funds, and fixed-income securities. Unfortunately, it isn't that simple. In the 1990s, you will also be required to check the safety of the institution holding your investment, as well as the profit potential of the investment itself.

So what's the solution? What can you do to both protect and build your wealth during the 1990s?

Foremost, every investor needs to have a road map of where he or she wants to be at the end of this decade. And before you can chart a safe path through the rest of this decade, you must first examine the hazards that lie ahead.

RECOVERY, DOUBLE-DIP RECESSION OR WORSE?

As the Dolans of CNBC's, *Smart Money,* put it: "Economic forecasting is the science that makes astrology respectable."

If you have been following the economic news lately, you are probably confused. This is completely understandable. One day the headlines read, "Economic recovery"; the next day they read, "The economy stalls."

Despite what the headlines read, we are facing an economic situation that few (even the economists) understand. Why? Because this recession is like no other we have faced.

In past recessions, the classic stimulant to the economy was to drop interest rates. Though interest rates have dropped to their lowest levels in over a decade, it has failed to spark the economy into a recovery as it has in the past. Why, you ask?

Because in this cycle, we have five factors that preclude the fiscal stimulus:

Loss of foreign investors

Tax hikes

Too much business and consumer debt

Federal debt has exploded

Shaky real estate deals

Loss of Foreign Investors

First, this recession may have been influenced more by foreign factors than anyone realized.

Figure 1.1 shows the amount of foreign investment in the United States over the last decade. In 1990, it was reported that the Japanese held $62 billion (or nearly ⅓) of our national debt. It was feared then that any sudden decision to withdraw this support could send our already vulnerable financial markets into a tail spin.

In addition, Japanese investments in the United States passed the $70 billion mark in wholly owned or joint-venture interest. Literally half of downtown Los Angeles is Japanese-owned. The capital-rich Japanese appetite for U.S. real estate, in many cases, drove the prices of real estate far out of reality.

We could go on. The point is that the Japanese currently have their own problems, and that has caused them to retreat in their acquisitions of U.S. properties and investments. In many cases, capital has been removed, and that may have created a more serious recession than most economists expected.

No wonder property values have dropped—especially in California, where Japanese investments were the highest. In fact, real estate values are still plummeting in California, and they have even started falling in Hawaii. William Seidman, former Federal Deposit Insurance Corporation (FDIC) chief, stated in October 1991 that "the recession has just begun to hit California."

**Figure 1.1.   Foreign Investment in the United States
(in billions)**

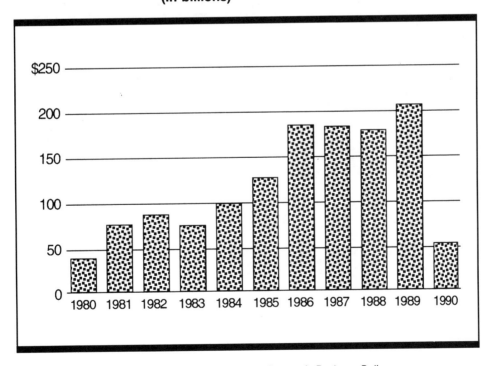

Source: Commerce Department, Investor's Business Daily

What will that do to the S&Ls, banks, and insurance companies that poured millions of dollars into California real estate properties and mortgages?

Investors from other countries have withdrawn capital from the United States as well. This is partly due to the political stability and free-market development occurring around the world (i.e., Eastern Europe and the Soviet Union). And, partly due to recessionary pressures and capital crunches that have hit many countries and resulted in their pulling their capital from the United States in order to support their problems at home.

Tax Hikes

The record tax hikes enacted by President Bush and Congress in 1990 are directly responsible for the United States' slide into a recession. The taxes were designed to raise $135 billion by 1995. But according to the Cato Institute (William C. Dunkelberg and John Skorburg), "the budget package enacted last year [1990] cannot reduce the deficit as advertised. Indeed, by ignoring the impact of taxes on the economy federal lawmakers have dramatically over-estimated the reduction in deficit spending that their grand compromise budget yields." Figure 1.2 shows how much the U.S. Deficit has risen in the past decade.

Whenever the tax burden rises above 20% of GNP, the nation enters an economic danger zone in which it runs a high risk of a recession. The study shows

Figure 1.2.   Federal Budget Deficit (by fiscal year, in billions)

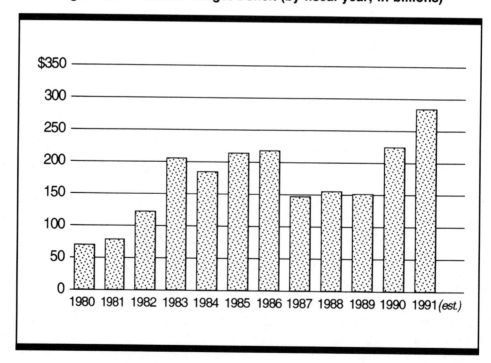

Source: Commerce Department, Investor's Business Daily

that taxes will rise to 20.0% of GNP in 1991, 20.7% in 1992, and 20.8% between 1993 and 1995.

Each 1% rise in federal tax burden leads to a 1.8% reduction in economic growth. GNP growth will therefore average 0.7% less between 1991 and 1995 than it would have without taxes.

The increases in income tax rates, gasoline taxes, and excise taxes will total more than $150 billion over the next five years and "raise the federal tax burden on American workers to an all-time peak."

The new tax increases will destroy 400,000 jobs. The unemployment rate will be 0.45% higher over the next five years.

Any realistic antirecession economic package, according to the Cato Institute, should contain three reforms: repeal of the new gas, excise, and income taxes.

Too Much Business and Consumer Debt

Businesses and consumers took on too much debt during the 1980s. Now, they are not interested in borrowing more—especially when the economy looks this shaky.

Federal, corporate, and private debt expansion was massive in the 1980s. It now stands at the highest level in history. In that 10-year period, governmental, business, and individual debt outstanding rose to nearly $11 trillion from less than $4 trillion. That is close to $43,000 for each person in the United States. Personal debt represented 83% of disposable income in 1991 versus 62% in 1983. Figure 1.3 shows how much consumer credit card (Visa and MasterCard) debt increased in the 1980s.

The Federal Debt Has Exploded

As the federal government enters fiscal year 1992, the deficit stands at a record $282.2 billion and climbing. The projection for 1992 is $348.3 billion.

The 1990 budget accord quietly raised the federal debt ceiling to $4.145 trillion in hopes that would be high enough to avoid another embarrassing vote until after the 1992 presidential election. But the latest projections suggest the debt ceiling must be raised sooner. By 1995, the interest alone is projected to be $390 billion (see Figure 1.4). That means that the interest on the debt will be the most expensive expenditure—even surpassing defense spending. That's $1 for every $5 the government spends.

Shaky Real Estate Deals (and Other Lousy Investments)

During the 1980s, S&Ls, banks, and insurance companies poured millions of dollars into shaky real estate deals and other lousy investments.

A report, prepared for the House Banking subcommittee, on the condition of U.S. financial institutions noted: *"This nation faces an almost unprecedented situation in having most of its largest banks operating on—or conceivably, over—the edge of insolvency."*

Figure 1.3.   Credit Card Debt: VISA and MasterCard

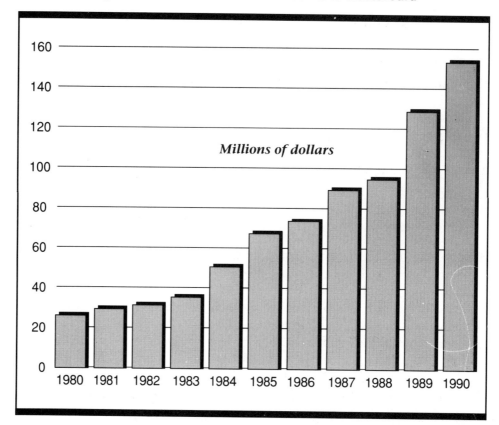

Millions of dollars

Source: BankCard Holders of America
© 1991 Communique Marketing & Associates, Inc.

On October 15, 1991, L. William Seidman retired as director of the FDIC and the Resolution Trust Corporation (RTC–the agency charged with the S&L cleanup). During his six-year tenure, over 1,000 banks failed. A decade of unwise loans to Third World countries, corporate buyouts, and leverage deals and speculative real estate ventures have many of this nation's largest banks still in trouble. As Seidman stated on his departure: *"The industry doesn't look like it's getting much worse, but it's not getting much better . . . if the economy does better, the insurance fund will recover rather quickly. If not, the problems will be much worse than we expected."*

At the end of 1991, the FDIC and the RTC were near insolvency. The FDIC is expecting a net loss of $12.2 billion to $16.7 billion by the end of 1992–previous projections were $4 billion to $11 billion. And the RTC was expected to exceed its $80 billion congressional outlay by $8 billion by the end of 1991.

While the vast majority of insurance companies are healthy, there are several insurers that are potentially at risk due to real estate and junk bond invest-

Figure 1.4. Paying the Interest on the Federal Debt

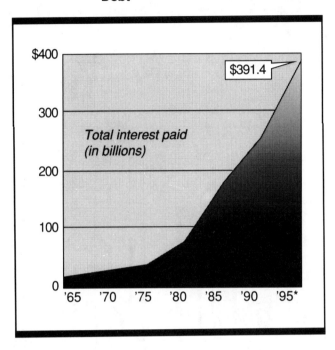

*projection

Compiled by Communique Marketing & Associates, Inc.

ments. If the recession continues (or deepens), this risk could grow to disturbing levels.

INFLATION—FAINT, BUT STILL LURKING

Politically, Washington has little choice but to avoid the worst effects of a recession or depression. Heading into the 1992 election, Bush wants to firmly put the recession behind him. Therefore, the Fed will not stand for any double-dip recession, like the one that sank President Nixon in 1960. The Fed will continue to walk a tight rope between controlling inflation and keeping interest rates down to stimulate the economy.

By reducing interest rates and increasing the money supply, the government decreases the real value of not only the U.S. dollar, but also the national debt.

More taxes aren't the answer. Another tax increase would only worsen the recession and the overall problem. After all, the 1990 tax increase assured us of the recession. Even if the U.S. public would put up with additional tax increases, Figure 1.5 shows that tax increases would stand little chance of slowing down the growth in the deficit.

Figure 1.5.   The More We Tax, The More We Spend

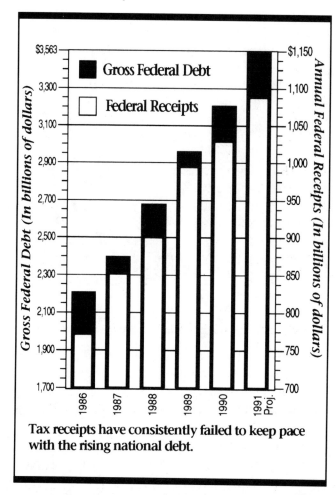

Tax receipts have consistently failed to keep pace with the rising national debt.

Additional budget cuts won't help either. The last bout of budget reductions was much ballyhooed, yet few people realize that the cuts only slowed the federal debt's *rate of growth.*

Thus, will the Fed attempt to reduce the federal debt by monetizing it through the inflation of the money supply? Who knows, but it is important that you understand the effects of inflation and how it severely reduces the yield on your investments.

NEGATIVE YIELDS ARE ERODING YOUR LIFE SAVINGS

In response to uncertainty in the U.S. economy and overseas, investors across the United States flock to the safety of cash: Treasury bills, bonds, certificates of deposit, and other interest-bearing instruments. But if you're in cash right now, you've invested in the right area, but probably in the wrong accounts. Here's why:

Let's use the Fed's 1991 (estimated) Consumer Price Index of an annual rate of 4.3%. Although the true rate of inflation was likely much higher, let's use the government's more conservative figure for a few simple calculations. (Use Table 1.1 to compare various inflation rates.)

Imagine that you invested in a one-year U.S. dollar CD yielding 5.25%. That would seem (based on the declining interest rates) to be a fair return at first glance. But as you can see in Figure 1.6, your REAL return with this CD (after accounting for a 4.3% rate of inflation and an income tax rate of 31%) is a *negative 0.68%*.

In the same way that a positive yield constantly increases your wealth, a *negative* yield constantly *decreases* your wealth.

In short, a 4.3% rate of inflation and a 31% income tax rate means that your cash investments must yield at least 6.23% *just to break even.*

Any yield less than that, and you are tossing more of your hard-earned wealth out the window every day.

Moreover, the cumulative effects of inflation and taxes over time are not only extremely destructive, but also deceivingly subtle.

CAPITAL GAINS TAX RATES ARE ERODING YOUR SAVINGS

Few people are aware that capital gains tax rates, after adjusting for inflation, now run at 75% for any investment held for 15 years or more. After paying a 28% tax on both the real and inflationary gains over the last 15 years, you are left with only 25% of your capital gain as measured in 1975 dollars! (See Figure 1.7.)

The bottom line is that the rate of inflation is very likely to be much greater

Table 1.1. The Yields You Need to Get Just to Break Even at Various Inflation and Tax Rates

Inflation Rate	Tax Rate	
	28%	31%
7.0%	9.7% yield	10.1% yield
8.0%	11.1%	11.6%
9.0%	12.5%	13.0%
10.0%	13.9%	14.5%
11.0%	15.3%	15.9%

**Figure 1.6.   Inflation and taxes can take a big
bite out of your wealth**

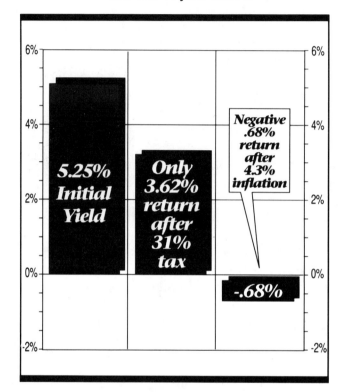

than what is now being reported. If your personal buying experience leads you to
believe that prices are rising much more quickly, consider these figures:

If the true rate of inflation is 7%, for example, you need a yield of 10.1% just
to break even after taxes. At 8% inflation, you need at least 11.6% yield; and at
9%, you need a 13.0% yield.

A NEED FOR HIGH YIELDS AND SAFETY

Today's investment markets present a combination of danger and opportunity that is virtually unparalleled in economic history. Accordingly, we have
designed *The Cash Book* to help you protect AND build your wealth during the
turbulent 1990s.

So, although the future looks uncertain, a properly diversified portfolio using
the strategies outlined throughout the book should be able to generate a wealth-
building *real return* for you no matter what happens in the economy.

RESOURCES

Cato Institute, 224 Second Street S.E., Washington, DC 20003; (202)

Figure 1.7. The Real Capital Gains Rate: 75%

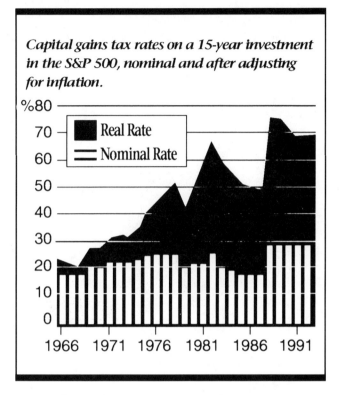

Source: Polyconomics, Inc., Wall Street Journal

546-0200. The Cato Institute provides many special reports on economics and investments. For a copy of the Institute's report on the economy, send $4 to the above address.

Dow Theory Letters, Editor: Richard Russell, P.O. Box 1759, La Jolla, CA 92038; (619) 454-0481. Richard Russell writes an excellent newsletter that provides tremendous insight into the theories of investing in the 1990s.

The Economist, P.O. Box 5044, Boulder, CO 80321-0400. If you plan to invest internationally, then this English-based magazine is a must.

Federal Reserve Bank of St. Louis, P.O. Box 422, St. Louis, MO 63166. This bank publishes several periodicals (available in most libraries) with good statistics and editorials on the economy.

Terry Savage, WBBM-TV, 630 N. McClung Court, Chicago, IL 60611. Terry Savage has several TV shows and newspaper columns and has written a very good book on investments: *Terry Savage Talks Money: The Common Sense Guide To Money Matters,* available in bookstores nationwide.

The Wall Street Journal. For subscription information call 1-800-841-8000.

— 2 —

High Yields with Safety in U.S. Dollar-Denominated Investments

---

"Money is indeed the most important thing in
the world; and all sound and successful
personal and national morality should have this
fact for its basis."
George Bernard Shaw

I n 1991, interest rates fell to their lowest levels in more than 18 years as the
U.S. economy struggled to recover from a recession. From December 4, 1990 to
December 20, 1991, the Federal Reserve lowered its discount rate an *unprece-
dented seven times* — lowering the rate to 3.5%. To put this in perspective, the
Federal Reserve had lowered the reserve requirement only 15 times since 1938.

As interest rates fell, yields on CDs and money market funds plummeted as well. As a result, the actual and real lower rates of return from fixed assets could now be the single greatest financial challenge you will face in the 1990s.

Some of this chapter's highlights include:

- How the power of compounding interest can make you a millionaire with an eight-year investment of only $2,000 per year,
- Six safe alternatives to low-paying certificates of deposit,
- The first adjustable-rate mortgage fund, yielding 7.44%, that will waive all fees and expenses,
- A safe, high-yielding bond fund that protects you whether interest rates rise or fall,
- Plus safety and yield tips on CDs, money market funds, U.S. government Treasuries, and corporate bonds.

A recession-induced drop in interest rates may be good news for the economy and mortgage owners (provided it eventually stimulates recovery), but it's painful for investors.

For a $10,000 investment, a 2% decline in yield means a difference of $200. Lower interest rates affect all investors:

Retirement savings grow at a slower pace,
Investment returns barely keep up with inflation, and
Less money is earned to meet everyday expenses.

The new risk for investors will now become their *reinvestment risk*. With actual rates of return at their lowest levels in almost two decades, the real rates of return from fixed assets could most likely become the greatest threat to your financial well-being.

There are many investment vehicles that provide higher yields. But the amount of income will rest primarily on the amount of investment risk you are willing to take and the safety of the institution in which you deposit those investment dollars.

(NOTE: In Chapter 8, we address the all-important topic of how to rate the safety of your financial institutions.)

Before we show you how to maximize your yields, let's go over a few necessary basics.

HOW INTEREST RATES WORK

The most simple form of interest is, not surprisingly, *simple interest*—when interest is paid only on principal. The earned interest is NOT included with the principal for calculating future interest payments.

For example, if you have $1,000 on deposit at 10% simple interest for one year, you would receive $100 for that year (or $8.33 a month). Fortunately for the investor, there are more profitable ways of calculating interest!

COMPOUND INTEREST: THE FAST LANE TO WEALTH

Compound interest refers to interest calculated on your basic principal PLUS all the interest accrued to that point in time (see Table 2.1).

In short, your principal earns interest, and your interest earns interest. The result is that a compound interest account can grow at a truly amazing rate over time, as Figure 2.1 shows.

The sooner you get your money working for you, the better the results. For example:

Mr. Pennysaver puts $2,000 a year into a tax-free fund, in each of eight years starting at age 19 (and ending at age 26). At age 65, assuming compounding of 10%, he has a million dollars, from an original investment of $16,000. If you have another man who began at age 27 and put in $2,000 every year from age 27 until he retires at age 65 (a total of $78,000), he would still have less money than Mr. Pennysaver with his $16,000 investment (see Table 2.2).

As you can see, the results are remarkable. Without question, this proves the power of compounding over time.

The moral of the story: *The sooner you plant the garden, the larger the harvest.*

TYPES OF INTEREST RATES

In addition to the *method* by which interest is computed, interest rates come in a variety of *types.*

Nominal interest is the most common rate you will see. It is simply the rate of interest you will earn. Your *nominal yield,* on the other hand, is the percentage of

Table 2.1. The Magic of Compounding

A regular investment of $100 per year, compounded annually, will at the end of each year, grow to:

Compounded at a rate of:	Years							
	5	10	15	20	25	30	35	40
6%	$564	$1,318	$2,328	$3,679	$5,486	$7,906	$11,143	$15,476
8%	587	1,449	2,715	4,576	7,311	11,328	17,232	25,906
10%	611	1,594	3,177	5,727	9,835	16,449	27,102	44,259
12%	635	1,755	3,728	7,205	13,333	24,133	43,166	76,709
14%	661	1,934	4,384	9,102	18,187	35,679	69,357	134,202
16%	688	2,132	5,166	11,538	24,921	53,031	112,071	236,076

Source: Encyclopedia of Banking and Financial Tables

Figure 2.1. Compounding Dramatically Increases Your Returns

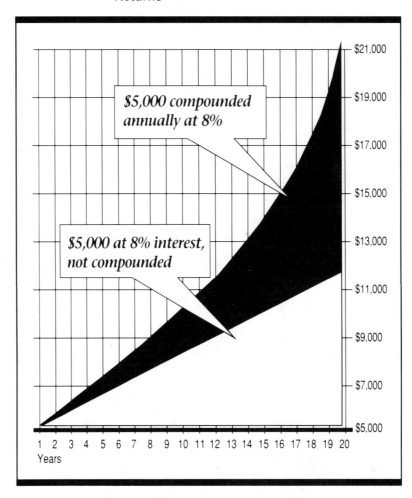

Table 2.2. Pennysaver's Progress

Age	Contribution	Year-end Value
19	$2,000	$ 2,200
20	2,000	4,620
21	2,000	7,282
22	2,000	10,210
23	2,000	13,431
24	2,000	16,974
25	2,000	20,872
26	2,000	25,159
27	0	27,675
28	0	30,442

Table 2.2. (continued)

Age	Contribution	Year-end Value
29	0	33,487
30	0	36,835
31	0	40,519
32	0	44,571
33	0	49,028
34	0	53,930
35	0	59,323
36	0	65,256
37	0	71,781
38	0	78,960
39	0	86,856
40	0	95,541
41	0	105,095
42	0	115,605
43	0	127,165
44	0	139,882
45	0	153,870
46	0	169,257
47	0	186,183
48	0	204,801
49	0	225,281
50	0	247,809
51	0	272,590
52	0	299,849
53	0	329,834
54	0	362,817
55	0	399,099
56	0	439,009
57	0	482,910
58	0	531,201
59	0	584,321
60	0	642,753
61	0	707,028
62	0	777,731
63	0	855,504
64	0	941,054
65	0	1,035,160

Source: Train Smith Investment Counsel

your principal that you *actually receive* as interest—your "return." In cash deposits, it is usually higher than your nominal interest rate. (As you are about to see, neither your nominal interest nor your nominal yield takes any extraneous factors into account.)

REAL interest and REAL yield are your bottom-line rate and return for an investment after adjusting for inflation and taxes.

For example, a CD might yield 6%. However, the 31% income tax bracket effectively takes away 1.86% of the 6%, leaving you with only 4.14% yield. Next you must subtract the rate of inflation, let's say 4.3%, to get your real yield.

From this example, it's obvious that a typical CD yield of 6% will generate a real return of NEGATIVE 0.16%.

By factoring inflation and taxes into your returns for various investments, you may find some real surprises, as Table 2.3 demonstrates.

But even these figures may be misleading. You see, this information was based on an inflation rate of only 4.1% (the government's consumer price index figures for 1991). In a moment, we will show why these figures may be grossly underestimated.

This is why it is so important to calculate your REAL yield for any cash investment today. Given the rate of inflation (and taxation), you could actually be *losing* money while believing that you are earning respectable gains.

Another commonly encountered term, *taxable equivalent yield,* refers to your yield on tax-free instruments. Investments such as municipal bonds are free of federal taxes (and often all taxes), and you pay for this feature with lower yields.

To give a fair comparison of these instruments with taxable investments, the taxable equivalent yield is computed. It shows what you would need to yield on a taxable investment to equal your bottom-line return from the selected tax-free

Table 2.3. Real Yield vs. Nominal Yield

INVESTMENT	1981		1991	
	Nominal yield (%)	Real yield %	Nominal yield (%)	Real yield %
Passbook Account	4.25	−7.31	4.50	−0.86
Money-Market Fund	16.82	−0.83	4.63	−0.77
Corporate Bond Fund	12.68	−3.07	11.80	−4.32
Municipal Bond Fund	9.12	−1.18	9.60	−2.81

1981 figures are based on a 10.5% inflation rate and a 43% marginal tax rate.
1991 figures are based on an estimated 4.1% inflation rate and a 28% tax rate.

investment. (For your convenience, Table 7.8 provides a worksheet for computing the taxable equivalent yield.

PREDICTING INTEREST RATES

In the final analysis, the Federal Reserve *decides* where interest rates should be by regulating the amount of money flowing into the Federal Reserve banking system. This manipulation by the Fed is what shows up in money supply figures.

The factors governing the Fed's decision to tighten or loosen the money supply are as follows:

- Inflationary fears will cause the Fed to tighten money, which causes interest rates to rise.

- Deflationary or recessionary fears will cause the Fed to ease the money supply, making money more plentiful and driving interest rates down—making it less expensive to borrow.

Predicting interest rates is simply a matter of looking at all the factors currently affecting rates, and deciding on an order of priorities for the Federal Reserve. For example, from 1990 to 1991 the Fed had to look at the following factors:

- America is the world's largest debtor, with a large portion of its enormous debt owned by foreigners. This is a reason to keep interest rates high. (While high interest rates alone do not encourage foreigners to buy a currency, new money can be attracted into the system if rates are kept a few points above the admitted rate of inflation and the currency is fairly sound.)

- U.S. inflation on the average has been higher than several other industrial nations over the past few years—a reason to keep rates high. For the short term, however, (reported) inflation rates have fallen, allowing the Fed to ease or lower interest rates.

- The economy is attempting to rebound from the recession. If leading indicators rise anytime during 1992, a case will be made for higher interest rates—especially to encourage foreign investors. If indicators fall, interest rates could remain at or near their lowest levels in years. The one thing that economists agree on is that, over the next 12 to 18 months, the economy will remain anemic. And remember, during an election year, the economy must show signs of recovery, or the President may find himself in political trouble.

- There is also a risk of a banking and credit collapse, which is another reason to maintain lower rates to inject much needed liquidity into the system.

When there are as many points for lower rates as against, which way will interest rates go? The answer lies in the fact that governments, like people, tend to deal with the urgent rather than the important. They tend to treat the immediate symptoms rather than deal with the longer-term underlying causes.

In 1991, the two most pressing problems facing the Fed were the banking crisis and the recession. In 1992, the Fed will continue to face a banking and insurance industry crisis, a weak economy, and a growing concern about the federal deficit along with a presidential election. Therefore, it is likely that the Fed will keep interest rates low through November 1992.

INTEREST RATE STRATEGIES

Most mutual funds regard the shorter term to be "safer" than the longer term—not so much because they believe that interest rates will rise, but because it is much easier to judge the credit-worthiness of a company or financial institution for the next few months than it is to judge it for the next several years. Many cash-equivalent mutual funds buy short- to intermediate-term instruments, more to protect themselves than their clients.

So as an individual investor, if you make long-term investments in the 1990s, you have to be very sure that the investment and the institution with whom you make this investment are both top quality.

In general, you can think in terms of locking in relatively high long-term rates in government paper of any industrialized nation. For other cash instruments, take an ever shorter view as the interest rates and yields increase. Chances are, the higher the yield, the riskier the investment is over the longer term.

Before you buy any fund, check what their payout is relative to current interest rates. In the more conservative vehicles—Treasuries and other government paper—you will likely make more money by buying longer-term individual securities for your own account than by paying a fund to do it for you.

In the more risky investments (most corporate bonds, junk bonds, and so on) you are better off with a fund, because you probably do not have sufficient funds to spread your risks through diversification.

CERTIFICATES OF DEPOSIT

As we mentioned earlier, one risk facing investors in the 1990s is reinvestment risk—especially for holders of CDs. For example:

Let's assume that you held a $10,000 CD that paid 8.6% and expired in September 1991. If you rolled it over, you would have received only 6.5% or a loss of $210 a year in interest income. Since most retirees prefer the safety of CDs, many have seen their retirement incomes drop substantially during the past year.

Low rates, therefore, force many holders to look at other investments that not only offer higher returns, but represent more risk—something most CD holders would prefer to avoid.

SAFETY TIP

BEWARE: The CD You Own May Not Be FDIC-Insured

With a rise in bank and S&L failures, it is more important than ever that you make sure the CD (or what you thought was a CD) is FDIC-insured.

When National Bank of Washington failed earlier this year, one depositor found that she had lost over $113,000—most of her life's savings. She had made two critical errors.

She had purchased CDs from the bank several years before. Each time the CDs matured, someone from the bank would call and ask if she wanted to roll them over. Each call was then followed up with a written confirmation. Unfortunately, she never looked at the confirmations, but rather put them away in a safe location, unopened.

When the bank failed, she was surprised to find that the bank representative had switched her federally insured CDs into uninsured commercial paper. If she had reviewed each of her confirmations, she most likely would have caught the problem. Instead, her $113,000 was left uninsured and it's doubtful she will ever recover her life's savings.

Even if she still owned FDIC-insured CDs, she would have lost $13,000. Again, since she paid little attention to her confirmations, she had not realized that her investment had exceeded the FDIC limit of $100,000.

To avoid this type of surprise, we recommend that you thoroughly (and carefully) review all correspondence you receive from your bank, as well as any papers you sign.

And most importantly, read and understand your initial CD agreement. These agreements generally specify that when your CD matures, the bank will contact you to determine whether you want to withdraw your funds or roll them over. If the bank can't reach you within a specified time, it will usually renew the CD automatically. Some agreements allow the bank to revert these funds to passbook rates, and some (though it is not common) allow the bank to invest your money in commercial paper.

If you have CDs maturing soon, the following are some alternatives you might consider:

- *Pay down debt.* Pay off credit card debt and other consumer debt. As you will learn in Chapter 11, this could result in earning an equivalent 28% to 30% yield.
- *Diversify maturities.* Split your CDs into five equal amounts. Then purchase a 6-month, 1-year, 2½-year, 3-year, and 5-year CD. This gives you protection against both rising and falling interest rates.
- *Consider short- to intermediate-term bond funds.* But understand (unlike

CDs and money market mutual funds) that the value of your investment—the net asset value of the funds' share—will vary with the market price of the bonds in the funds' portfolios.

- *Buy some Treasury notes.* Seven-year notes yield more.

- *Seek out-of-state CDs.* Many investors have found higher yields out of state. But before you send any money, call the bank to confirm the interest rate. Banks can change rates without notice, so ask if the bank guarantees the rate until your check arrives. Also know the particulars of the deposit agreement—minimum deposit, penalties for early withdrawal, and fees levied on the account. Don't forget to ask if the account is insured by the federal government—and get it in writing.

- *Buy your CDs through a brokerage firm.* Brokerage firms often pay *higher rates of interest* than banks because they can buy in bulk from banks, thus giving you the higher rate of interest that banks normally give to only their larger clients. Table 2.4 provides a list of top yielding FDIC insured banks.

Table 2.4. Top-Yielding Federally Insured
Certificates of Deposit

Institution	City & State	Telephone	Quoted Rate	Actual Yield
30-Day CD				
Merchants Bank	Kansas City, MO	816-471-1700	5.90	6.08
Dartmouth Bank	Manchester, NH	800-888-1152	5.84	6.00
Westside Bank-So. Ca.	Los Angeles, CA	213-473-1531	5.80	5.97
Fireside Thrift	Newark, CA	415-490-6511	5.80	5.96
First International	Chula Vista, CA	619-425-5000	5.75	5.90
60-Day CD				
Merchants Bank	Kansas City, MO	816-471-1700	5.90	6.08
Westside Bank-So. Ca.	Los Angeles, CA	213-473-1531	5.85	6.02
Dartmouth Bank	Manchester, NH	800-888-1152	5.84	6.00
First International	Chula Vista, CA	619-425-5000	5.75	5.90
Gateway Bank	San Francisco, CA	415-268-8108	5.65	5.80
3-Month CD				
East-West. Fed. Savings	San Francisco, CA	415-397-6800	6.05	6.24
Piedmont Federal Savings	Manassas, VA	800-541-6301	6.00	6.14

Table 2.4. (continued)

Institution	City & State	Telephone	Quoted Rate	Actual Yield
Fireside Thrift	Newark, CA	415-490-6511	5.95	6.11
Merchants Bank	Kansas City, MO	816-471-1700	5.90	6.08
Westside Bank-So. Ca.	Los Angeles, CA	213-473-1531	5.90	6.08
6-Month CD				
East-West. Fed. Savings	San Francisco, CA	415-397-6800	6.25	6.45
Gateway Bank	San Francisco, CA	415-268-8108	6.20	6.38
Chevy Chase Savings	Chevy Chase, MD	800-825-9000	6.20	6.35
Fireside Thrift	Newark, CA	415-490-6511	6.10	6.27
Columbia First Bank	Arlington, VA	703-247-5000	5.98	6.25
One-Year CD				
East-West. Fed. Savings	San Francisco, CA	415-397-6800	6.60	6.82
Gateway Bank	San Francisco, CA	415-268-8108	6.50	6.70
MBNA America	Newark, DE	800-441-7787	6.45	6.66
Chevvy Chase Savings	Chevy Chase, MD	800-825-9000	6.40	6.56
Potomac Savings	Silver Spring, MD	301-236-0070	6.35	6.56
2½-Year CD				
Citibank, S.D.	Sioux Falls, SD	800-248-4669	6.95	7.30
Standard Federal	Gaithersburg, MD	301-670-6119	7.00	7.19
Green Point Savings	Flushing, NY	718-670-7615	6.93	7.18
Western Federal Savings	Marina Del Rey, CA	213-306-6500	6.88	7.12
Oak Tree Savings	New Orleans, LA	504-588-9313	6.85	7.09
5-Year CD				
Merchants Bank	Kansas City, MO	816-471-1700	7.70	8.00
United Savings Bank	San Francisco, CA	415-928-0700	7.70	8.00
Continental Savings	San Francisco, CA	415-861-5554	7.70	8.00
Eastern Savings Bank	Hunt Valley, MD	800-777-7372	7.67	7.95
Fireside Thrift	Newark, CA	415-490-6511	7.65	7.92

Current as of 9/91

Source: Income & Safety

SAFETY TIP

What do you do if you find your bank is getting into difficulties? Break your time deposit or CD, of course, and move the money someplace else. However, most banks and savings and loans will charge you a hefty penalty for this.

But if you purchase through your broker, *chances are you won't be charged any penalty at all.* Since brokerage firms make secondary markets in CDs, they would likely sell your CD to another broker if you wished to cash it in before maturity.

YIELD TIP

To slow the yield decline when interest rates fall, fund managers will stretch the average maturity. During 1991, these maturities stretched to 61 days—the longest in over a decade. To keep investors, one fund extended its maturities to 88 days, while others have waived part of their expenses—which has the effect of boosting yield.

YIELD TIP

When shopping for a money market account, look for one with *frequent compounding.* If you can get daily compounding as opposed to weekly, monthly or quarterly compounding, you obviously earn a higher effective rate of interest, even though two funds may offer the same rates.

If you live in a high-tax state, *then you should consider a state-tax-exempt money market fund,* because it can mean as much as 0.5% to 1% more interest to you.

MONEY MARKET FUNDS

A money market fund is a mutual fund of short-term debt obligations of the U.S. government, large corporations, and other large financial institutions.

Before the introduction of money market funds, only investors with $100,000 or more could enjoy the extra yield that is given to large blocks of money. Money market funds operate very much like any mutual fund, except they confine their activities to short-term cash equivalent instruments.

The first money fund, the Reserve Fund, was established in 1972. Today, there are 630 money funds in operation with total assets of approximately $460 billion. The specific types of debt that these funds buy are usually among the following:

- *Short-term obligations* issued by U.S. government agencies.
- *Repurchase agreements:* Short-term agreements offered by banks and U.S. government securities dealers to raise temporary funds (often merely for an overnight period).
- *Banker's acceptances:* Issued by banks promising to pay at a given maturity date, usually 180 days or less.
- *Commercial paper:* Unsecured IOUs offered by big corporations and institutions to finance day-to-day operations, usually for 91 days or less and in amounts of $100,000 or more.
- *Certificates of deposit:* Large demoninations sold by banks for a minimum time deposit (e.g., 14 days, 91 days, etc.).
- *Eurodollar CDs:* These are like U.S. CDs, except they are sold by foreign branches of U.S. banks or by foreign banks (payable outside the United States). The minimum is generally $1 million, usually for at least two weeks.

As previously mentioned, money market funds can pay higher rates of interest to you than your local checking or savings account. This is a result of the fund managers pooling your money into large block amounts, thus giving you the advantage of the higher rates of interest afforded only to their wealthier institutional clients. Table 2.5 shows the money market fund performance for 1991. Table 2.6 lists the seven highest 12-month money market fund yields.

Table 2.5. 1991 Money Market Fund Performance

(Average Actual 30-Day Calendar Yields)

	Tax	Tax-Free
January	6.89%	4.75%
February	6.41	4.18
March	6.09	4.22
April	5.84	4.20
May	5.58	4.07
June	5.49	3.78
July	5.47	3.70
August	5.36	4.03
September	5.21	4.26
October	5.03	3.90
November	4.78	3.73

Source: IBC/Donoghue's Money Fund Report

Table 2.6. Highest 12-Month Money Market Fund Yields

(3rd Quarter 1991)

AVERAGE Yields		6.31%
Dreyfus Worldwide Dollar	800-782-6620	7.12%
Evergreen Money Market Trust	800-235-0064	6.94%
Vanguard MMR Prime	800-662-7447	6.86%
Fidelity Spartan	800-544-8888	6.86%
Dreyfus 100% U.S. Treasury	800-782-6620	6.85%
INVESCO Treasurer's MM Reserve	800-525-8085	6.82%
Fidelity Spartan U.S. Government	800-544-8888	6.81%

Source: IBC/Donoghue's Money Fund Report

HOW SAFE IS YOUR MONEY MARKET ACCOUNT?

In general, your money market account is safe because it is SHORT-TERM credit, and it is less likely that the borrower will renege in a shorter span of time.

The safest money market funds are those that invest only in U.S. government securities. However, these usually pay up to a percentage point lower than most other funds. Also, since these are funds, not direct credit to an institution, there is a fee involved to cover expenses, usually around 0.75% of the interest the fund receives.

You probably have a money market fund attached to your brokerage account, but if you are expecting to keep large amounts of money in a highly liquid state over weeks (or months), the following funds have higher-than-average yields and are also the safest:

Benham Government Agency Fund, minimum investment $1,000; 1-800-472-3389.

Fidelity U.S. Treasury Money Market Fund, minimum investment $20,000; 1-800-544-8888.

Dreyfus U.S. Guaranteed Money Market Account LP, minimum investment $2,500; 1-800-782-6620.

Blanchard Government Money Market Fund, minimum investment $1,000; 1-800-922-7771.

U.S. GOVERNMENT ISSUES

If you plan to keep your money in U.S. dollars, the safest place is in U.S. government issues. Although the federal debt continues to balloon, it is unlikely that the U.S. government will ever renege on its debt.

YIELD TIP

If money market funds are too low yielding for your income needs, here's a safe higher-income parking place as recommended by Richard Band, editor of *Profitable Investing.*

"With interest rates at near record lows, many investors may be facing an income crunch. Unfortunately, many of investors are now compounding their mistake by "reaching" for yield. They're buying lower-grade junk bonds, or going out to the long end of the maturity spectrum — 20 to 30 years — which is another form of risk. Don't panic.

"Start rolling some of your maturing CDs into this no-load bond fund: Vanguard Fixed Income — Short-Term Corporate Bond Portfolio. *1-800-662-7447. Vanguard has one of the lowest overheads of any fund group in the nation. As a result, more income flows into your pocket, not theirs. Current yield is 6.45%. Minimum investment is $3,000. Maturities average 2.5 years.*

"If you are in the upper income bracket, you can draw tax-free income from Vanguard Municipal Bond Limited-Term Portfolio *(with an average maturity of 2.9 years) or* Intermediate-Term Portfolio *(an average maturity of 8.7 years). The current intermediate yield of 5.56% works out to more than 8% for highly taxed investors.*

"For those who can live with more risk, but still well below that of long-term bonds or 'junk,' I recommend Scudder Short-Term Bond Fund *1-800-225-2470. This fund, which also has no sales load or redemption fee, currently yields 9%. The minimum is $1,000. The fund invests a portion of its money into high-yielding foreign currencies, CMOs (collateralized mortgage obligations) and other asset-backed securities, which generally provide higher yields than conventional bonds. By charter, at least 65% of the portfolio must consist of paper rated AA or better. Average maturity is 2.7 years."*

BUYING THROUGH TREASURY DIRECT

Treasury Direct is a system in which the records of ownership of government securities are held in book-entry by the U.S. Treasury itself. Since 1986, Treasury bills and bonds have been part of Treasury Direct, and since 1987, Treasury notes as well.

Securities held in a Treasury Direct account are paid at maturity, unless the purchaser chooses to reinvest the proceeds into new securities.

Treasury Direct book-entry accounts are designed primarily *for investors who plan to hold their securities until maturity.* It is NOT for people who want to trade their securities or, in the case of bonds, hold them for only a year or two.

If you purchase through the Treasury Direct system and decide to sell, you must give the Treasury at least 20 days' notice, either before an interest payment date or before the maturity date. You will receive a statement of account each time you make a transaction within your account.

You also have a choice of registration options: Single ownership, joint ownership with right of survivorship, or co-ownership. Check out the program thoroughly with your local Federal Reserve bank to make sure that the program is for you.

You can purchase any government security through any of the Federal Reserve banks listed at the end of this chapter, or from the *Bureau of Public Debt,* Division of Customer Service, 300 13th Street SW, Washington, DC 20239-0001.

You also can call the U.S. Treasury's continuous recorded line at (202) 874-4000 and receive the following information (you must have a Touchtone phone to dial the specific extensions):

Service Available	Extension
Treasury bill offerings	211
Treasury note and bond offerings	212
Treasury bill auction results	221
Treasury note and bond auction results	222
General information on Treasury bills	231
General information on Treasury notes and bonds	232
General information on the Treasury Direct system	233
Savings bond information	004
Requesting forms	241
Information on how to purchase Treasury securities	251
Information on how to redeem Treasury securities	254
To get specific questions answered	003

YIELD TIP

To get the maximum yield on all government issues—U.S. government bonds, notes or bills—buy them at auction (when issued) rather than in the secondary market.

If you purchase these instruments in the secondary market, your broker will charge you up to a half point on your first year's interest in commission fees. If you buy "when issued," your broker will charge you only about $50. If you buy directly from the Treasury, the transaction is free of charge.

THE FOUR TYPES OF TREASURY SECURITIES

There are four instruments that the U.S. government uses: bonds, notes, bills and EE savings bonds.

1. *Treasury Bonds:* These are long-term debt obligations issued in the following denominations: $1,000, $5,000, $10,000, $100,000 and $1 million. Maturity is between 10 and 30 years. A fixed rate of interest is paid every six months, and this interest is exempt from state and local taxes. If you live in a high-tax state, the tax-free interest is a big consideration.

2. *Treasury Notes:* Notes are issued in $1,000 and $5,000 denominations and mature in two to 10 years. The interest is paid every six months and, like Treasury bonds, is exempt from state and local taxes.

3. *Treasury Bills:* There is a minimum requirement of $10,000 for purchase of Treasury bills, but after that you can purchase $5,000 lots. Treasury bills are the most important tool the Treasury uses to finance its operations. They are sold at a discount for maturities of three, six and 12 months. Unlike other government instruments, T-bills are sold at auction, with no fixed-rate interest. They also do not pay annual or semiannual interest. They are redeemed at face value, and the "interest" you make over the life of the bill is the difference between your purchase price and your selling price. Because of this, they are not taxable until you sell and, like EE savings bonds, are technically "zero coupon" instruments.

4. *Series EE Savings Bonds:* EE savings bonds are exempt from state taxes, eligible for deferral of federal taxes, and available without commissions. They also present virtually no risk and can be bought through any private or Federal Reserve bank.

   EE savings bonds sell for half their face value and mature in 12 years from date of purchase. They can be bought in small increments, beginning at $50. If you hold them for at least five years, then 85% of the average yield on five-year Treasuries will be paid to you.

REFCORP BONDS

In 1987, when the U.S. government first started to deal with the S&L crisis, it formed the Financing Corporation that issued $10.8 billion in 30-year bonds. By 1989, it was evident that the $10.8 billion was hopelessly inadequate, so Congress created the Resolution Funding Corporation (RefCorp) to issue $30 billion in bonds.

Although these bonds are not federally guaranteed the way T-bills are, they yield at least 0.25% more than Treasuries and are backed by zero-coupon Treasuries.

The interest payments on the first $10.8 billion worth of bonds are met from the premiums S&Ls pay to the government for deposit insurance. The interest on the $30 billion worth of bonds is paid out of the Federal Home Loan Bank system's earnings from loans to savings institutions and proceeds from the sale of failed thrifts' assets.

YIELD TIP

With the yields on bank CDs and money markets declining, series EE savings bonds are becoming more attractive. For example, in November 1991, the average money fund was yielding 4.97%, a six-month CD 5.18% and a five-year CD 6.62%. The rate for a series EE savings bond was 6.38%.

The series EE rate is adjusted each November 1 and May 1 to 85% of the average yield on five-year Treasury securities for the *previous* six months. If you hold a bond five years or more, then you are guaranteed a minimum of 6% while you owned it.

In addition, series EE bonds are not taxable by states. So a 6.38% rate is equivalent to 6.86% if you are in a 7% state-income-tax bracket. Federal tax is deferred until you cash the bonds. If you use them to pay for your child's college education, they are tax free (provided your income is below $62,900 for joint returns and $41,950 for single filers).

YIELD TIP

If you are interested in buying U.S. government Treasury bonds and holding them to maturity, always buy those at the lowest price below par (100). No matter what the basic dividend is, in the secondary market, rates adjust to approximately the same yields.

Buying the cheapest bonds and holding them to maturity locks in the current interest rates on these bonds and builds in capital gain, since bonds are always paid out at "par" (i.e., $1,000 per bond).

Interest payments are also NOT backed by the Treasury on RefCorp bonds. However, the law directs the Treasury to make up the shortfall if the funds available are not enough to meet interest payments—as was true in April and July 1990.

REFCORP BONDS COME IN TWO FORMS:

1. Bonds that pay interest every six months.
2. Zero-coupon bonds that make no periodic payments, but sell for much less than the face value you receive at maturity. Interest-paying bonds come with maturities of 30 or 40 years, but the zeros have maturities ranging from three months to 40 years. Like Treasuries, they are exempt from state and local taxes.

YIELD TIP

Benham Capital Management Group has launched a no-load **Adjustable-Rate Mortgage Fund,** the first adjustable-rate government securities fund without a sales charge. The typical fund of this type charges a sales commission of about 4%. With a yield of around 7.44%, this is a great alternative for money market fund and CD investors who have seen their income drop sharply.

The fund is rated AAA by Standard & Poor's and invests only in securities issued by the U.S. government or its agencies. The fund invests primarily in adjustable-rate mortgages, whose values fluctuate far less than those of traditional fixed-rate mortgages.

"This makes it a much more suitable alternative for money market fund shareholders looking for extra yield than most government bond funds," Benham says. *"As a rule, a $10 share should move up or down only 15 to 25 cents for each 1% change in interest rates, while 'garden variety' Ginnie Maes investing in fixed-rate mortgages would normally move 45 cents. If interest rates continue to fall, money fund shareholders will see their yields drop even further. But if they rise, investors in long-term bonds will be hurt the most. The adjustable-mortgage fund is positioned between one and two years, a fair balance of risk and reward."*

As an added bonus, the fund will waive all fees and expenses until March 1992. Once imposed, fees and expenses will not exceed 0.75%. There are no 12b-1 fees and the minimum initial investment is $1,000.

For more information, contact Benham Capital Management Group, 1665 Charleston Road, Mountain View, CA 94043; 1-800-472-3389.

RefCorp bonds are sold by stockbrokers in minimum amounts of $1,000. However, we suggest that you buy at least $20,000 worth at a time to minimize your costs. For that amount, the cost is about 1% of the face value, or $200.

ZERO-COUPON INSTRUMENTS

While other cash-equivalent investments sell for par and then pay interest on a regular basis, zero-coupon investments such as zero-coupon bonds and compound-interest bonds (CIBs) sell for a discount, and then are redeemed at par. The difference in the two prices is the interest on the instrument.

In other words, the interest is added to the principal each month and allows you to earn "interest on interest" versus being paid out on a regular basis.

Therefore, zeros provides you with the benefits of compound interest. They have been "stripped" of their interest coupons, so that the interest is compounded and paid out in a balloon payment at maturity.

YIELD TIP

Double Your Money on Zero-Coupon Bonds

When interest rates fall, the prices of coupon bonds rise to adjust to the going interest rate. On regular bonds (bonds that pay interest at regular intervals), this is generally a gain of a few points if rates fall 1%. But with zero-coupon bonds, prices rise much further to reflect the 1% rate change all the way to maturity.

To see how this works, turn to the Treasury bonds, notes and bills page in the financial section of your newspaper and note the difference between a coupon bond that was issued at 10% and one issued at 9%. Then check the same two bonds in the U.S. Treasury STRIPS section. You will see that the spread in the coupon bonds is perhaps 5% to 10%, while it can be *100% or more* in the Treasury STRIPS.

Besides differences in interest, several other factors also affect prices for bonds of varying maturities. A conservative rule of thumb is that for every 1% drop in interest rates, a Treasury zero will rise 1% to 2% for every year until maturity. There is also a high probability that it would rise even more.

If you buy zeros for this interest-rate play, then remember that you are buying for the short to medium term. When you judge that interest rates have bottomed out, then you should sell.

Government Zeros: In 1982, Merrill Lynch created "Treasury Zeros" by buying long-term government bonds, putting them in an irrevocable trust, and issuing receipts against the interest payments. That is, Merrill Lynch separated the "interest coupons" from the principal of the Treasury bonds and sold them as "Treasury Investment Growth Receipts," or TIGRs.

Salomon Brothers followed suit with a similar investment, which they called "Certificates of Accrual on Treasury Securities," or CATS. CATS are also on Treasury securities that are callable before the 30-year maturity (usually about four years before).

Separate Trading of Registered Interest and Principal of Securities (STRIPS) are Treasury notes or bonds that have been stripped of their interest-paying coupons. They are available on Treasury securities that are non-callable for 30 years from their issue date.

A very good broker for the purchase of fixed-income securities is *Tom Hill,* Merrill Lynch, Pierce, Fenner & Smith (Liberty Center, 14th Floor, Pittsburgh, PA 15222-3720; 1-800-937-0761). Tom is a very knowledgeable broker and will not try to talk you into trading short-term.

ZEROS VERSUS COUPON BONDS

Many securities specifically designed as compound-interest vehicles calculate their interest less frequently than if you bought a simple-interest vehicle and did your own compounding (i.e., reinvested the interest as it was paid).

The various stripped bonds tend to be far more volatile in price than their equivalent simple-interest vehicles. Yet, because they are more volatile than their coupon cousins, they can move up faster as well.

There is no tax advantage to buying zero-coupon bonds because, whether you actually receive interest or not, you have to pay tax on it as if you did. Municipal zeros are the tax-free exception to this rule.

TARGET MATURITY FUNDS

Benham Target Maturity Funds (1-800-472-3389) invest in zero-coupon bond holdings. But unlike other bond funds, they have a fixed lifetime—when the target maturity date is reached, the fund is liquidated. Benham currently offers such funds with maturities of 1995, 2005, 2010, 2015, and 2020.

These funds are pooled zero-coupon investments. Unlike regular bond funds (where the manager tries to outguess interest rates and moves between bonds, depending on how he thinks interest rates are going to move), Benham Target Maturities are *simply a long-term play on interest rates*.

By buying the fund instead of an individual bond, you are spreading your risks among several bonds, which you could most likely not afford to do yourself.

DEFERRED INTEREST SECURITIES

Deferred Interest Securities (DINTS) are bonds issued by Exxon Shipping Company and General Motors Acceptance Corporation before 1983—the year the IRS ruled that corporate zero interest was taxable. Their maturities range between 2012 and 2015, and they are taxable only upon maturity or sale.

MUNICIPAL ZEROS

Issued by state and local governments, municipal zeros are exempt from federal taxes and usually from state taxes in the state where issued. Their main attraction is the huge tax break. (See Chapter 7 for more information about these and other municipal bonds.)

CORPORATE BONDS

If you want to set up a steady stream of income, then corporate bonds, rather than stocks, may be the answer.

Bonds, unlike stocks, represent debt. This is like an IOU. When you buy a bond, you lend money to the issuer; and in return you receive a certificate that says, "I'm going to pay you back with a set amount every year." When the bond reaches maturity, on a set date, you are paid back the full purchase or face value of the bond. That is, if everything goes well from start to finish. So, under no circumstances should you buy any bond rated less than A-, unless you are aggressively seeking a high-risk situation with high-profit potential.

If the company fails, you may lose everything. That's why bond funds are better for most investors than individual bonds. Bond funds provide more diversification than you can typically get on your own. The average investor probably doesn't own more than five to 10 individual bonds, while the average bond fund can own over 100 issues. Funds can also have a variety in the average maturity of bonds that are held in the portfolio.

Another advantage of purchasing bond funds rather than individual bonds is that you get better liquidity. To sell your individual bonds before maturity, you must pay commissions—which can be substantial.

Rule of thumb: If you plan to hold for less than four years, then buy a no-load zero-coupon bond fund. If you plan to hold for longer than that, buy the individual bonds. The same holds true if you are buying individual Treasury securities, such as Treasury bills, notes or bonds.

PRICE RISK

As Table 2.7 reveals, bond funds did extremely well in 1991. But the risks may be rising.

Unlike money market funds that maintain a fixed $1-per-share net asset value, bond funds fluctuate in value as interest rates rise or fall. When rates go down, the value goes up; but when rates rise, the value declines.

The mistake most investors make is that they focus only on yield and seldom focus on the price risk. Investors believe that when they need their money, it will be there. It might not be. (At least not all of it, depending on how sensitive the bonds in a particular fund's portfolio are to interest rate moves.)

For example: If interest rates rise just 1%, an investor who puts $10,000 into a Treasury bond fund yielding 7.7% would be left with $9,820, according to calculations by Vanguard Group. (See Table 2.8.)

Long-term funds are four to five times as risky as short-term funds, because the price for short-term bonds fluctuate far less in response to interest rate changes. If you think interest rates are going to go down, and if you are deliberately playing that move, then long-term bond funds are a good place to be. If interest rates go up, then short-term is where to be.

BOND FUND RECOMMENDATIONS

- *Alex Green or Michael Spartz* (International Assets, 201 West Canton Avenue, Suite 100, Winter Park, FL 32789; (407) 629-1400, Fax (407) 629-2470) recommend the following bond funds:

Table 2.7. Bond Fund Performance 1991

Fund Category	Total Return	
	Third Quarter	Twelve* Months
Zero Coupon Bonds	9.27%	23.88%
Global Bond	7.61	12.02
Convertible Bonds	6.92	26.38
High Current Yield	6.64	25.22
Corporate Bond-A Rated	5.86	16.00
Flexible Income	5.80	19.54
Corporate Bond-BBB Rated	5.76	16.00
U.S. Government	5.69	14.75
Intermediate U.S. Government	5.30	13.66
GNMA	5.12	14.69
Intermediate Taxable	5.07	13.97
General Municipals	4.01	12.86
Insured Municipals	3.75	12.79
High Yield Municipals	3.72	11.13
Short-Term Global	3.66	6.27
Short-Term Taxable	3.48	10.89
Short-Term U.S. Government	3.45	11.14
Intermediate Municipals	3.14	10.64
Adjustable Rate Mortgage	2.89	9.37
Short-Term Municipals	2.16	8.04
Institutional Money Market	1.43	6.73
Inst. Gov't Money Market	1.40	6.47
Money Market Funds	1.34	6.36
Government Money Market	1.33	6.18
Tax-Exempt Money Funds	1.00	4.60
AVERAGE TAXABLE BOND FUND	5.44%	16.39%

*Sept. 1990–Sept. 1991

Source: Lipper Analytical Services Inc.

- *Summit Tax-Exempt Bond Fund.* Summit is a limited partnership traded on the NYSE that invests in first mortgages issued by state and local governments. At its current price of $10 a share, the fund is yielding 9% tax-free (after-tax equivalent is 13% for investors in a 31% tax bracket) and makes distributions quarterly.

Table 2.8. How Interest Rate Changes Affect Bond Funds

Hypothetical performance of some Vanguard Group funds*

| | | *One Year Total Returns* | | |
Fund	Yield 10/91	Rates Fall 1 Percentage Point	Rates Unchanged	Rates Rise 1 Percentage Point
Municipal (long-term)	6.5%	15.0%	6.5%	–2.0%
U.S. Treasury	7.7	17.2	7.7	–1.8
GNMA	8.4	13.4	8.4	2.9
High-yield	11.5	15.3	11.5	4.5
Short-term	6.9	9.1	6.9	4.7
Money Fund (Prime Port.)	5.5	5.0	5.5	6.0

*Returns assume portfolio holdings are unchanged, interest-rate movements are uniform for all securities and maturities, some default risk in high-yield portfolio and some prepayment risk in GNMA fund.

Sources: Vanguard Group, The Wall Street Journal

Mortgages are all in a senior position, no properties are mortgaged at more than 85% of their appraised value, and the occupancy rate on the commercial properties is currently averaging 95%. In addition, the fund is trading at almost a 40% discount to its net asset value (NAV). Aggressive income investors seeking high tax-free income should give Summit serious consideration.

- *Freeport-McMoRan Copper and Gold Liquid Yield Option Notes*. These unique zero-coupon notes are currently yielding 6.8% and mature in July 2011. Of particular interest, the notes are convertible, at the option of the holder, into 7.5 shares of the company's common stock or 0.6 ounces of gold.

  The earnings prospects for the company are exceptional. Due in part to enormous reserves discovered in Indonesia, the company's earnings are likely to triple by 1995. The bonds offer three separate possibilities for the investor to profit: If gold rises, if the shares of the company's stock rise, or if interest rates decline. Currently offered at $270 a bond, these convertibles are an excellent vehicle for the conservative hard-money investor.

- *Magma Copper Indexed Bonds*. These notes mature in November 1998, trade on AMEX, and are unique in that the interest they pay is indexed to copper prices. They may pay as much as 21% and in no case less than 12% (currently trading at 107, they are paying 14%, with distributions quarterly). Magma Copper is the second largest copper producer in the United States and is quite profitable. The rating on the bonds was recently upgraded by Standard & Poor's to B+.

Mark Skousen (*Forecasts & Strategies,* Phillips Publishing, 7811 Montrose Road, Potomac, MD 20854; 1-800-722-9000) recommends the following bond fund:

- *Putnam High-Income Convertible Bond Fund.* This closed-end fund has responded favorably to lower interest rates. The yield was 10.6% in October 1991, and if the stock market takes off (since this fund holds convertibles), the upside potential looks good.

JUNK BONDS

In the 1991 edition of *The Cash Book* we said, "It may seem strange to have a section on junk bonds in a book on conservative, high-yield investments. But with interest rates about to fall, and junk bonds so out of favor, there is a case to be made for investing in selected junk bonds at this time."

That, indeed, was the case. As the panic somewhat subsided, the market for junk bonds increased, fueling a 21% total return for the junk market in the first half of 1991. But the opportunities are over, and we recommend staying away from junk bonds for several reasons:

1. Whether risk on junk bonds has increased or declined, the declining yields make them less attractive. The original attraction that led investors to junk bonds could just as likely cause them to dump their junk for other mutual funds.
2. The continued weakness of the economy could lead to increased erosion of profits for issuing companies and increase defaults. Most of the decline so far in the junk bond market has come not from actual defaults, but merely from *fear* of defaults.

A continued sluggish economy and poor earnings records by the strongest of U.S. companies could fuel this fear even more. At the beginning of 1991, it was estimated that about one-third of the junk bond market would actually default by the end of 1992–provided the recession continued throughout 1991.

And it remains to be seen whether insurance companies and thrifts have finished their dumping of junk bonds that could further injure the market.

WHAT IS A JUNK BOND?

Junk bonds are those bonds rated by Standard & Poor's at "BB" or lower, and by Moody's as "Ba" or lower. Some are so risky they have no rating at all. Junk bonds are issued by companies with uncertain earnings; and therefore, the risk is that they may not be able to cover their bond interest payments, let alone pay off the principal when it comes due.

Junk bonds are issued by small companies that are trying to survive, and by large companies that need to fund a leveraged buy-out or raise large amounts of money to prevent a hostile takeover.

Junk bonds are not an investment for the fainthearted. This is a specialized investment; and if you invest personally instead of through a fund, then you have to find out if the company under consideration has very real prospects for earnings improvement.

If you insist on investing, you should not invest anything that you cannot afford to lose. We recommend a junk fund versus investing in specific bonds. Take a hard look at what funds are buying and what they are paying. Don't get greedy. The higher the yield, obviously the higher the risk.

According to *Forbes'* Annual Fund Survey, the junk bond funds listed in Table 2.9 have performed well during up or down markets.

A FINAL THOUGHT

Just remember, it is unlikely that interest rates will remain down very long. This is only a short-term situation so don't panic. And don't put yourself into a situation where you invest in long-term investments that hurt you as interest rates rise—especially long-term bonds.

RESOURCES

Davis/Zweig Bond Fund Timer, P.O. Box 360, Bellmore, NY 11710; 1-800-633-2252. A good bond-timing newsletter.

Forecasts & Strategies, Editor: Mark Skousen, Phillips Publishing, 7811 Montrose Road, Potomac, MD 20854; 1-800-722-9000. Mark Skousen is good at finding safe, high-yield funds and other unusual investment situations. He also provides a brief, but incisive commentary on markets.

Table 2.9. High-Performance Junk Bonds

	5-Year Total Annualized Return	Risk Level	Phone
Merrill Lynch High Income A	8.75%	Low	800-637-1022
Vanguard Fixed Income High Yield	6.50%	Low	800-662-7447
Kemper High Yield Fund	8.20%	High	800-621-1048
Fidelity Capital & Income Fund	5.50%	Very Low	800-544-8888
T. Rowe Price High Yield Fund	5.40%	Low	800-638-5660

IBC/Donoghue Inc., 290 Eliot Street, Box 91004, Ashland, MA 01721; 1-800-343-5413; in MA (508) 429-5930. IBC/Donoghue publishes the *IBC/Donoghue's Money Fund Report.*

Income & Safety, Institute for Econometric Research, 3471 N Federal Highway, Fort Lauderdale, FL 33306; 1-800-327-6720. This is a newsletter that rates money funds according to average maturity, volatility of their holdings, diversification, and disclosure to shareholders.

Merriman's Fund Exchange, Editor: Paul Merriman, 1200 Westlake Avenue North, Seattle, WA 98109; 1-800-423-4893. A newsletter that gives advice on trading bond funds and money market funds. Paul Merriman has also recently introduced a mutual fund that uses his bond fund timing system.

Profitable Investing, Editor: Richard Band, Phillips Publishing, Inc., 7811 Montrose Road, Potomac, MD 20854; 1-800-777-5005. Richard Band writes an extremely insightful newsletter.

Train Smith Investment Counsel, John Train, 667 Madison Ave., New York, NY 10021; (212) 888-7676. Train Smith is one of the nation's largest firms dealing only with private individuals. John Train has published 10 books on financial subjects. The most recent is *The New Money Masters,* which deals with the methods (such as compounding, and so on) used by the great investors to build their massive fortunes.

FEDERAL RESERVE BANKS

Walk-in addresses, phone numbers and mailing addresses of Federal Reserve Banks:

Atlanta, GA, 104 Marietta Street NW, P.O. Box 1731, Atlanta, GA 30303; (404) 521-8657.

Baltimore, MD, 502 South Sharp Street, P.O. Box 1378, Baltimore, MD 21203; (301) 576-3300.

Birmingham, AL, 1801 Fifth Ave. N, P.O. Box 10447, Birmingham, AL 35202; (205) 252-3141, Ext. 215 or 264.

Boston, MA, 600 Atlanta Ave., P.O. Box 2076, Boston, MA 02106; (617) 973-3805 or 3810.

Buffalo, NY, 160 Delaware Ave., P.O. Box 961, Buffalo, NY 14240; (716) 849-5046.

Charlotte, NC, 401 South Tryon Street, P.O. Box 30248, Charlotte, NC 28230; (704) 336-7100.

Chicago, IL, 230 South LaSalle Street, P.O. Box 834, Chicago, IL 60690; (312) 322-5369.

Cincinnati, OH, 150 East Fourth Street, P.O. Box 999, Cincinnati, OH 45201; (513) 721-4787, Ext. 334.

Cleveland, OH, 1455 East 6th Street, P.O. Box 6387, Cleveland, OH 44101; (216) 579-2490.

Dallas, TX, 400 South Akard Street, Securities Dept., Station K, Dallas, TX, 75222; (214) 651-6362.

Denver, CO, 1020 16th Street, P.O. Box 5228, Terminal Annex, Denver, CO 80217; (303) 572-2473 or 2470.

Detroit, MI, 160 West Fort Street, P.O. Box 1059, Detroit, MI 48231; (313) 963-0080 or (313) 964-6157.

El Paso, TX, 301 East Main Street, P.O. Box 100, El Paso, TX 79999; (915) 544-4730.

Houston, TX, 1701 San Jacinto Street, P.O. Box 2578, Houston, TX 78295; (713) 659-4433.

Jacksonville, FL, 515 Julia Street, P.O. Box 2499, Jacksonville, FL 32231-2499; (904) 632-4245.

Kansas City, MO, 925 Grand Ave., P.O. Box 440 Kansas City, MO 64198; (816) 881-2783 or 2109.

Little Rock, AR, 325 West Capital Ave., P.O. Box 1261, Little Rock, AR 72203; (501) 372-5451, Ext. 288.

Los Angeles, CA, 409 West Olympic Blvd., P.O. Box 2077, Terminal Annex, Los Angeles, CA 90051; (213) 683-8546.

Louisville, KY, 410 South 5th Street, P.O. Box 32710, Louisville, KY 40232; (502) 568-9236 or 9238.

Memphis, TN, 200 North Main Street, P.O. Box 407, Memphis, TN 38101; (901) 523-7171, Ext. 225 or 641.

Miami, FL, 9100 NW 36th Street, P.O. Box 520847, Miami, FL 33152; (305) 593-9923.

Minneapolis, MN, 250 Marquette Ave., Minneapolis, MN 55480; (612) 340-2075.

Nashville, TN, 301 8th Ave. N, Nashville, TN 37203; (615) 259-4006.

New Orleans, LA, 525 St. Charles Ave., P.O. Box 61630, New Orleans, LA 70161; (504) 593-3200, Ext. 3291.

New York, NY, 33 Liberty Street, Federal Reserve, P.O. Station, New York, NY 10045; (212) 791-6619, (212) 791-5823 (24-hour-recording).

Oklahoma City, OK, 226 Dean A. McGee Ave., P.O. Box 25129, Oklahoma City, OK 73125; (405) 235-1721, Ext. 182.

Omaha, NE, 2201 Farnam Street, Omaha, NE 68102; (402) 221-5633.

Philadelphia, PA, 10 Independence Mall, P.O. Box 90, Philadelphia, PA 19105; (215) 574-6680.

Pittsburgh, PA, 717 Grant Street, P.O. Box 867, Pittsburgh, PA 15230-0867; (412) 261-7988.

Portland, OR, 915 SW Stark Street, P.O. Box 3436, Portland, OR 97208; (503) 221-5921 or 5931.

Richmond, VA, 701 East Byrd Street, P.O. Box 27622, Richmond, VA 23261; (804) 643-1250.

Salt Lake City, UT, 120 South State Street, P.O. Box 30780, Salt Lake City, UT 84130; (801) 322-7911 or (801) 355-3131.

San Antonio, TX, 126 East Nueva Street, P.O. Box 1471, San Antonio, TX 78295; (512) 224-2141, Ext. 303 or 305.

San Francisco, CA, 101 Market Street, P.O. Box 7702, San Francisco, CA 94120; (415) 392-6640 or 6650.

Seattle, WA, 1015 Second Ave., P.O. Box 3567, Seattle, WA 98124; (206) 442-1650.

St. Louis, MO, 411 Locust Street, P.O. Box 442, St. Louis, MO 63166; (314) 444-8602.

— 3 —

Mutual Funds: The Ultimate Compounding Vehicle

"A study of economics usually reveals that the
best time to buy anything is last year."

Marty Allen

Mutual funds could be considered the ultimate compounding vehicle. Nowhere else has an investment vehicle taken more advantage of the principles of compounding and the use of reinvestment dividends to further enhance its returns.

Not all mutual funds have done well, but a few have performed remarkably. In this chapter we will show you:

- Eleven advantages mutual funds have over other investment vehicles,
- The advantages of a no-load fund versus a load fund,
- A hidden charge that *some* mutual funds charge that will dramatically affect your profits,
- A market-timing program that can boost the yield of even the best mutual funds by 125%,
- Another mutual fund program that has consistently yielded 20% per year,

• And *yield* and *safety* tips on mutual funds, managed accounts and telephone switch programs.

A mutual fund is an investment company that combines the investment dollars of many investors, its shareholders. This pool of investment dollars is then deposited in a diversified portfolio of securities—stocks, bonds or money market instruments. Each shareholder owns a proportionate share of the fund. Investors who invest $1,000 get the same rate of return as those who put in $10,000.

The first mutual fund was organized in Boston in 1924 and the first no-load fund, Scudder Income, was formed in 1928. Since then, mutual funds have enjoyed unhampered growth. By the end of 1991, there were more than 3,400 mutual funds, with assets of more than $900 billion.

ADVANTAGES OF MUTUAL FUNDS

Mutual funds have 11 distinct advantages over other investment vehicles:

1. *Ease of Investment:* Buying a fund is easy. With many funds you can open or add to your account via mail, telephone or bank wire. You can also arrange an electronic transfer from your checking account on predetermined dates.

2. *Affordability:* Each fund sets the minimum amount it takes to get into the fund. The best thing about mutual funds is that initial investments are very reasonable—most funds range from $250 to $1,000 minimums. Once you have purchased the minimum initial investment, you can usually buy subsequent shares for as little as $50.

3. *Diversification:* Since money is pooled, you can enjoy the same advantages usually available only to large investors. In other words, you have the ability to invest in a broad range of investments—a market basket of securities. The average fund is diversified with holdings in 200 to 300 issues. That makes owning mutual funds far safer than owning a handful of stocks or bonds.

4. *Dollar-Cost-Averaging:* Mutual funds can be purchased in small amounts at periodic intervals, making them ideal for dollar-cost-averaging. Do you remember our story about the "Rich Man, Poor Man"? The poor man was always buying at the wrong times. By dollar-cost-averaging, you invest a portion of income at regular levels without trying to guess the market highs and lows. It's a great way to protect you from the extremes of the market.

   For example: Let's assume you purchase $100 per month for six months:

	Amount Invested	**Cost/ Share**	**Shares Purchased**
Month 1	$100	$10	10.00
Month 2	$100	$9	11.11
Month 3	$100	$12	8.33
Month 4	$100	$13	7.69
Month 5	$100	$10	10.00
Month 6	$100	$8	12.50
Totals	$600		59.63

Your average cost per share is $10.06, even though you paid as high as $13 per share for some shares. (In Chapter 7, we will show you the tax advantages associated with dollar-cost-averaging as well.)

5. *Low Trading Costs:* Small investors may have to pay commission rates equal to several percent of the amount of their investment when buying or selling securities. Mutual funds buy and sell in large blocks and obtain lower trading costs. These costs are usually passed along to the shareholder via management fees.

6. *Professional Management:* Mutual fund managers are the best security pickers in the world. It's their chosen profession, so they are much more in tune with today's complex and volatile markets. They have access to the latest market information and are able to execute trades on the largest and most cost-effective scale.

    But remember: They are only "professional" if they generate a reasonable return on your investment.

7. *Retirement plans.* Most funds offer several accounts including Keoghs and IRAs.

8. *Reinvestment of Dividends:* The power of compounding can be magic. As shown in Chapter 2, by reinvesting your interest, or in the case of mutual funds, your dividends and capital gains, the results can be tremendous. Figure 3.1 shows the results of compound investing $10,000 at different rates of growth.

    And if you prefer, you can receive all your dividends in cash.

9. *Telephone Switching.* There are literally dozens of mutual funds for every market segment. Since most funds offer the telephone switching privilege, you can easily switch funds to capture the uptrends and dodge the

**Figure 3.1.   Mutual Funds: The Power of
Compound Growth**

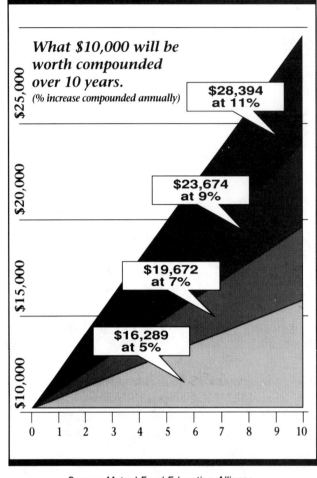

Source: Mutual Fund Education Alliance

downtrends. Many funds allow you to switch between their funds, usually at no charge.

10. *Liquidity:* Mutual funds are completely liquid. You can easily redeem your shares at any time by letter, bank wire or check. (Note: This is for open-end funds; see closed-end funds below.)

11. *Automatic Withdrawal Plans:* Many funds also allow investors to sell their shares gradually in an amount and frequency of their choosing, and will mail a check for the proceeds monthly or quarterly.

NO-LOAD VERSUS LOAD FUNDS

A *load* is the sales charge or commission charged to purchase shares of a mutual fund. Load funds charge commissions of up to 8.5%. So, for every $1,000 you pay into a fund with an 8.5% load, you actually invest only $915. This commission (which really amounts to 9.3% of the $915) goes to your broker and the brokerage firm.

With a *no-load* fund, all your money goes to work for you. As Figure 3.2 shows, the difference between a load and a no-load fund can make as much as a $2,205 difference in 10 years.

OTHER COSTS ASSOCIATED WITH MUTUAL FUND INVESTING

Besides determining whether a fund is a load or a no-load fund, you should read the prospectus for other charges that may be passed along to you:

Figure 3.2.   No-Load vs. Load Funds

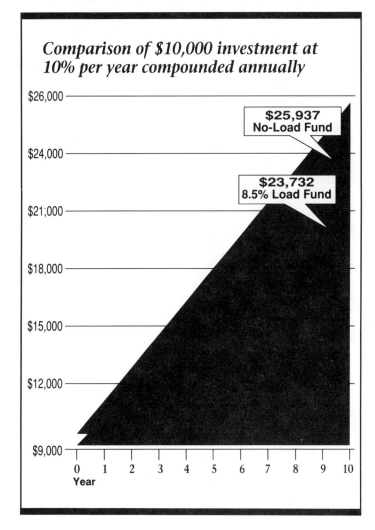

Source: Mutual Fund Education Alliance

1. *Redemption Fee.* A few funds may charge you a redemption fee (or sales charge) when you redeem shares. These charges can be as little as 1%, or up to 5.3% of the amount of the sale.

2. *Reloading Charge.* Nearly all funds automatically allow you to reinvest all your capital gain and income distributions into new shares at no sales charge. However, a few funds levy what is called "reloading" charges. The maximum permissible quoted reload charge is 7.25% of the total amount of investment.

3. *Transaction Costs.* As a fund buys and sells securities, it will incur brokerage commissions that are passed along to shareholders.

4. *Operating Expenses.* Day-to-day operating costs such as rent, telephone, employee salaries, and so on, may be passed along to the shareholders.

5. *Portfolio Management Fees.* These are payments to the portfolio manager of the fund. This amount usually ranges from 0.25% to 1.25% of the fund's assets per annum. Generally, the larger the fund, the lower the fee.

6. *12b-1 Charges.* The most controversial charges that some funds assess are 12b-1 fees (commonly referred to as "hidden loads"). Rather than levy sales charges on new investments, some funds take sales and promotion expenses out of the assets belonging to existing shareholders. In other words, a percentage (1.25% for example) is used to pay a commission to the salesman on all future sales of a fund. As a rule, 12b-1 fees vary from 0.25% to a high of 1.25%. The preceding table shows some of the higher maximum annual 12b-1 fees in effect as of mid-1991. Table 3.1 shows the highest 12b-1 fees among all funds.

YIELD TIP

Watch Out for Hidden Loads

The problem with hidden loads or 12b-1 fees is that, depending on the performance of the fund, you could incur charges that exceed your initial investment. Here's an example provided by Norman Fosback, editor of *Mutual Fund Forecaster* (3471 N. Federal Highway, Fort Lauderdale, FL 33306; 1-800-327-6720):

"A mutual fund implemented a 12b-1 Plan and ostensibly became a no-load fund. Under this plan, all shareholders will pay up to 1.25% of their investments on an annual basis. The worst part of this plan is that existing shareholders, in addition to having paid a sales charge (when the fund was a load fund) are also forced to pay the 12b-1 charge on their investments. This means that investors who paid the fund a 9.25% sales charge in the pre-no-load days will have their investments reduced by a further sales charge of up to the 1.25% per year as long as they remain in the fund."

Table 3.1. Highest 12b-1 Fees Among All Funds

Berger - One Hundred One	1.00%	Bull & Bear Funds	1.00%
Composite Growth	1.00%	Dean Witter Funds	1.00%
IDS Strategy Aggressive	1.00%	IDS Strategy Equity	1.00%
Kaufmann	1.00%	Kemper Inv Pt-Equity	1.25%
Kemper Inv Pt-Total	1.25%	Keystone Funds	1.25%
Legg Mason Value Trust	1.00%	Merrill Lynch Balanced B	1.00%
Merrill Lynch Fd Tomorrw B	1.00%	Merrill Lynch GR Inv & Ret	1.00%
PaineWebber Asset B	1.00%	Prudential Funds	1.00%
Rightime	1.20%	Royce-Value	1.00%
Selected American Shares	1.00%	Selected Special Shares	1.00%
Shearson Funds (i)	0.75% to 1.00%	Southeastern Growth	1.00%
SunAmerica-Capital Apprec	1.25%	Thomson-Growth B	1.00%
Wood Struthers-Winthrop	1.00%		

Gold & Hard Asset Funds

Bull & Bear Gold Investors	1.00%	Keystone Precious Metals	1.25%
Shearson Port Prec Metals	1.00%		

International Funds

Dean Witter Worldwide Inv	1.00%	Keystone International	1.25%
Shearson Global	1.00%		

(i) Shearson's Appreciation, Fundamental Value and Small Capital funds have no 12b-1 fees.

Source: Information compiled from Mutual Fund Forecaster by Communique Marketing Associates, Inc.

Mutual Fund Forecaster calculated the amount that shareholders could lose over a 10-year period. The results are shown in Table 3.2 and are based on various performance scenarios.

Compare these figures to a load fund that charges 9.25%, in which you would pay only $92.50 over the lifetime of the fund for every $1,000 invested.

EXPENSE RATIO

A common phrase used in mutual funds is the *expense ratio*. This is the ratio of total expenses to the net assets of the fund. The expenses include each of the six associated expenses listed above.

Table 3.2. Potential Loss for Mutual Fund Shareholders Over a 10-year Period

Performance	Change of Initial $1,000 Investment Before Loads	Net Value After All Loads	Total Cost of Loads
Flat	$1,000 to $1,000	$882	$118
Good	$1,000 to $5,000	$4,409	$591
Super	$1,000 to $10,000	$8,818	$1,182

UNDERSTAND WHAT YOU ARE DOING

Before you invest in any fund, order (and read) the prospectus. Though the formats vary, a prospectus will include a brief description of the fund's investment objectives, minimum investment requirements, and the identification of all fees and charges in a standardized table. In addition SEC rules require that a hypothetical example is included on how a $1,000 investment would be affected by expenses over one, three, five and 10 years, assuming a 5% rate of return.

Some excellent sources of information on mutual fund investing are:

Investment Company Institute, 1600 M Street NW, Suite 600, Washington, DC 20036; (202) 293-7700. See the end of the chapter for a list of available brochures.

Mutual Fund Education Alliance, 1900 Erie Street, Suite 120, Kansas City, MO 64116; (816) 471-1454. They publish an excellent *Investor's Guide to Low Cost Mutual Funds.* It costs $5 and lists the no-load funds by fund type. See page 55 for a sample page.

And finally, when you research mutual funds, look at their performance over time. Do not rely simply on a one-year performance. A fund may do exceptionally well in certain market conditions (in the short term), but do miserably over the longer term.

CLOSED-END VERSUS OPEN-END FUNDS

The typical mutual fund is an open-end fund. That means the fund can sell as many shares as an investor wants to buy.

Closed-end (or publicly traded) funds amount to only a small fraction of the mutual funds in existence. They are similar to stocks because they only have a limited number of shares available for trading. You will not find these funds listed in the mutual funds tables, but rather in the stock tables. As a result, you will find that closed-end funds are not as liquid as open-end funds.

Caveat: Though there are many excellent closed-end mutual funds, you need to be careful. Some struggling funds may trade at a discount in hopes that it will convert to profit.

YIELD TIP

The Top Mutual Fund for the '90s Earning 37% in 1991

James Stack, editor of *InvesTech Market Analyst* (2472 Birch Glen, White-fish, MT 59937-3349; (406) 862-7777), prefers small-to-middle capital stock funds for the 1990s. According to a study by Ibbotson Associates, small capital stocks (between 1961 and 1983) outperformed large blue chip stocks 18 out of 23 years—up 3,605.8% for small stocks, compared to 598.1% for blue chips. Since 1984, however, the typical small stock has gained only 19% as compared to 140% for the average blue chip stock. According to Stack, "Safety, higher yields, and blue chip status is what investors have sought since 1984. That same migration is also true of many professional fund managers. As a result, these big-capitalization stocks have outperformed smaller stocks in six of the past seven years. But histori-cally, the migration toward large capital stocks runs in cycles, and the year-end 1991 stock performance suggests a solid move toward the small to middle capital stocks for the '90s."

Whether a migration toward small-capital stocks occurs or not, Stack strongly recommends Fidelity's OTC Portfolio. This fund invests primarily in securities traded on the over-the-counter (OTC) market. Ordinarily, OTC securities will account for at least 65% of the fund's total asset value, and the fund may invest up to 30% in foreign securities as well.

While small stocks gained a return of only 19% during the past seven years, Fidelity OTC has gained a hefty five-year return of 115%. The year-to-date 1991 return (as of mid-December) was 37%.

For more information, contact: Fidelity OTC Fund (Fidelity Investments, General Distribution Corporation, 82 Devonshire Street, Boston, MA 02109; 1-800-544-8888).

MUTUAL FUNDS THAT INVEST IN CASH EQUIVALENTS

Every mutual fund follows specific investment objectives. By carefully exam-ining your investment goals, you can choose a fund to match. As with any invest-ment, results are never guaranteed; and the higher the yield, most likely, the higher the risk.

Generally, mutual funds fall into the following categories: Aggressive growth, growth, growth and income, income (which includes equity income, fixed income and balanced funds), municipal bond, money market, and specialty funds (i.e., biotech, utilities, precious metals, or international and country funds).

However, for the purpose of this book, we will discuss only mutual funds that invest in cash equivalents:

Corporate Bond Funds seek a high level of income by buying bonds of corporations for most of their portfolio. However, they also may hold U.S. Treasury bonds or bonds issued by a federal agency.

Flexible Portfolio Funds may be 100% in stocks, bonds, money market instruments, or a combination of all three, depending on market conditions.

Ginnie Mae Funds invest in mortgage debt backed by the Government National Mortgage Association (GNMA).

Global Bond Funds invest in debt instruments of governments and companies worldwide.

Global Equity Funds and *International Funds* invest in securities traded worldwide. In times healthier for the U.S. dollar, we would not regard these as cash equivalents. But these days, by investing in an overseas stock or government instrument, you are investing in the currency as well. And in the last few years, all major currencies have been strong against the U.S. dollar.

(See Chapter 4 for specific recommendations in this category.)

High-Yield Bond Funds keep at least two-thirds of their portfolios in corporate bonds of Baa or lower (Moody's) or BBB (Standard & Poor's). They are almost, but not quite, junk bond funds.

Income Bond Funds always invest in a mix of corporate and government bonds.

Long-Term Municipal Bond Funds invest in bonds issued by states and municipalities. In most cases, income earned on these funds is not taxed at the federal level, but may be taxed on state and local levels. Check with your tax advisor for whether these funds would be a good tax-advantaged investment for you. These are usually multistate investments, but there are funds that specialize in the securities of just one state. (See Chapter 7 for more information on municipal funds and specific recommendations.)

Short-Term Municipal Bond Funds invest in municipal securities of shorter-term maturities. They are also known as tax-exempt money market funds. Like long-term municipal funds, there are multistate and single-state funds.

U.S. Government Income Funds. These funds invest in several different government securities, including U.S. Treasury bonds, federally guaranteed mortgage-backed securities, and other government notes.

A Treasury bond mutual fund is constantly buying and selling its portfolio to spread maturity dates. As it brings new, lower-yielding bonds into its portfolio, your payments will go down.

Table 3.3 shows you the type of mutual fund you should invest in.

SPECIFIC FUND RECOMMENDATIONS
Benham Capital Management Group

The Benham Group began in 1972 when Jim Benham opened the first money market fund designed for the individual investor.

The Benham Group offers:

GNMA Income Fund: Invests in GNMA (Ginnie Mae) certificates guaranteed by the full faith and credit of the U.S. government.

Table 3.3. Selecting a Mutual Fund

If Your Basic Objective Is	You Want The Following Fund Type	These Funds Invest Primarily In	General Characteristics		
			Potential Capital Appreciation	Potential Current Income	Stability of Principal
Maximum Capital Growth	Aggressive Growth	Common Stocks with potential for very rapid growth. May employ certain aggressive strategies.	Very High	Very Low	Low to Very Low
High Capital Growth	Growth, Specialty	Common Stocks with long-term growth potential.	High to Very High	Very Low	Low
Current Income & Capital Growth	Growth & Income	Common stocks with potential for high dividends and capital appreciation.	Moderate	Moderate	Low to Moderate
High Current Income	Fixed Income, Equity Income	Both high-dividend-paying stocks and bonds.	Very Low	High to Very High	Low to Moderate
Current Income & Protection of Principal	General Money Market Funds	Money market instruments.	None	Moderate to High	Very High
Tax-Free Income & Protection of Principal	Tax-Exempt Money Market	Short-term municipal notes and bonds.	None	Moderate to High	Very High
Current Income & Maximum Safety of Principal	U.S. Government Money Market	U.S. Treasury and agency issues guaranteed by the U.S. government.	None	Moderate to High	Very High
Tax-Exempt Income	Municipal Bonds, Double & Triple Tax-Exempt	A broad range of municipal bonds.	Low to Moderate	Moderate to High	Moderate

Source: Mutual Fund Education Alliance

Treasury Note Fund: Invests exclusively in U.S. Treasury securities for high yields and longer maturities.

Both funds have $1,000 initial minimum investments with no sales or 12b-1 fees.

For more information contact: Benham Capital Management Group, 1665 Charleston Road, Mountain View, CA 94043; 1-800-472-3389.

Fidelity Family of Funds

Fidelity started its first fund, Fidelity Puritan Fund, in 1946. In 1974, Fidelity Daily Income Trust was the first money market fund to offer check writing. In 1989, with the introduction of its Spartan Funds, it offered a new approach to high yields by reducing fund operating expenses and letting individual shareholders pay only for the service they use.

Fidelity now offers a Spartan Fund with no sales charge in the following funds:

Cash Reserves Money Market Fund: Seeks to obtain as high a level of current income as is consistent with the preservation of capital and liquidity by investing in money market instruments.

U.S. Government Reserves Money Market Fund: Invests only in obligations issued or guaranteed as to principal and interest by the U.S. government, its agencies or instrumentalities, and in repurchase agreements secured by these obligations.

Fidelity's Tax-Free Bond Funds: Fidelity has five municipal bond funds, each of which seeks to provide as high a level of income as possible, free from federal income taxes. They include: Fidelity Aggressive Tax-Free Portfolio, High Yield Tax-Free Portfolio, Municipal Bond Portfolio, Insured Tax-Free Portfolio, and Limited Term Municipals. The titles describe their objectives (e.g., Aggressive Tax-Free Portfolio seeks high-yield, lower-quality municipal bonds).

As the Spartan name implies, these are no-load funds with $2,500 minimum initial investment.

For more information contact: Fidelity Investments, General Distribution Corporation, 82 Devonshire Street, Boston, MA 02109; 1-800-544-8888.

Neuberger and Berman Income Funds

Neuberger and Berman was established in 1939 as a stock exchange firm and now has over $7 billion under management. Their income funds are as follows:

Government Money Fund: A money market fund that invests only in U.S. Treasuries (no repurchase agreements). This not only makes the fund ultra-safe, but since many state and local governments that do not tax dividend income from U.S. government securities do tax dividend income from repurchase agreements, the tax advantage of this fund is also a plus.

Cash Reserves: Invests in diversified high-quality money market instruments and seeks to maintain a constant $1 net asset value.

Ultra-Short Bond Fund: Invests in a diversified, high-quality portfolio combining the investment features of money market instruments and short-term bonds.

Limited-Maturity Bond Fund: Seeks high yield at reduced risk by investing in debt instruments with maturities of 5½ years or less.

Municipal Money Fund: Invests only in high-quality, short-term tax-exempt municipal securities.

Municipal Securities Trust: Seeks high, tax-free yields by investing in short- to intermediate-term municipal securities. The average maturity in this fund is 10 years or less.

The Limited-Maturity Bond Fund and Municipal Securities Trust require a minimum initial investment of $5,000. The balance of the funds require a $2,000 investment. There are no sales, redemption or 12b-1 charges.

For more information contact: Neuberger and Berman, 342 Madison Avenue, New York, NY 10173; 1-800-877-9700.

Templeton Funds

The Templeton's approach to money management has been used very successfully for the last 49 years. These funds are not newcomers of the 1980s. They began in an age of high growth, but have survived the chaotic 1960s and the inflationary 1970s, and generally have performed superbly.

Their philosophy is summed up by founder John M. Templeton:

"We are essentially long-range investors and we don't think it pays to play the market. When we buy a stock we have no idea whether we will own it for one month or 20 years, but it averages out to about five years."

The Templeton Funds that are relevant to this book are:

Templeton Income Fund: Seeks current income with capital appreciation and growth of income primarily through debt securities of companies, governments and government agencies of various nations throughout the world, and in dividend-paying equities.

Templeton Tax-Free Money Fund: Seeks current income exempt from regular federal income tax, stability of principal, and liquidity by investing in high-quality municipal securities and maturities not exceeding one year.

Templeton Money Fund: Objectives are current income, stability of principal, and liquidity by investing in short-term, high-grade money market instruments.

Templeton Insured Tax-Free Fund: Seeks the highest level of income exempt from regular federal income tax, liquidity, and safety of principal by investing in a diversified portfolio of insured municipal securities.

Except for the Insured Tax-Free Fund (which requires a minimum investment of $2,500), the above Templeton Funds require a minimum initial investment of $500. These are load funds not to exceed 4.5% of the offering price.

For more information or to receive a prospectus contact: Templeton Funds Distributor, Inc., 700 Central Avenue, St. Petersburg, FL 33701; 1-800-237-0738.

Blackstone Income Trust

Blackstone Income Trust: This closed-end bond fund is made up of 51% mortgage pass-throughs, 3% money markets, 12% multiple-class mortgage pass-throughs, 11% stripped mortgage-backed securities and 23% CMO residuals. It offers a higher proportion of AAA credit-quality assets than many closed-end bond funds.

If you want additional information on this fund, contact:
Pru-Bache at (908) 417-7666 for a copy of the annual or semi-annual report, or
Andy Clipper, Bear Stearns & Company, Inc., 245 Park Avenue, New York, NY 10167; (212) 272-7215.

MANAGED ACCOUNTS

Managed accounts are recommended only for large investors. If you are a smaller investor, you are better off sticking with mutual funds. For those who have sufficient funds, the rewards can be tremendous.

For managed accounts, we recommend the following:

Merriman Investment Management Company

Shearson Lehman Brothers

Telephone Switch Newsletter

Merriman Investment Management Company

Merriman offers a family of internally timed mutual funds that have had tremendous success using a unique market-timing concept. This idea, developed by Paul A. Merriman, a noted market-timing technician, is intended to reduce the risks of declining market segments and to improve the overall returns.

Merriman Market-Timing. According to Merriman, the buy-and-hold concept will beat market-timing in *most* years, because the market goes up most of the time. But over the long haul, good timing can beat buy-and-hold strategies, with considerably less risk, even if you use the best funds.

For example: Suppose you put $10,000 into Fidelity Magellan back in 1970, and reinvested all dividends and capital gains. Your investment would have been worth an impressive $342,000 by 1989. Yet your nest egg could have soared to $770,000 by switching back and forth from Magellan to 90-day U.S. Treasury bills, using Merriman's timing system. That is an increased return of 125%.

You can see how much better Fidelity Magellan did with market timing in Table 3.4.

Table 3.4. Fidelity Magellan: Even Better with Timing

Year	Buy/Hold		Market Timing	
1970	−15.7%	$8,430	24.5%	$12,450
1971	35.1	11,389	31.7	16,397
1972	30.1	14,817	28.9	21,135
1973	−42.1	8,579	−7.5	19,550
1974	−28.3	6,151	7.9	21,094
1975	44.4	8,882	23.5	26,051
1976	35.5	12,035	32.4	34,492
1977	16.3	13,997	4.4	36,010
1978	31.7	18,434	26.4	45,517
1979	51.7	27,964	26.9	57,761
1980	69.9	47,511	74.3	100,677
1981	16.4	55,303	20.4	121,215
1982	48.1	81,904	43.1	173,459
1983	38.6	113,519	35.8	235,557
1984	2.0	115,789	10.3	259,819
1985	43.1	165,694	40.5	365,046
1986	23.7	204,963	16.5	425,279
1987	1.0	207,013	23.8	526,495
1988	22.7	254,005	8.7	572,300
1989	34.6	341,891	34.6	770,316
1990	−4.6	326,164	−3.3	744,896

This performance reflects actual results since mid-1983, when Merriman started managing funds. Earlier results are hypothetical, using the same timing model. Also, these are pretax profits. Because capital gains taxes are relatively high with market timing, it is particularly suitable in a tax-deferred account.

Source: Executive Wealth Advisory

The minimum investment is $1,000 and there are no sales loads, redemption fees or 12b-1 fees.

Managed Margin Program (MMP). Using a proprietary timing model developed by Stan Lipstadt (PSM Investors, Inc.) it may be possible to achieve an annualized 25% compound rate of return. That, in effect, would double your money every 37 months. Here's how the model works:

When the model generates a buy signal, Merriman account managers purchase mutual funds on a 50% margin basis (a $10,000 account would purchase $20,000 worth of mutual fund shares). On the next sell signal, the mutual fund shares would be liquidated and moved to a money market account, anticipating the next buy signal.

Though the 13+ year performance resulted in exceptional returns, there were many losing periods that some investors may find unacceptable. The ideal MMP investor should have a long-term growth objective and the ability to withstand short-term losses. The minimum investment for this program is $20,000; but because it is aggressive in nature, no more than 10% of an investor's portfolio should be invested in this program.

For more information on either market-timing or MMP, contact: Merriman Investment Management Company, 1200 Westlake Avenue North, Suite 700, Seattle, WA 98109-3530; 1-800-423-4893. Ask for either Paul or Jeff Merriman.

Shearson Lehman Brothers

Other investment advisors we recommend for managed accounts are Martin Truax, Ron Miller and C. Taylor Walet, Jr. of Shearson Lehman Brothers.

They have two recommendations:

Robinson-Humphrey Company Best Buys, a division of Shearson Lehman Brothers, Inc. For the seven-year period ending June 30, 1991, the results have been an amazing 42% per year. An investment of $100,000 in July 1984, would have grown to $1,280,000 by June 30, 1991. That is an appreciation of 1,180% versus the S&P performance of 211%–over five times better.

Of course, past performance is not a guarantee of further results, but based on those results, it is worth consideration. The minimum investment is $50,000. The account is a no-load with a 0.75% management fee charged quarterly.

Equity Income Account. This managed account is for investors who are looking for high income *now,* but with long-term capital growth potential. The dividend yield is between 8% and 8.5% and realized total returns of over 26% in the first six months of 1991. The minimum investment is $50,000.

For more information on these Shearson recommendations, contact: Martin Truax or Ron Miller, 400 Perimeter Center Terrace NE, Suite 290, Atlanta, GA 30346; 1-800-825-7171; or C. Taylor Walet, Jr., 909 Poyydras, Suite 1600, New Orleans, LA 70112; 1-800-227-6121.

Telephone Switch Newsletter

Doug Fabian, President and Co-Editor of *Telephone Switch Newsletter,* recommends the Fabian Compounding Plan that was originally developed by his father, Dick Fabian. Often called the wealth-building plan, this plan is based on a simple mathematical formula that scientifically identifies market trends. This allows you to switch in and out of funds to take advantage of maximum gains, but limit your losses as well.

Although past performance is no guarantee of future results, so far they have remained closely on the target of 20% since the plan's inception in April 1977. For example, based on past performance, a monthly contribution of $1,000 could grow to $98,671 in five years, $344,061 in 10 years and $2,472,202 in 20 years.

To use Table 3.5, first decide the monthly, yearly, or lump sum contributions you can make to work for your goal. Then, follow these amounts across horizontally to see what the future values of your contributions will be in 5, 10, 15 years or longer.

If you would like more information (or to subscribe to the newsletter) contact: *Telephone Switch Newsletter,* P.O. Box 2538, Huntington Beach, CA 92747; 1-800-950-8765.

RESOURCES

Mutual Fund Forecaster, Editor: Norman G. Fosback. This newsletter is also published by the Institute for Econometric Research. (See Resources: Chapter 4.) It provides monthly profit projections and risk ratings on many mutual funds.

InvesTech Market Analyst, Editor: James Stack, 2472 Birch Glen, Whitefish, MT 59937-3349; (406) 862-7777. Stack publishes an excellent, technically based, mutual fund newsletter.

Investment Company Institute, 1600 M Street NW, Suite 600, Washington, DC 20036; (202) 293-7700. Call or write for a complete-catalog of their publications and audiovisual materials on mutual funds. One of the most helpful brochures they offer is *An Investor's Guide To Reading The Mutual Fund Prospectus.*

Mutual Fund Education Alliance, 1900 Erie Street, Suite 120, Kansas City, MO 64116; (816) 471-1454. They have an excellent *Investor's Guide to Low Cost Mutual Funds.* It costs $5 and is printed twice each year. See the next page for a sample of what they offer. In addition, they offer a mutual fund investor starter kit for $10 or an *Investor Series Module* (includes a book with audio tape) for $12.50.

Mutual Fund Investing, Editor: Jay Schabacker, Phillips Publishing, 7811 Montrose Road, Potomac, MD 20854; 1-800-722-9000. Jay Schabacker has one of the best newsletters in the business. He also operates managed accounts and can be reached at 1-800-346-0138.

National Institute of Business Management, Inc., 1328 Broadway, New York, NY 10001; 1-800-543-2054. They publish *Winning Mutual Fund Strategies for Uncertain Times,* an excellent guide to mutual funds. It was written by Sheldon Jacobs and sells for $6.95. They also publish an investment newslet-

Table 3.5. 20% Annualized Compounded Growth Table

Future Values

Monthly Deposits	5 Years	10 Years	15 Years	20 Years	25 Years
$ 100	$ 9,867	$34,406	$95,432	$247,201	$624,639
200	19,734	68,812	190,865	494,402	1,249,278
300	29,601	103,218	286,298	741,604	1,873,918
400	39,468	137,624	381,730	988,805	2,498,557
500	49,335	172,030	477,163	1,236,100	3,123,196
1,000	98,671	344,061	954,327	2,472,201	6,246,392

Yearly Deposits	5 Years	10 Years	15 Years	20 Years	25 Years
$ 1,000	$8,929	$31,150	$86,442	$224,025	$606,377
2,000	17,859	62,360	172,884	448,051	1,132,755
3,000	26,789	93,451	259,326	672,077	1,699,132
4,000	35,719	124,601	345,768	896,102	2,265,510
5,000	44,649	155,752	432,210	1,120,128	2,831,886
10,000	89,299	311,504	864,421	2,240,256	5,663,772

Large Sum Deposits	5 Years	10 Years	15 Years	20 Years	25 Years
$10,000	$24,880	$61,910	$154,070	$383,370	$953,962
20,000	49,766	123,834	308,140	766,752	1,907,924
30,000	74,649	185,752	462,210	1,150,128	2,861,886
40,000	99,532	247,669	616,280	1,533,504	3,815,849
50,000	124,410	309,580	770,350	1,916,880	4,769,811
100,000	248,800	619,100	1,540,700	3,833,700	9,539,622

Note: This table is provided to help you set a personal financial goal and is not a guarantee of your investment results.

The future values represent tax-deferred growth (as with an IRA, Keogh, or variable annuity) or growth with income taxes paid separately.

Source: Telephone Switch Newsletter

ter, *Executive Wealth Advisory,* edited by Philip Springer (212) 971-3300. It covers no-load funds, plus tax tips and other investment-related information.

The No-Load Fund Investor, Editor: Sheldon Jacobs, P.O. Box 283, Hastings-on-Hudson, NY 10706; (914) 693-7420. This newsletter covers 550 no-load and low-load mutual funds, and provides fund recommendations and market-timing.

Paul Merriman's Fund Exchange, Editor: Paul Merriman, Merriman Investment Management Company, 1200 Westlake Avenue North, Suite 700, Seattle, WA 98109-3530; 1-800-423-4893. For information on managed margin or timing accounts, contact either Paul A. or Jeff Merriman. Paul's newsletter gives advice on trading bond funds and money market funds.

Forecasts & Strategies, Editor: Mark Skousen, 7811 Montrose Road, Potomac, MD 20854; 1-800-722-9000. Mark Skousen is good at finding safe, high-yield funds and other unusual investment situations. He also provides a brief, but incisive commentary on markets.

Telephone Switch Newsletter, Co-Editor: Doug Fabian, P.O. Box 2538, Huntington Beach, CA 92747; 1-800-950-8765. An excellent newsletter that advises how to invest in no-load mutual funds, following a mathematical trading model that predicts market cycles.

Standard & Poor's/Lipper Mutual Fund Profiles. This publication is available in most libraries. It provides monthly profiles, rankings and volatility ratings of over 750 mutual funds.

4

Foreign Currency Investments Available in the United States

"The new electronic interdependence recreates
the world in the image of a global village."

Marshall McLuhan

F oreign currency equivalents offer you the opportunity to enhance return
potential and provide currency diversification. They protect you against the
weakness of the U.S. dollar, plus they give you the opportunity to take
advantage of the opening of once-communist nations to trade, free enterprise,
and democracy. The ideal ways for you to exploit today's overseas markets are
discussed in this chapter. Among them:

- How to invest in the foreign currency markets,
- A list of U.S. banks that offer foreign currency accounts with returns as
  high as 12.6%,
- How to keep emergency cash handy and still collect *real* returns of 10% or
  more,
- A *triple-play* opportunity that could earn you 20% or more in 1992,

- How to earn 9.9% virtually risk-free, and
- The top global income and foreign currency funds for 1992.

William Stack, the Chief Investment Officer for Lexington Management Corporation, believes a global perspective will be the key ingredient for successful investing in the 1990s:

"The savvy investor of the '90s will capitalize on attractive investment opportunities wherever they may be found throughout the world.

"As companies become more globalized in their operation and the world's markets become more interconnected, a global approach to investing will become a way of life for investors seeking growth of capital. Opportunities for superior returns in overseas markets may be achieved by exploiting the 'open windows of inefficiency' in the world's markets today."

While overseas markets are offering tremendous opportunities, here at home we are seeing declining strength in our economy and the once-strong U.S. dollar.

You may not realize it, but over the past three years, your global purchasing power has declined approximately 50% to 60%.

That may be hard to believe, especially if you earned generous profits from your investment portfolio in recent years. But the fact remains that the dollar's value has plummeted against major world currencies since 1985. Granted, the Gulf War gave the dollar some support (approximately a 17% gain) in early 1991, but this gain quickly disappeared.

As the Fed continues its balancing act between a weak economy and inflation, the dollar will continue to be volatile. It is, therefore, prudent to diversify into nondollar-denominated investments.

WHAT MAKES THE DOLLAR RISE AND FALL?

It is estimated that over $675 billion exchanges hands in the world's currency markets per day. Twenty-four hours a day, the world's currency traders exchange one currency for another in order to trade goods internationally and to search for profits from fluctuating currency markets.

Originally, in the 19th century, the exchange rate (the price of one currency in terms of another) was tied to the "old standard." But shortly after World War II, the dollar was established as the exchange benchmark.

Thus, the U.S. dollar rises and falls on the basis of foreign currency traders' opinions of world interest rates, the U.S. economy, and global trade (mainly oil) transacted in U.S. dollars.

Interest rates are one of the biggest factors. When U.S. interest rates are higher than those available in other countries, foreign investors buy U.S. government securities. This buying of U.S. securities tends to lift the value of the dollar.

A rise or fall in the dollar is also an indication of currency traders' opinions of the U.S. economy. They sell the dollar when the economy looks weak and buy when it looks strong.

Finally, the dollar has been a refuge for investors when world events look threatening. The relative strength and safety of the U.S. government makes the dollar appealing when the world is in turmoil.

In recent years, though the dollar remains the principal currency, more countries have looked to other stronger currencies as their basis for comparison. It comes as no surprise that the dollar's value has diminished worldwide, over the years.

LOST PROFITS

Not only is the eroding value of the U.S. dollar robbing you of purchasing power, but it is robbing you of profits as well.

The United States is an aging and maturing economy. Because of this fact, many economists see continued slow growth. In contrast, some overseas markets are offering up to three and four times the U.S. growth rate. The Pacific Basin is an excellent example.

If you have been sitting in U.S. dollars, the value of each individual dollar has diminished against certain foreign currencies. And you have most likely earned several percentage points less in interest-rate income besides.

As indicated by Tables 4.1, 4.2, and 4.3, interest rates in several currencies have been far higher than in the U.S. dollar.

So the question is: Can you really afford to hold *only* U.S. dollars?

Table 4.1. Key International Rates

	3-month interbank	6-month interbank	Discount rate	Prime equivalent
United States	5.06	5.06	4.50	7.50
Japan	6.25	6.06	5.50	7.00
Canada	7.56	7.56	7.73	8.50
U.K.	10.56	10.43	9.75	10.50
Germany	9.43	9.43	7.50	11.50
Switzerland	8.00	8.00	7.00	10.00
France	9.75	9.68	9.00	10.00
Italy	11.50	11.50	11.50	12.50

As of 11/91

Available in American Banker, WSJ, Euromoney Magazine

Table 4.2. International Growth and Inflation Estimates

Economic Growth

(Yearly Averages)	1989	1990	1991E	1992E
United States	+2.5%	+1.0%	−0.3%	+2.7%
Japan	+4.7	+5.7	+4.1	+3.0
United Kingdom	+2.2	+0.8	−2.0	+2.0
West Germany	+3.8	+4.7	+3.2	+1.6
France	+3.9	+2.8	+1.0	+2.0
Switzerland	+3.9	+2.2	−0.6	+1.2
Netherlands	+4.1	+3.5	+2.0	+1.7
Spain	+4.8	+3.7	+2.8	+3.1
Italy	+3.2	+2.0	+0.8	+2.1
Canada	+2.3	+0.2	−0.8	+3.1

Consumer Price Index

(Yearly Averages)	1989	1990	1991E	1992E
United States	+4.8%	+5.4%	+4.3%	+3.7%
Japan	+2.3	+3.0	+3.2	+2.3
United Kingdom	+7.8	+9.5	+5.8	+4.2
West Germany	+2.8	+2.7	+3.5	+4.0
France	+3.5	+3.4	+3.0	+3.0
Switzerland	+3.2	+5.4	+5.8	+4.1
Netherlands	+1.1	+2.4	+3.7	+3.7
Spain	+6.8	+6.7	+5.9	+5.4
Italy	+6.6	+6.1	+6.4	+5.7
Canada	+5.0	+4.8	+5.9	+3.6

Source: Investment Strategy, Pictet & Cie Banquiers, Geneve, November 1991

INVESTING IN FOREIGN CURRENCIES WITHOUT EVER LEAVING THE UNITED STATES

Investing in foreign currencies offers you two ways to profit: The availability of high yields in many foreign currency markets, and the potential of capital gains as currencies fluctuate in value—which we touched on earlier. So, why are so many American investors hesitant to venture into the overseas markets?

Table 4.3. World Interest Rates Government 10 years—End of December

	1989	1990	Current level	March 1992E
ECU	9.60%	10.09%	8.85%	8.60%
United States	7.93	8.07	7.62	8.00
Japan	5.75	7.09	5.85	5.50
United Kingdom	10.70	11.18	9.86	9.25
Germany	7.15	9.00	8.35	8.20
France	8.92	10.00	8.76	8.45
Switzerland	4.67	6.60	6.45	6.00
Netherlands	8.26	8.91	8.66	8.55
Denmark	10.40	10.58	8.92	8.60
Spain	14.50	14.50	11.40	10.90
Italy	14.02	13.05	12.60	12.00
Australia	13.00	12.00	10.02	10.00
Canada	9.50	10.10	9.10	9.00

Source: Investment Strategy, Pictet & Cie Banquiers, Geneve, November 1991

LIKE BUYING A FOREIGN CAR . . .

Noted market analyst David Fuller makes the following observation:

"Do you hold foreign currency positions? If not, why not? This is the world's largest market area. Indeed, the word 'foreign' should not be used any more than you would ask for a 'foreign' car when what you want is a BMW. Americans ask for foreign consumer goods by name, without even thinking about their being foreign, but suggest that they put their cash into a D-Mark or a Yen account, and they get scared."

Opening a yen account should be emotionally no different than buying Sony electronic equipment—or a D-mark account than buying a Mercedes or a Volkswagen.

But logical or not, the fear of foreign money is still in the minds of many investors. At least part of this fear is that many people equate investing in foreign currencies with having to open an account abroad, and they suspect that foreigners are not to be trusted.

HIGHER REAL YIELDS

Rich rewards in the currency markets are abundant, if you can find them. For example, compare the various government 10-year rates in the accompanying chart.

Figure 4.1 shows how much you would have made on your money if you had invested in a global short-term money market portfolio versus U.S. dollar CDs. A $10,000 investment in short-term global bonds in 1983 would have grown to $23,916 by September 1990, while an equal investment in the three-month U.S. CDs grew to $17,396 in the same seven-year period. Both cases assume reinvestment of interest payments. The average annual return for the short-term global bond portfolio was 13.79%, compared with an average return for the U.S. dollar CD investment of 8.55%.

HOW TO INVEST IN FOREIGN CURRENCIES

There are now many ways you can invest in foreign hard currency equivalents *in the United States.* You can switch individual currencies, make deposits and withdrawals, or conduct any other transaction with the convenience of a domestic phone call.

(It also means that, in many foreign currency deposits, *your money is insured by the FDIC.*)

Or, you can buy into the ever-growing number of currency funds or managed currency accounts. Currency funds, for example, offer the small investor simple and efficient ways to enter the world's major currency markets while limiting your risk.

Managed currency portfolio accounts offer the large investor a basket of cur-

Figure 4.1. Composite Global Money Market Portfolio vs. U.S. Dollar CDs

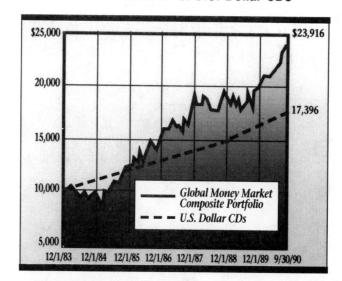

Source: Salomon Brothers International Money Market Performance Indices, Mitchell Hutchins Asset Management Inc. and PaineWebber

rencies. These accounts attempt to maximize the U.S. dollar value of the portfolio's holdings while carefully managing the overall currency exposure for the investor.

ADVANTAGES OF FOREIGN CURRENCY BANK ACCOUNTS

The advantages of foreign currency investments (as opposed to an international fund) are that you can choose the currency or currencies you want. You are not at the mercy of an institutional fund manager's judgment on where currencies are headed. In addition, most international funds keep about 25% of their assets in U.S. dollars, no matter where else they invest.

In some instances, a U.S. bank offering foreign currency accounts does not actually go into the international market to buy these currencies. Instead, the bank uses hedging and other trading techniques to "create" the foreign currency from your U.S. dollars. Your dollars are left in the bank for normal day-to-day transactions.

Then when you decide to withdraw your foreign currency, or to switch currencies, the bank does not have to go into the international money market and bid for U.S. dollars. So you are not penalized as much by the spread between bid and ask on foreign currencies.

But the greatest advantage is that, if the bank holds the funds within the United States, *your deposit is FDIC-insured exactly as any other U.S. deposit.* All foreign currency accounts can be used in IRA or Keogh accounts, or anywhere you would normally buy a U.S. dollar CD.

SAFETY TIP

Be aware that the liquidity in the foreign currency markets can dry up occasionally. During the latter half of 1991, some banks that offer foreign currency term deposits raised their minimums, shortened maturities, and discouraged accounts because of their liquidity concerns.

RISKS OF FOREIGN CURRENCY ACCOUNTS

Certainly, there is some risk in buying foreign currencies. For example:

Let's assume you purchased a $10,000 deutsche mark CD. If the U.S. dollar rallies 10%, you would lose 10% if you sold out your CD *and did not roll it over.*

However, it is very likely that the dollar will remain weak over the long term. It will continue to depreciate against the stronger currencies, such as the British pound, German mark, and Swiss franc. On a short-term basis, many experts are predicting a strong dollar. Assuming this is the case, you can always opt to continue rolling over your CD until you can convert it back into U.S. dollars at a hefty profit.

REDUCING YOUR RISK

There are three ways to reduce the risk involved in foreign currency accounts:

1. *Keep maturities shorter.* This allows you greater freedom to convert your CD back into U.S. dollars at the appropriate time without a costly penalty. A shorter term will often force you to accept a lower rate, however.

2. *Diversify.* Obviously, diversification into several currencies lessens your exposure to any single, adverse currency move.

3. *Buy through a fund.* You can always choose to leave it up to the professionals, who are paid to watch the markets and make the right moves at the appropriate times.

YIELD TIP

In August 1991, Germany's central bank raised the key interest rates in a move to curb inflation pressures brought on by the cost of reunifying East and West Germany. The Bundesbank's discount rate was raised to 7.5% from 6.5%. The Lombard rate, used for short-term emergency borrowing, rose to 9.25% from 9%. These rates represent a nine-year high.

Because of the mark's prominent weighting within the European Monetary System, other European countries are expected to follow suit. For example, the Dutch central bank increased its discount rates by 0.25% to 8%.

With U.S. interest rates at their lowest levels in 18 years, this strengthens the opportunities for currency profits in these European countries.

U.S. BANKS OFFERING FOREIGN CURRENCY ACCOUNTS

Although the Federal Reserve recently gave U.S. banks approval to offer foreign currency accounts, only a handful of banks have taken advantage of this opportunity. The following is the most comprehensive list of banks yet compiled:

American Security Bank

Bank of America

Central Fidelity Bank

Citibank

First Union National Bank

First Wachovia Bank & Trust Company

Mark Twain Bank

Northern Trust Bank

Security Pacific Asian Bank

Union Bank

American Security Bank

Rex Evans of American Security Bank recommends investing in the ECU – the market basket of Euro-currencies. Japan is struggling and must go through considerable banking and securities reform. When they resolve these problems, significant capital will flow into Japan and the yen will raise against the dollar.

American Security Bank started offering foreign currency accounts the day the Fed said they could. However, these accounts are available only at the main office, because foreign currency accounts are considered more risky than a U.S. dollar account. (This is true despite the fact that, over the last few years, the "supposedly safe" dollar has lost up to 60% against "risky" foreign currencies.)

The minimum investment is $100,000 and, provided they feel you are qualified financially, you can invest by wire transfer from anywhere in the United States.

Their account works as a "time deposit," with deposit periods of one, two, three, six, and 12 months. The investor purchases the currency and then puts it on deposit with the bank.

They offer all the major currencies, such as British pound, Swiss franc, German mark, French franc, Canadian dollar, Japanese yen, Belgian franc, Australian dollar, and ECUs. They will offer other currencies to astute investors upon request.

For more information, contact: American Security Bank, Attn: Rex Evans, Trading Department, 730 15th Street NW, Washington, DC 20013; (202) 371-0006.

Bank of America

Any U.S. investor can call the Bank of America trading department and set up a foreign currency account over the phone or through the mail. These accounts are referred to as Grand Cayman deposit accounts. As the name indicates, deposits are held offshore in the Cayman Islands, so they are not federally insured.

They offer term deposits in almost any foreign currency you want, with a minimum of $100,000 for maturities of one day to 12 months. To open a foreign currency account, you must establish a checking account with them. Give them two days' advance notice to purchase the currency for you, debit your account, and open a term deposit.

For more information, contact: Bank of America, Attn: Foreign Trading Department, 315 Montgomery St., Mezzanine, San Francisco, CA 94104; (415) 622-2414. Make sure to ask for the foreign trading department. It will save you some time.

Central Fidelity Bank

Central Fidelity offers a "Euro-Time Deposit" that is similar to a normal CD. The maturity can be anywhere from one day to several years, and they can tailor them to your particular needs. Currencies include: French franc, Swiss franc,

German mark, Italian lira, British pound, and Japanese yen. The minimum is $100,000.

While they feel more comfortable providing the service to existing customers or investors who can set up the account in person, they will service the needs of out-of-state investors over the phone (and through wire transfer).

For more information, contact: Central Fidelity Bank, Investments Department/Foreign Exchange, Attn: Robert Brockmeier, 1021 East Cary Street, Richmond, VA 23219; (804) 697-6776.

Citibank

Only the main Citibank office in New York can offer foreign CDs; branch offices cannot. To reach someone who understands this service, you must contact the foreign trading department. Once you have made contact, you can set up an account through the mail.

Citibank offers two MultiMoney accounts:

Money Market Deposits. These are liquid deposits that pay daily interest on daily balances. There is a $25,000 minimum deposit and you can spread your deposit across as many currencies as you wish.

Time Deposits. CDs are available for terms of one, two, three, six, nine, and 12 months. A minimum $25,000 deposit is required and this amount is limited to a *single* currency.

For more information, contact: Citibank International Personal Banking, MultiMoney Service Center, 666 Fifth Avenue, 7th Floor, New York, NY 10103; 1-800-755-5654 or (212) 307-8323.

First Union National Bank

This is the only bank we know of that offers a foreign currency *money market account*. The account is offered in your choice of eight currencies: German mark, British pound, Swiss franc, French franc, Japanese yen, Italian lira, Canadian dollar, and Australian dollar. These accounts are FDIC insured. The minimum investment is $25,000 for individuals, or $10,000 for corporations.

They also have a Eurocurrency deposit account, which is held offshore and is note FDIC-insured. You can hold money in these Eruo accounts for any time from overnight to one year. The minimum investment is $400,000.

For more information, contact: First Union National Bank, One First Union Center, Charlotte, NC 28288; 1-800-736-5636. Ask for Pat Weaver.

First Wachovia Bank & Trust Company

Wachovia Bank offers foreign currency accounts through its Corporate Services Departments at the First National Bank of Atlanta and Wachovia Bank and Trust in Winston-Salem, North Carolina. The minimum opening balance is $5,000 (or equivalent). However, these accounts were primarily offered for commercial needs rather than for individuals, and therefore they do not pay interest on these accounts. They offer accounts in 21 currencies.

For more information, contact: First Wachovia Bank & Trust Company, P.O. Box 3099, Winston-Salem, NC 27102; (919) 770-5000.

Mark Twain Bank

Mark Twain Bank offers two foreign currency vehicles:

Foreign Currency Certificates of Deposit. CDs are available for periods of 3, 6, 9, or 12 months in 10 currencies: Australian dollars, English pounds, New Zealand dollars, Belgian francs, Canadian dollars, French francs, German marks, Japanese yen, Dutch guilders, and Swiss francs.

If you would like an account in a currency not listed here, discuss it with them. Mark Twain representatives are so service-oriented that they are willing to customize an account to your particular needs. The interest they currently pay on these accounts is quoted in Table 9.1.

World Currency CD. This CD offers a mix of currencies for time periods similar to those of the single country CDs. The minimum amount necessary to open an account is $20,000.

For information, contact: Mark Twain Bank, Frontenac Bldg., 1630 South Lindbergh Blvd., St. Louis, MO 63131; 1-800-926-4922 or (314) 997-7444. Ask for Frank O. Trotter III, Vice President.

SAFETY TIP

The Mark Twain Bank has three separate charters: Mark Twain St. Louis, Mark Twain Kansas City, and Mark Twain Illinois. As a result, you can have *FDIC insurance of up to $300,000* by splitting your deposits into three $100,000 lots, one for each separately chartered bank.

Northern Trust Bank

Northern Trust offers accounts to clients at any of their branch offices. There is a $100,000 minimum per currency. They regularly handle the British pound, German mark and Swiss franc, but can probably make arrangements if you require other foreign currencies. Northern Trust offer CDs held in their London branch (which means no FDIC coverage). Maturities are up to the client.

For more information, contact: Northern Trust Bank, 50 South LaSalle, Chicago, IL 60675; (312) 630-6000.

SECURITY PACIFIC ASIAN BANK

If you live in the Los Angeles area, you can go to any branch of Security Pacific Asian Bank to set up a foreign currency CD. However, to set up an account by mail, you must contact the foreign exchange trading department.

Security Pacific Asian Bank offers foreign currency time deposits in Australian dollars, British pounds, Canadian dollars, German marks, Japanese yen,

New Zealand dollars, Swiss francs, and ECUs. The minimum investment is $250,000 for terms of one to 12 months. These accounts are not insured by the FDIC, as the deposits are held offshore in the Bahamas.

They will purchase the currency and create a time deposit for you, but they will also accommodate investors who already have the foreign currency. In other words, you don't have to buy the currency from them, you can simply deposit foreign currency with them to open an account.

NOTE: Security Pacific Asian Bank is a wholly owned subsidiary of Security Pacific Corporation in Los Angeles. They have several offices in California, as well as in Asia.

Walk-In Service: Security Pacific Asian Bank (Main office), 977 North Broadway, Los Angeles, CA 90012; (213) 680-9000.

Mail-In Service: Security Pacific Asian Bank, Foreign Currency Exchange, 609 South Grand Ave., Los Angeles, CA 90017; (213) 229-1165. Contact a representative in the foreign currency trading department for the paper work and details.

Union Bank

Union Bank offers currency deposits for terms of seven days to one year in British pounds, Canadian dollars, German marks, Japanese yen and Swiss francs. The minimum investment is $100,000 and they are FDIC-insured.

Any branch of Union Bank should be able to open such an account for you. However, they will open it only in person—you cannot mail in your check. Also, the bank does not guarantee to buy back your foreign currency for U.S. dollars at maturity.

For more information, contact: Union Bank, Attn: Reiko Carnes, Financial Services Officer, 370 California St., San Francisco, CA 94104; (415) 445-0224.

TALK TO YOUR BANK . . .

As investor interest grows in foreign currency deposits, other banks may begin to offer this type of service. We suggest that you contact your local bank and ask if they offer this service. We believe that by the end of the 1990s, all American banks (all those who survive the next few years, that is!) will offer one-stop international investment services, just as European banks already provide.

EMERGENCY CASH THAT OFFERS REAL RETURNS

In case of a bank closure (or banking holiday), you should always have some cash on hand. A great way to ensure against such closures—and get your money to increase in value while it is "stuffed in the mattress"—is to buy traveler's checks denominated in one or more of the hard currencies.

Even though traveler's checks won't earn interest, chances are you could enjoy greater gains through appreciation of your hard currencies than you would by keeping that same money in an interest-bearing U.S. dollar savings account.

Depending on the currency, you could enjoy gains of 10% or more AND have instant liquidity.

Foreign currency traveler's checks are available at many banks, but shop around to get the best exchange rate and the lowest purchase fees. Three firms

---

YIELD TIP

Foreign currency traveler's checks are generally sold commission-free. However, you will pay the exchange rate, which can run as high as 2% or 3% over the price at which the currency trades.

Usually, the exchange rates in Europe are more favorable to the U.S. dollar than if you exchange dollars into foreign currencies in the United States. Therefore, if you are planning a trip to Europe any time soon, buy your foreign "folding money" while there. Even if you buy foreign traveler's checks, you will get a better rate in a European bank than from any U.S. bank or currency dealer. If you must buy stateside, shop around!

YIELD TIP

A Triple-Play Opportunity to EARN 20% or More in 12 Months

The German 10-year Treasury Bond (called the "bund") is particularly attractive right now. As with U.S. Treasuries, the principal is guaranteed against loss by the German government. The combination of German unification, the crumbling of the Soviet empire, and the Bundesbank's near-fanatical fear of inflation gives you a rare, *triple-play* opportunity in these ultra-safe government bonds:

1. High yield. In 1991, the bund was yielding over 8.5%.
2. When interest rates fall, bond values rise. As the world economy slows, interest rates should drop. You can expect German interest rates to fall at least 1%. This in turn will cause the value of any 10-year German bond you buy now, to rise at least 6% beyond the 8%-plus guaranteed interest you'll be collecting.
3. Besides high yields and rising value of your bunds, you'll also gain from appreciation on the D-mark against the U.S. dollar. Because the mark is the world's most inflation-proof currency now, you could estimate another 10% or so in appreciation from this one factor alone.

Overall, it is the safest way we know to make 20%+ on your money in the coming months.

that sell foreign currency traveler's checks, in case you cannot find them locally (or wish to compare fees) are:

1. Thomas Cook Currency Services, Inc.
2. Guardian Safe Deposit
3. Reusch International

Thomas Cook Currency Services, Inc.

Thomas Cook is the second largest issuer of foreign currency traveler's checks, with 1,600 offices in 120 countries. They offer Thomas Cook traveler's checks in nine major currencies: Australian dollar, British pound, Canadian dollar, German mark, Hong Kong dollar, Japanese yen, Spanish peseta, Swiss franc, and U.S. dollar.

For more information, call 1-800-582-4496.

Guardian Safe Deposit

Guardian sells Thomas Cook, Swiss banks', and American Express foreign currency traveler's checks. They also offer drafts in foreign currency for payments abroad. (For example, if you wanted to open a brokerage account in London in British pounds, you could purchase a foreign currency draft, or check, from Guardian for the desired amount.) They charge $3 over the exchange rate for this service. All their products may also be purchased by phone or mail.

For more information, contact: Guardian Safe Deposit, 2499 North Harrison, Arlington, VA 22206; (703) 237-1133.

Reusch International

Reusch sells Thomas Cook and Swiss banks' traveler's checks in nine currencies. They may be purchased only by mail. Reusch also has branch offices in New York, Chicago, and Los Angeles.

For more information, contact: Reusch International, 1350 I Street NW, Washington, DC 20005; (202) 408-1200.

THE GLOBAL BOND MARKET

As we enter the 1990s, many experts see international bonds stealing the investment spotlight. Over the past seven years, many foreign bond markets have far outperformed the U.S. bond markets. See Figure 4.2 and Table 4.4.

Many overseas bonds can be purchased directly through your local broker, but shop around. The commissions (the spread between bid and ask) on foreign bonds, particularly for smaller quantities, are usually quite high and can largely offset the advantage of being in a high-real-yield currency.

If you want to buy foreign stocks or bonds, we recommend that you consider doing so through one of the funds listed later in this chapter.

Figure 4.2. Global Government Bond Markets Average Annual U.S. Dollar Returns

	France	21.1%
United Kingdom		
Denmark		
Netherlands		17.4%
Germany		17.0%
Japan		
Canada		14.6%
Australia		14.1%
Switzerland		13.8%
United States		11.3%

Source: Salomon Brothers World Government Bond Market Index and PaineWebber Global Income Fund

Table 4.4. 10-Year Government Bonds

	Current Yields	Projected 6 Month Yields
Spain	11.40%	10.70%
Italy	11.16	10.60
Finland	10.95	10.00
Australia	9.82	9.50
Britain	9.88	9.10
Canada	8.73	8.10
Denmark	8.93	8.10
France	8.76	8.10
Germany	8.35	7.70
U.S.	7.50	7.40
Japan	5.91	5.25

Source: Lombard Odier International Portfolio Mgt. Ltd.

YIELD TIP

Earn 9.9% Virtually Risk-Free

A 30-year Canadian T-bond yields 9.9% and a three-year T-note yields 9.2%. Canadian securities are backed by the Canadian government's "full faith and credit" just as U.S. government securities are.

The risk you must consider is in converting your dollars to Canadian dollars when you buy the bonds, and back to U.S. dollars when you sell them. If the dollar rises in value, you could lose some money converting your currency, because your Canadian dollars would buy fewer U.S. dollars. Still, Canadian bond yields are quite attractive.

THE EUROPEAN CURRENCY UNIT (ECU)

It is also possible to invest in bonds denominated in ECUs–(European Currency Units)–the "market basket of currencies"–which Europe hopes will ultimately mature into a single currency. Investing in the ECU is safer than most individual currencies because, if any individual currency becomes weak, the other currencies in the "basket" act as a cushion.

All currencies within the ECU are forced to conform to low inflation rates. Each currency is allowed to diverge by only 2.25% (6% for the Spanish peseta) to either side of its fixed central rate against any other member currency.

This means that not only is the ECU a sound "currency" in its own right, but *so are the member currencies.*

In particular, the currencies that had higher inflation before joining the European Community (such as the British pound) are particularly good buys. Their interest rates are higher than many other European currencies; and as their inflation rates are brought down, they should enjoy greater appreciation against the U.S. dollar.

Some big American companies that feel uncomfortable with issuing bonds in U.S. dollars (such as J.P. Morgan, G.E., Ford Motors, and Pepsi) are already issuing ECU bonds. In fact, *the growth of ECU-denominated bonds has outstripped that of all other bond markets.* And in terms of straight Eurobonds outstanding, the ECU now ranks fifth.

If you are interested in diversification of currencies and safety, then ECUs are a good bet.

ECU bonds can be bought through American brokerage houses. However, most brokerages ask for a minimum of $20,000 before they will invest in the ECU market for you.

One very knowledgeable broker on ECUs is Robert S. Berlin, Bear Stearns & Company, 245 Park Ave., 9th Floor, New York, NY 10167. You can call him at 1-800-926-0124.

Wealthy investors who have substantial assets in a foreign bank account can arrange to buy foreign bonds directly. Most international banks offer a securities account and can recommend specific bonds for your portfolio.

YIELD TIP

One of the fastest growing and top-yielding global income funds is the new Blanchard Short-Term Global Income Fund. Unlike other global income funds, the Blanchard Fund has no front-end load, no "back-end" redemption fees, and no administrative costs.

Yielding above 9%, this new fund invests in short-term (three years or less) money market instruments denominated in U.S. dollar and foreign currencies. The Blanchard Fund is flexible and uses hedging techniques that can reduce the risk of a dollar rally, while earning high yields in foreign currencies in the meantime.

For more information, contact Blanchard Short-Term Global Income Fund, 41 Madison Ave., New York, NY 10010; 1-800-688-7904.

INVESTING IN INTERNATIONAL BOND FUNDS

For those investors with more modest means or less international know-how, there are many very good international bond funds and global income and equity funds. They all can be purchased through your local broker. Some are available without any sales loads. Table 4.5 lists 1991's top 10 international bond funds.

Be aware that international bond funds are fairly new to U.S. investors. Therefore, it is impossible to determine a long-term return for these funds. However, on the average, these funds delivered a 13.6% return in 1990 and approximately 9.9% in 1991.

In the first three quarters of 1991, Global bond funds yielded an average return of 9.9% compared to 13.6% in 1990. Remember, these funds do best when interest rates decline abroad and the U.S. dollar is weak against foreign currencies.

INVESTING IN FOREIGN STOCKS: OPPORTUNITIES ABOUND

Martin Truax of Shearson Lehman Brothers says there are substantial opportunities available in international economies.

"Some of these markets are the equivalent of the U.S. market in 1982 or perhaps even 1932. The year 1992 will mark the official end of tariffs, custom and trade barriers in the European Economic Community as they also work toward just one unified currency over the next decade. Inefficient plants are closing, mergers are starting to take place, and many companies are presently selling at bargain levels.

Table 4.5. Top 10 International Bond Funds in 1991

	Total % Return (12 Months)	Total Assets (Millions)	Maximum Sales Charge	Annual Expenses per $100
Global Bond Composite Index	9.9%			$1.42
First Australia Prime Income (b)	20.1%	$886	n/a	$1.54
Kleinwort Benson Australian (b)	17.7%	$70	n/a	$1.68
Scudder International Bond	14.9%	$144	n/a	$1.35
Putnam Global Governmental Income	14.0%	$287	4.75%	$1.65
Capital World Bond Fund/ American Funds	12.4%	$60	4.75%	$1.52
Putnam Master Income Trust (b)	12.3%	$446	n/a	$1.08
Fidelity Global Bond Fund/ Fidelity	12.2%	$130	1.43%	
ACM Managed Multi-Market Trust (b)	12.1%	$111	n/a	$2.90
Templeton Global Income Fund (b)	11.7%	$966	n/a	$0.82
PaineWebber Global Income Fund	10.8%	$1,470	5.00% (a)	$1.86

(a) Includes back-end load that reverts to distributor

(b) Closed Funds

Source: Forbes Annual Fund Survey September 1991

"The U.S. has gone from representing the majority of all the stock markets' total value to now accounting for less than 30% of world stock market capitalization. Out of the more than 30 stock markets, the U.S. has been in the top five for performance only once during the '80s, and has ranked only 12th over the past 10 years."

The greatest growth over the next 10 years is expected to come from countries that are just beginning to industrialize. Some have the cheapest labor today (e.g., Mexico). Some are extremely rich in untapped natural resources, while others have stock markets that are almost elementary when compared with those of the U.S. market during its formation. (See Tables 4.6 and 4.7.)

The Pacific Rim stock markets have collectively grown sixfold over the last 10 years.

Table 4.6. World Stock Market

(Year-to-date change from 12/31/90 to 11/29/91)

Country	% Increase (U.S. dollars)	Country	% Increase (U.S. dollars)
Hong Kong	37.86%	Britain	3.41%
Singapore	31.01%	Germany	3.04%
Australia	27.41%	Spain	2.03%
U.S.	9.91%	Japan	−0.51%
Canada	8.25%	Italy	−8.14%
France	5.22%	Switzerland	−12.39%
Netherlands	4.99%		

Source: Morgan Stanley Capital International

And as of December 1992, 12 Western European countries will combine their economic strengths to create the world's largest commercial market. The new European Community, with over 320 million consumers, will be one-third larger than the United States and twice the size of Japan. Add the changes occurring in the Eastern Bloc, and there will be tremendous investment opportunities available to anyone who seeks them out.

DON'T GET FOOLED BY SHORT-TERM PERFORMANCES

Global and foreign stock funds were down during 1991, reflecting not only the price movements of foreign stocks, but also the strength of the dollar against most foreign currencies. But long-term, they will continue to outperform most domestic markets.

GLOBAL STOCK RECOMMENDATIONS

Today, there are several ways you can make international stock investments. You can invest directly in foreign companies either through American Depository Receipts (ADRs), or by purchasing regular shares of international companies that are traded through the foreign trading departments of many security firms. The most popular method, however, is through mutual funds that specialize in global investment portfolios.

AMERICAN DEPOSITORY RECEIPTS

ADRs are negotiable receipts that represent the ownership of shares in a foreign corporation, and they trade in the U.S. securities market—just like U.S. stocks (see Table 4.8 for a partial listing of ADRs). The actual shares that back

Table 4.7. Top-Peforming Markets

Year	1st	2nd	3rd	4th	5th
1981	Sweeden +39	Denmark +25	Singapore +18	Japan +16	Spain +13
1982	Sweden +24	U.S.A. +22	Neth. +17	Germany +10	Belgium +10
1983	Norway +82	Denmark +69	Australia +56	Sweden +50	Neth. +38
1984	Hong Kong +17	Spain +41	Japan +17	Belgium +13	Neth. +12
1985	Austria +177	Germany +137	Italy +134	Switz. +108	France +83
1986	Spain +123	Italy +109	Japan +100	Belgium +81	France +79
1987	Japan +43	Spain +38	UK +35	Canada +15	Denmark +14
1988	Belgium +55	Denmark +54	Sweden +49	Norway +43	France +39
1989	Austria +105	Germany +47	Norway +46	Denmark +45	Singapore +42
1990	UK +10	Hong Kong +9	Austria +7	Norway +1	Denmark 0

The U.S. stock market has been among the five best performers only once since 1980.

Source: Morgan Stanley Capital International and G.T. Global Growth Funds

ADRs are held by the foreign bank or the agent of an American bank, and the ADR is issued by the American bank.

There are about 880 of these dollar-denominated receipts for foreign stocks (in 38 countries) that you can buy through your local broker. They are bought, sold and pay dividends in U.S. dollars, so you don't have to worry about converting foreign currency.

If you are concerned about the liquidity of ADRs, consider the fact that in 1990 the listed trading volume was 3.8 billion shares, an all-time high.

There are two types of ADRs. Sponsored ADRs have only one U.S. depository bank that is appointed by the issuer. Unsponsored ADRs may have more than one depository bank, and there is no agreement between banks and the foreign corporation that clearly defines the rights and responsibilities. Therefore, there is more risk involved in unsponsored ADRs.

Some ADRs with especially good potential for 1992:

Tubos de Acero de Mexico. This is Mexico's only producer of seamless pipe and tubing and the country's leading manufacturer of steel ingot. Petroleos Mexicanos (Pemex) is one of Tubos de Acero's biggest customers—which offers tremendous upside potential. Pemex is one of the early beneficiaries of Mexican President Salina's privatization campaign, and it has begun an ambitious capital-spending program. Without a doubt, one of Mexico's largest industries in the years to come will be oil and gas.

Telefonos de Mexico. This company is the world's fastest-growing telephone company and a good long-term bet. It has also been criticized for being one of the world's notoriously unreliable telephone systems. Regardless, Telemex dominates the Mexican telephone market as AT&T does in the United States, so it has tremendous potential. (This ADR made big moves in 1991, so check with your broker before you invest in this security.)

Royal Bank of Scotland is the sixth largest bank in the United Kingdom, with assets of $58 billion.

Barclays Bank is Britain's second largest bank, with assets of $203 billion.

Akzo is a Netherlands chemical producer, with sales of $10 billion. Two-thirds of Akzo's earnings come from commodity and specialty chemicals, the rest from pharmaceutical.

Fletcher Challenge is a $7.9 billion New Zealand natural resources company.

BCE is the $19 billion holding company for Bell Canada.

Hanson Trust is a $14 billion British conglomerate that owns, among other things, Consolidated Gold Fields, Kaiser Cement, and SCM.

COUNTRY CLOSED-END FUNDS

More recently, several closed-end investment companies have emerged that specialize in the companies of a particular country or region of the world. These are referred to as *country funds* (see Table 4.9 for examples).

These funds can be somewhat risky. Just remember that not all foreign countries are equally safe.

(To get an idea of the risk factor of several emerging countries see Table 4.10.)

Also, if a country suddenly becomes a "hot prospect," be careful. Usually these funds will trade at a premium to their net asset value (NAV). As a rule, these funds trade at a 10% to 20% discount to the underlying asset value of their portfolios, so be wary of a premium. It probably won't last. When a country gets

Table 4.8. Selected ADRs

Country	Company	Industry	Exchange: Symbol
Australia	The Broken Hill Proprietary Co., Ltd.	Mining and oil	OTC:BRKNY
Denmark	Novo Industries A/S	Industrial enzymes, drugs	NYSE:NVO
Great Britain	Courtaulds plc	Rayon yarn	AMEX:COU
	Glaxo Holdings plc	Drugs, foods	OTC:GLXOY
	The Plessey Company plc	Telecommunications	NYSE:PLY
	The Rank Organization plc	Electronic equipment	OTC:RANKY
Ireland	Elan Corp. plc	Drug research and technology	OTC:ELANY
Israel	Teva Pharmaceutical Industries, Ltd.	Veterinary products	OTC:TEVIY
Japan	Canon Inc.	Cameras	OTC:CANNY
	Fuji Photo Film Co., Ltd.	Photo products	OTC:FUJIY
	Hitachi, Ltd.	Electrical manufacturing	NYSE:HIT
	Honda Motor Co., Ltd.	Motorcycles and autos	NYSE:HMC
	Kubota, Ltd.	Agricultural machinery	NYSE:KUB
	Matsushita Electric Industrial Co.	Electronics equipment	NYSE:MC
	Pioneer Electronic Corp.	Audio equipment	NYSE:PIO
	Sony Corporation	Electronic products	NYSE:SNE
	TDK Corporation	Video and audio tapes	NYSE:TDK
	Tokyo Marine-Fire	Insurance	OTC:TKIOY

Mexico	Tubos de Acero de Mexico, S.A.	Steel	AMEX:TAM
South Africa	Anglo-American	Gold, diamonds	OTC:ANGLY
	Blyvooruitzicht Gold Mining	Gold, uranium	OTC:BLYVY
	DeBeers Consolidated Mining	Diamond mining	OTC:DBRSY
	Free State Consolidated Gold	Gold producer	OTC:FREEY
	St. Helena Gold Mines	Gold mining	OTC:SGOLY
	Western Deep Levels	Gold mining	OTC:WDEPY
Sweden	Gambro, Inc.	Medical devices and systems	OTC:GAMBY
	Ericsson (L.M.) Telephone Co.	Telecommunications	OTC:ERICY
	Pharmacia A.B.	Medical science products	OTC:PHABY

Source: Foreign Stocks and Bonds

Table 4.9. A Sampling of "Country Funds"

Symbol	Fund Name	Fund Management Group
APB	Asia Pacific FD	Baring Intl Inv
OST	Austria FD	Alliance/Girozentrale Cap Mgt. Beratungs
BZF	Brazil FD	Scudder/Banco Icatu SA
CH	Chile FD	Bea Associates/Celsius Agente de Valores
GTF	Europe, GT Greater	G T Capital Group
NEF	Europe, Scudder New	Scudder, Stevens & Clark
FRF	France Growth FD	Indosuez Intl Inv Ser/Banque Indosuez
GER	Germany FD	Deutsche Bank Capital Corp
FRG	Germany FD, Emerging	Asset Mgt Advisor of Dresdner Bank
GF	Germany FD, New	Deutsche Bank Capital/DB Cap Mgt Intl
IGF	India Growth FD	Unit Trust of India Inv Adv Ser
IRL	Irish Investment FD	Bank of Ireland Asset Mgt Ltd
ITA	Italy FD	Shearson Lehman Global Asset Mgt
JGF	Jakarta FD	Nomura Capital Mgt Inc
JOF	Japan OTC FD	Nomura Capital Mgt Inc
KF	Korea FD	Scudder/Daewoo Securities Co Ltd
MF	Malaysia FD	Morgan Stanley/Arab-Malaysian Mrch Bank
MXF	Mexico FD	Impulsora del Fondo Mexica, S A de C V
FPF	Philippine FD, First	Bea Associates/Socifa & Beta S A
PGF	Portugal FD	Clemente Capital/Philippine Natl Bank
SGF	Singapore FD	DBS Asset Mgt/Daiwa Intl
SNF	Spain FD	Alliance/Banco Bilbao Vizcaya
GSP	Spain, Growth FD	Kemper/BSN Gestion de Patrimonies, S A
SWZ	Swiss Helvetia FD	Helvetia Capital/Wilkinson & Hottinger
TWN	Taiwan FD	China Securities Inv Trust Corp
TTF	Thai FD	Morgan Stanley/The Mutual Fund Co (Thai)
TKF	Turkish Invest. FD	Morgan Stanley/Teb Ekonomi Arastir A S
UKM	United Kingdom FD	Warburg Inv Mgt Intl
MGC	Morgan Grenfell SM CAP	Morgan Grenfell Capital Mgt
TY	Tri-Continental FD (US)	J & W Seligman & Co

Source: Shearson Lehman

"hot," as Germany did recently, enthusiastic buyers push the premiums to 25% or more before they eventually slide back to a discount. If you get caught in such an upswing, you could lose as much as 40% of your assets after underwriting fees and the swing from premium to discount in the market price.

Finally, when investing abroad, realize that you are taking an exchange-rate risk that can greatly add to or detract from your results.

THE TOP GLOBAL INCOME FUNDS, FOREIGN CURRENCY FUNDS AND MANAGEMENT FIRMS FOR 1992

"Probably the best way for the individual investor to participate in foreign markets is through a mutual fund."

――Standard & Poor's

Many people feel more comfortable investing in foreign currencies and markets through a professionally managed fund. There are basically four types of funds to choose from:

1. *Foreign Currency Funds.* A simple and efficient way to gain access to the world's major currency markets—a "market basket" of currencies that does not depend upon rising financial markets. The portfolio can benefit from the dollar rising as well as falling.
2. *Global Bond Funds.* These funds buy bonds from foreign governments and bonds and commercial paper from overseas corporations.
3. *Global Stock Funds.* These funds buy a mix of foreign and U.S. securities.
4. *Foreign Stock Funds.* These are U.S.-based stock funds with primarily foreign stock portfolios.

Fortunately, there are several excellent options available (see Table 4.11). The best funds we found are:

Fidelity Investments

Scudder Fund Distributors

T. Rowe Price

Dean Witter

Huntington Advisors International Cash Portfolios

PaineWebber

Shearson Lehman Brothers

Shearson's Managed Accounts

G.T. Global

Templeton Foreign Funds

Blanchard Group of Funds

Table 4.10. A Global Ranking

What follow are the International Risk Guide's August Rankings for 129 countries. The maximum, or least risky, score is 100 for the political category and 50 each for financial and economic risk.

Country	Political Risk	Financial Risk	Economic Risk	Composite Risk
1. Switzerland	93.0	50.0	39.5	91.5
2. Luxembourg	93.0	49.0	36.0	89.0
3. Norway	87.0	47.0	42.0	88.0
4. Austria	88.0	47.0	39.5	87.5
5. Germany	83.0	50.0	38.5	86.0
5. Netherlands	85.0	46.0	40.5	86.0
7. Brunei	81.0	48.0	41.5	85.5
8. Japan	80.0	50.0	39.0	84.5
9. Singapore	79.0	48.0	39.5	83.5
9. U.S.	78.0	49.0	39.0	83.5
11. Canada	81.0	48.0	37.0	83.0
12. Belgium	82.0	45.0	36.5	82.0
12. Denmark	86.0	41.0	37.0	82.0
14. Sweden	81.0	47.0	35.0	81.5
14. Taiwan	71.0	49.0	43.0	81.5
16. United Kingdom	76.0	50.0	36.0	81.0
17. Finland	85.0	44.0	32.0	80.5
18. France	79.0	46.0	34.5	80.0
18. Ireland	80.0	42.0	37.5	80.0
20. New Zealand	78.0	46.0	35.0	79.5
21. Australia	76.0	45.0	37.0	79.0
21. Iceland	82.0	42.0	33.5	79.0
23. Malasia	71.0	45.0	38.5	77.5
24. Italy	72.0	47.0	35.0	77.0
25. Venezuela	75.0	40.0	36.0	75.5
26. Portugal	69.0	42.0	38.5	75.0
27. South Korea	63.0	47.0	36.5	73.5
28. Botswana	70.0	34.0	42.0	73.0
44. Qatar	56.0	33.0	42.0	65.5
45. Gabon	57.0	33.0	39.0	64.5
45. Mongolia	65.0	36.0	28.0	64.5
47. Greece	65.0	33.0	29.5	64.0
48. Jamaica	65.0	37.0	24.0	63.5
49. Saudi Arabia	60.0	31.0	35.5	63.5
50. Israel	58.0	33.0	34.5	63.0
50. Trinidad/Tobago	59.0	35.0	31.5	63.0
50. U.A.E.	53.0	33.0	39.5	63.0
53. Bahrain	54.0	30.0	40.5	62.5
54. Brazil	67.0	34.0	23.0	62.0
54. Hungary	68.0	32.0	24.0	62.0
56. Gambia	53.0	33.0	35.5	61.0
56. Poland	62.0	29.0	31.0	61.0
58. China	58.0	24.0	38.0	60.0
59. South Africa	56.0	30.0	32.5	59.5
60. Bolivia	52.0	34.0	32.0	59.0
60. Cote d'Ivoire	66.0	29.0	23.0	59.0
62. Algeria	54.0	30.0	32.5	58.5
63. Argentina	63.0	30.0	23.0	58.0
63. Senegal	53.0	29.0	33.5	58.0
65. Bulgaria	61.0	28.0	25.5	57.5
66. Ecuador	58.0	29.0	26.0	56.5
66. Egypt	54.0	30.0	29.0	56.5
66. Libya	52.0	27.0	34.0	56.5
66. Nigeria	49.0	29.0	35.0	56.0
70. Syria	53.0	23.0	36.0	56.0
71. Iran	56.0	28.0	26.5	55.5
87. Madagascar	57.0	20.0	26.0	51.5
88. Togo	41.0	26.0	35.0	51.0
89. Guyana	51.0	29.0	20.5	50.5
90. Burkina Faso	41.0	23.0	36.0	50.0
90. Kenya	48.0	26.0	26.0	50.0
90. Zimbabwe	51.0	25.0	23.5	50.0
93. Romania	55.0	29.0	15.0	49.5
93. Turkey	52.0	19.0	27.5	49.5
95. Niger	45.0	24.0	29.0	49.0
96. Guinea	48.0	21.0	28.0	48.5
97. Guatemala	41.0	24.0	30.5	48.0
97. Jordan	45.0	20.0	30.5	48.0
99. Peru	45.0	28.0	21.5	47.5
99. Sri Lanka	36.0	26.0	32.5	47.4
99. Surinam	44.0	23.0	28.0	47.5
102. Philippines	41.0	22.0	29.5	46.5
102. Yugoslavia	45.0	24.0	23.5	46.5
104. Kuwait	38.0	24.0	29.0	46.0
104. New Caledonia	44.0	13.0	34.5	46.0
106. North Korea	59.0	15.0	16.0	45.0
106. Mali	40.0	19.0	30.5	45.0
106. Zambia	45.0	19.0	25.5	45.0
109. Nicaragua	44.0	27.0	17.0	44.0
109. Pakistan	34.0	22.0	32.0	44.0
109. Vietnam	50.0	18.0	20.0	44.0
112. El Salvador	37.0	18.0	32.0	43.5
113. India	34.0	25.0	27.0	43.0
113. Mozambique	44.0	26.0	15.5	43.0

No. Country				
29. Cyprus	69.0	39.0	38.0	73.0
30. Bahamas	66.0	39.0	36.5	71.0
30. Spain	65.0	42.0	35.0	71.0
32. Malta	64.0	34.0	43.0	70.5
32. Mexico	71.0	41.0	28.5	70.5
32. Oman	65.0	34.0	42.0	70.5
35. Chile	67.0	42.0	30.5	70.0
36. Czechoslovakia	73.0	36.0	30.0	69.5
37. Costa Rica	71.0	35.0	32.0	69.0
38. Indonesia	57.0	44.0	35.5	68.5
38. Uruguay	66.0	39.0	32.0	68.5
40. Thailand	57.0	42.0	37.0	68.0
41. Columbia	60.0	41.0	34.0	67.5
41. Hong Kong	58.0	42.0	35.0	67.5
43. Paraguay	59.0	39.0	34.5	66.5

No. Country				
71. Morocco	52.0	28.0	30.5	55.5
71. U.S.S.R.	53.0	36.0	21.5	55.5
74. Ghana	53.0	30.0	27.0	55.0
75. Namibia	47.0	24.0	38.0	54.5
75. Panama	47.0	28.0	34.0	54.5
75. Tunisia	54.0	23.0	32.0	54.5
78. Cameroon	47.0	27.0	34.0	54.0
78. Papua	54.0	26.0	28.0	54.0
80. Dominican Rep.	53.0	23.0	30.5	53.5
81. Congo	52.0	20.0	33.5	53.0
81. Tanzania	56.0	27.0	23.0	53.0
83. Angola	45.0	19.0	41.0	52.5
83. Honduras	49.0	28.0	28.0	52.5
85. Albania	55.0	33.0	16.0	52.0
85. Malawi	51.0	28.0	25.0	52.0

No. Country				
115. Yemen	49.0	23.0	12.0	42.0
116. Cuba	54.0	16.0	12.0	41.0
117. Bangladesh	33.0	18.0	29.0	40.0
118. Lebanon	32.0	11.0	35.0	39.0
118. Sierra Leone	37.0	20.0	20.5	39.0
120. Guinea-Bissau	46.0	19.0	12.0	38.5
121. Zaire	30.0	18.0	20.0	34.0
122. Haiti	28.0	12.0	26.5	33.5
123. Ethiopia	22.0	16.0	25.0	31.5
124. Uganda	36.0	21.0	5.0	31.0
125. Burma	27.0	9.0	22.5	28.5
126. Iraq	19.0	4.0	25.5	24.5
127. Sudan	15.0	10.0	22.5	24.0
128. Somalia	22.0	12.0	5.0	19.5
129. Liberia	10.0	8.0	12.0	15.0

**Table 4.11. International Recommended Funds
at a Glance**

	1-Year	5-Year	10-Year or Since Inception
Fidelity Global Bond (ii)	8.82%		10.25% Since 12/86
Scudder International Bond (ii)	8.10%		11.34% Since 07/88
Scudder International (i)	15.90%	11.29%	15.52%
T. Rowe International Bond (ii)	8.79%		7.52% Since 09/86
T. Rowe Stock Fund (i)	9.62%	12.78%	15.41%

(i) 12-month returns as of December 1991.

(ii) 30-day yields as of December 1991.

Fidelity Investments

Single-Currency Portfolios. Fidelity began offering single-currency portfolios in the British pound, German mark, and Japanese yen in November 1989.

These single-currency funds seek to maintain stable principal in which the portfolio will approximate the performance of its currency, as well as earn income at the money market rates prevailing in that currency. Required initial minimum is $5,000 for any one currency and $1,000 for subsequent investments. Purchases of $25,000 and under carry a load of 0.4%; for $25,000 to $100,000 the load is 0.3%; and for investments of $100,000 or more, the load is 0.2%.

This is a growth fund, not an income fund, so you don't receive dividends. Instead, the fund grows in net asset value. Because this is a limited-partnership fund, you cannot use it for an IRA.

Fidelity Global Bond Fund. This fund seeks a high total investment return by investing primarily in debt securities issued worldwide. A $2,500 minimum investment is required and there is no sales charge. Yield as of December 1991: 8.82%.

For more information, contact: Fidelity Investments, 82 Devonshire St., Boston, MA 02109; 1-800-544-8888 or (617) 523-1919.

Scudder Fund Distributors

Scudder International Bond Fund. This fund seeks high income by investing in high-grade bonds denominated in foreign currencies. The 30-day yield as of December 1991 was 8.1%.

Scudder International Fund. This fund seeks long-term growth by purchasing a diversified portfolio of foreign equity securities. The 12-month return as of November 1991 was 15.9%.

Both funds have a $1,000 minimum investment. They are no-load funds and do not have 12b-1 fees.

For more information, contact: Scudder Fund Distributors, 175 Federal Street, Boston, MA 02110; 1-800-225-2470 or (617) 439-4640.

T. Rowe Price

T. Rowe Price International Bond Fund. Also called the International Bond Fund, this fund invests primarily in an international portfolio of nondollar-denominated, high-quality government and corporate bonds that include Western Europe, Japan, Australia, New Zealand and Canada. The 30-day yield as of December 1991 was 8.79%.

T. Rowe Price International Stock Fund. This is the only international stock fund to make the *Forbes* honor roll for 1990 and 1991. And based on its performance since its inception in May 1980, it was ranked the No. 1 international fund by Lipper Analytical Services. The fund pursues capital growth by investing in common stocks of established foreign companies and has shown an *average annual return of 20.4% since September 30, 1982.* The 12-month return as of October 1991 was 9.62%.

Both T. Rowe funds have $2,500 minimum ($1,000 for IRAs). They are both no-load funds and have no 12b-1 marketing fees.

For more information, contact: T. Rowe Price, 100 East Pratt St., Baltimore, MD 21202; 1-800-638-5660 or (301) 547-2308.

Dean Witter

Dean Witter Global Short-Term Income Fund. This fund seeks as high a level of current income as is consistent with prudent investment risk. It invests in short-term debt issued by the governments and agencies of the United States and nations around the world. The portfolio also contains money market instruments, including bank certificates of deposit and the high-quality debt of U.S. and foreign corporations, such as commercial paper. The 30-day yield as of December 1991 was 10.18%.

You can find the latest quotes on this fund in *Barron's,* or *The Wall Street Journal.* Minimum investment is $1,000. This is a load fund. For more information, contact: Dean Witter, Two World Trade Center, New York, NY 10048; 1-800-869-FUND or (212) 392-2550.

Huntington Advisors International Cash Portfolios (ICP)

Huntington Advisors offers seven single-currency cash portfolios, a global cash portfolio, a high-income portfolio, and a hard-currency portfolio.

Single-Currency Portfolios are in Australian dollars, Canadian dollars, German marks, British pounds sterling, Japanese yen, Swiss francs, and U.S. dollars. These are basically money market funds, where check-writing privileges and same-day wire redemption are available, if you require it. You also may exchange your holdings between any of the International Portfolios at net asset value (NAV). The weighted average maturity in ICP is typically under 30 days to keep risk at a minimum.

The Global Cash Portfolio (GCP) includes Australian dollars, Austrian schilling, British pound sterling, Canadian dollars, Dutch guilder, European Currency Unit, French franc, German marks, Japanese yen, Swedish krona, Swiss francs, and U.S. dollars. GCP has the flexibility to invest in any of these currencies, including the U.S. dollar, as market conditions change.

Donald Gould, the founder of the fund, pioneered the "basket of currencies" approach to money market investing when he started this fund in 1986. It invests in high-yield, low-inflation currencies to strike the most advantageous balance between currency appreciation and interest income in both U.S.-dollar- and non-dollar-denominated assets. Since its inception (June 1986), the fund has had a total return of 61.48% and as of November 1991, the yield was 5.06% with an effective yield of 5.19%. The fund carries a load of 1.5%.

High-Income Currency Portfolio invests in money market instruments denominated in three to five of the highest-yielding major currencies. To protect against capital loss, the fund can invest in U.S. and Canadian dollar instruments as well. However, the focus here is higher yields, and this fund will take a higher risk to achieve them. Since its inception (November 1989), the fund has had a total return of 27.35% and as of November 1991, the yield was 7.66% with an effective yield of 7.95%.

Hard-Currency Portfolio invests in money market instruments denominated in three to five of the least-inflated currencies. It does not invest in any U.S. dollar instruments. Its goal is long-term protection against U.S. inflation and currency depreciation. Since its inception (November 1989), the fund has had a return of 29.71% and as of November 1991, the yield was 5.49% with an effective yield of 5.64%.

All the portfolios invest in money market instruments denominated in the world's major currencies. Specifically, each portfolio invests strictly in high-quality, liquid, short-term debt securities. These securities include bank CDs, government bills, and corporate paper. As with other funds, they stick to instruments rated AA, Aa or better. The average maturity is 30 days.

For more information, contact:
Huntington Advisors, 251 South Lake Ave., Suite 600, Pasadena, CA 91101; 1-800-354-4111 or (213) 681-3700.

PaineWebber

PaineWebber Global Income Fund is a professionally managed mutual fund that holds an internationally diversified portfolio of high-quality bonds (Standard & Poor's AAA and AA or Moody's Aaa and Aa). The fund seeks to provide investors with a high level of current income, and secondarily, long-term capital appreciation. The minimum investment is $1,000. The 30-day yield as of December 1991 was 8.4%.

PaineWebber Short-Term Global Income is an open-end mutual fund designed for clients who want a yield higher than a traditional money market fund might offer, with less fluctuation in net asset value than an investment in a longer-term global bond fund entails. The fund focuses on high-quality debt securities from around the world denominated in various currencies, U.S. dollars or multinational currency units, with maturities no longer than three years. Minimum investment is $1,000. The 30-day yield as of December 1991 was 7.72%.

Note: PaineWebber offers two options for each of their funds: "A" Shares and "B" Shares. "A" Shares is a front-end load fund, while "B" Shares is a no-load fund with 12b-1 fees. The 30-day yields were based on the "B" Shares option.

For more information, contact:

PaineWebber, 1285 Avenue of the Americas, New York, NY 10019; 1-800-521-8840 or (212) 713-2000.

Shearson Lehman Brothers

Shearson Lehman Brothers Short-Term World Income Fund. Their short-term income fund includes four separate mutual funds: Canadian Dollar, Deutsche Mark, British Pound Sterling and Yen Performance Funds L.P. The investment objective is to maintain relative stability of principal in terms of its underlying currency with no attempt to minimize the effects of currency exchange fluctuations relative to the U.S. dollar. Eighty percent of the portfolio's net assets must be invested in the currency suggested by its name.

This fund offers a low investment minimum, daily liquidity at net asset value, and monthly income to be taken as cash for current needs or reinvested to take advantage of compounding.

Shearson Lehman Brothers Global Currencies Portfolio. This fund is a collection of five foreign-currency funds (one managed basket of currencies and four single-currency portfolios) designed to allow investors to make their own single-foreign-currency investments, or to delegate the currency selection process to professional managers.

These currency funds are made up of money market instruments denominated in the portfolio's underlying currency in combination with forward contracts. Dividends are declared monthly and capital gains annually. These are no-load funds and the minimum investment is $2,500.

Short-Term World Income Fund. There is a 3% load with this fund (which declines with the size of the account), and it is managed to keep the principal within a 3% fluctuation. It invests in high-grade, short-term Treasuries, CDs, and corporate paper. It is always at least 25% in U.S. Treasuries, plus it is always hedged to prevent any big loss from a U.S. dollar run-up. The 10-month average yield through October 1991 was 9%.

Single-Currency Portfolio. These funds are available in British pounds, Canadian dollars, German marks, and Japanese yen. Income distributions are paid according to prevailing interest rates.

YIELD TIP

Investment Advisor's Top Picks

Sheldon Jacobs' (*No-Load Fund Investor,* P.O. Box 283, Hastings-on-Hudson, NY 10706; 1-800-252-2042) best recommendation is *T. Rowe Price's New Asia Fund.* Since its inception on September 28, 1990, it has yielded 18.43%. It invests in both large and small companies located in Asia, the Pacific Basin, Australia and New Zealand (excluding Japan).

Mark Skousen (*Forecasts & Strategies,* Phillips Publishing, 7811 Montrose Road, Potomac, MD 20854; 1-800-722-7000) recommends:

Blanchard's Global Income Fund.
According to Skousen, *"[Blanchard's Global Income Fund] is the best 'cash' investment in the world today, with an average annualized yield of over 9%."* This fund invests primarily in foreign short-term and medium-term obligations. Minimum investment of $3,000 required. 1-800-688-7904.

Shearson's Managed Accounts

Managed Currency Portfolio. This fund takes long or short positions in any currency to enhance the rate of return on the portfolio, regardless of the U.S. dollar's strength or weakness. Like the single-currency portfolio, it invests in securities of two-year maturity or less. It is managed by Shearson Lehman Global Asset Management, which is based in London.

Global Equity Account: This is a managed account that buys closed-end country funds listed on the NYSE. Their approach is to track the performance of 30 or more country funds. The Global Equity fund has the advantage of efficiently focusing investment dollars into specific industries and companies that are carefully researched and closely followed by experienced portfolio managers and research analysts of major investment organizations from around the world. GEA then focuses your investment into only the top-performing country funds.

The minimum account is $50,000, but you may be able to establish a relationship for only $25,000. An annual management fee of 3% to 4% is charged quarterly.

G.T. Global

G.T. Global Government Income Fund. This fund is managed for high current income by investing in government-guaranteed high-quality bonds worldwide.

G.T. Global Bond Fund. This fund is managed for moderate quarterly income and capital growth through investments in high-quality global bonds.

G.T. Global Growth Funds. There are six unique mutual funds that offer a broad range of choices: G.T. Worldwide offers access to several major world markets, including the United States; G.T. International offers the same markets as

G.T. Worldwide, but excludes North America; G.T. Europe and G.T. Pacific offer regional exposure to Europe and the Far East; and G.T. Japan and G.T. America offer single-country exposure.

Each fund seeks long-term capital growth and normally invests at least 80% of its assets in the securities of issuers domiciled in that fund's primary investment area. Minimum investment is $500.

For more information, contact your local broker or G.T. Global, 50 California Street, 27th Floor, San Francisco, CA 94111; 1-800-824-1580.

Templeton Foreign Funds

Templeton World Fund. This fund seeks long-term capital growth through a flexible policy of investing in stocks and debt obligations of companies and governments of any nation—including the United States.

Templeton Foreign Fund. This fund is similar to the World Fund, except it invests wholly in securities of foreign companies outside the United States. The Templeton Foreign Fund consists of a range of overseas common stocks, utilities, and foreign cash-equivalent paper, all in the bluest of blue chips. It is a fairly safe way to buy foreign securities and obtain a monthly dividend income.

Other global funds include: Templeton Smaller Companies (formerly Templeton Global Fund) and Global Opportunities Trust.

Shares from these funds may be purchased at a price equal to their net asset value (NAV) plus a sales commission not exceeding 8% of the offering price. The minimum investment if $500.

For a prospectus or additional information, contact Templeton Foreign Funds, 700 Central Avenue, St. Petersburg, FL 33733-8030; 1-800-237-0738.

The Blanchard Group of Funds

Global Growth Fund. This fund divides its total assets among four strategic investment sectors: U.S. equity securities, foreign securities, precious metals, and fixed-income securities. It has been designed to emphasize investments in the sector that has the best potential for appreciation, though all four sectors have investments at all times. The strategy is to shift assets among the sectors at the most advantageous time and price.

Short-Term Global Income Fund. This fund (considered one of the best funds available) invests in high-quality, short-term (three years or less) debt obligations denominated in various currencies. The fund also may invest in repurchase agreements, cash or cash equivalents, or other high-quality debt instruments—rated AA or better or, if unrated, determined to be of comparable quality.

To guard against currency risks and reduce volatility, the fund may use sophisticated hedging strategies that can include the purchase and sale of options. The fund also offers free check writing to shareholders, which gives you instant access to your cash, plus a monthly statement (and statements any time they conduct a transaction on their account). The fund is managed by Lombard

Odier International Management, Ltd., the London-based subsidiary of one of Switzerland's oldest and largest private banks.

The minimum initial investment is $3,000 ($2,000 for IRAs). There are no front- or back-end sales commissions. They do charge a one-time-only account-opening fee of $75. The average 1991 yield for this fund was 9.5%.

For a prospectus or additional information, contact The Blanchard Group of Funds, 41 Madison Avenue, 24th Floor, New York, NY 10010; 1-800-922-7771.

CURRENCY FUTURES

For the more speculative and sophisticated investor, the currency futures market offers a way to capitalize on the sinking dollar and the rise in hard currencies.

This is the market that some banks that offer hard-currency time deposits use to hedge hard-currency CDs, rather than buy them outright. Also, some funds that offer single-currency portfolios use hedging operations to cover your choice of currency.

WHAT IS A CURRENCY FUTURES CONTRACT?

A currency futures contract is an agreement on the rate of exchange of U.S. dollars to another currency, for a transaction to take place at some pre-agreed time.

When you BUY (or "go long") a futures contract, you secure the purchase price in dollars for a specified amount of the other currency. Plus you agree to take delivery on that currency at a specified time in the future.

When you SELL (or "short") a futures contract, you secure a sale price for the transaction in U.S. dollars, for a specific point in time.

In other words, whether you buy or sell a futures contract, you are betting that a particular currency will reach a specific exchange rate within the time of the contract. If you think the dollar will strengthen against a foreign currency, you *sell* a futures contract. If you think it will weaken, then you *buy* a futures contract.

But the delivery of the underlying currency almost never takes place. Instead, both the buyer and the seller, acting independently of one another, usually liquidate their long and short positions before the contract expires.

Using futures, it is possible to hedge as well as speculate. You can buy or sell a futures contract simply in hope of making a profit. Or, if you have a large holding in a currency, you might hedge that exact amount with a currency future to seal in your exchange rate. International traders do this constantly to seal in a purchase price on overseas goods.

The big advantage to currency futures, as opposed to simply buying the full amount of the currency, is that you need to put up only $1 for every $20 of contracts that you enter.

Margin requirements on currency futures vary between 5% and 10%, depending on the currency. This means that if you are correct on the direction of a particular currency, then your profits are multiplied by leverage. However, if you are wrong, then the swings against you (the losses) are equally dramatic. To limit your potential losses, make sure you have a stop-loss order.

In addition, it is now possible to buy options on currency futures contracts that sometimes allow you to trade with strictly limited risk and no margin requirements.

For more information, contact Robert Meier, Fox Instruments, 141 W. Jackson Blvd., Suite 1800A, Chicago, IL 60604; 1-800-621-0265.

Additionally, there are several newsletters and hotlines that have good track records with currency futures. A partial list includes:

Davis/Zweig Futures Hotline, Davis/Zweig Futures, Inc., P.O. Box 360, Bellmore, NY 11710; (516) 785-1300. One year, 24 issues, $295 plus $1 per minute access to hotline.

Taurus, Taurus Corporation, P.O. Box 767, Winchester, VA 22601; (703) 667-4827. 52 issues per year, $700—includes nightly hotline.

The Elliott Wave Currency & Commodity Forecast, P.O. Box 1618, Gainesville, GA 30503; 800-336-1618, (404) 536-0309. $249 per year, $270 per year overseas.

The Timing Device, 1020 E. English, Wichita, KS 67211; (316) 685-6034. One year, 24 issues, $295.

Wellington's Tradeline, Wellington Financial Corp., 6600 Kalanianaole Hwy., Suite 114C, Honolulu, HI 96825; 1-800-922-9989. $450 per year by phone, $800 per year by fax.

RESOURCES

Executive Wealth Advisory, National Institute of Business Management, P.O. Box 25338, Alexandria, VA 22313; 1-800-543-2054. This is an excellent newsletter that covers investing overseas without leaving the United States.

Forbes Annual Fund Survey, September 2, 1991 issue available at your library. Provides performance ratings on global and foreign stock funds and global bond funds.

Fullermoney, David Fuller, Chart Analysis Ltd., 7 Swallow Street, London, WIR 7HD, United Kingdom; 011-4471-439-4961.

Mutual Fund Forecaster, Norman Fosback, Editor, 3471 N Federal Highway, Fort Lauderdale, FL 33306; 1-800-327-6720.

Standard & Poor's/Lipper Mutual Fund Profile, available in most libraries.

— 5 —

Tax-Advantaged Investing Through Guaranteed-Return Annuities

"The Eiffel Tower is the Empire State Building
after taxes."

Anon

Recently, there has been some negative news regarding annuities as, in a few situations, policyholders were unable to withdraw their savings from insurance companies. Despite the headlines, however, it is still easy to invest safely in annuities if you follow a few basic guidelines.

For many investors, provided you stick to sound insurance companies, annuity programs remain a good choice for retirement planning. Annuities are one of the few tax-advantaged investments to survive tax reform. As a result, they offer some extraordinary benefits, such as tax-deferred compounding, no hidden costs and, with most annuities, no maximum investment.

Therefore, in this chapter you will find:

- Faster accumulation through tax-deferred compounding,

- How a variable annuity will protect you against an insurance company failure,
- Five *safety* guidelines to buying annuities today, and
- Seven advantages that Swiss annuities have over U.S. annuities.

Annuities are among today's fastest growing investment areas. According to the Life Insurance Marketing and Research Association, annuity sales increased 22% in 1990 to $60.3 billion.

But with the recent events surrounding the health and integrity of this nation's insurers, many Americans are concerned about the safety of insurance companies and the investments they offer. According to an NBC News poll, of the 1,510 adults polled, about 46% believed the nation's insurers were "just somewhat sound" or "not at all sound." About 8% said they had moved their insurance policies or cashed them in, specifically because of their worries.

Yes, there are problems within the insurance industry; but, as in any situation, a "few bad apples can always spoil the broth." By carefully checking out the insurance company with the various ratings services (see Chapter 8), you can still safely invest in the various insurance and investment products they offer. And that includes annuities. By following the guidelines found later in this chapter, you can further protect yourself and your family from financial disaster.

Furthermore, there are guaranteed funds and various mechanisms to protect the investor. All states have laws to protect you.

U.S. DOLLAR ANNUITIES

An annuity is a contract between you and an insurance company where you can make either a single, lump sum deposit or flexible, scheduled deposits and earn competitive interest. Up to this point it is like a CD or a savings account. However, as one of the few investment vehicles to survive the 1986 Tax Reform Act (almost intact), annuities are a good way to accumulate tax-deferred savings for your retirement years.

FASTER ACCUMULATION THROUGH
TAX-DEFERRED COMPOUNDING

When you invest money into an annuity, it will grow on a tax-deferred basis until you begin receiving it—usually after age 59½. Until you begin withdrawing money from your annuity, you get to enjoy the advantages of compound interest, *tax-deferred.* See Figure 5.1 for a comparison of taxable and tax-deferred plans.

(The IRS allows withdrawals without penalties [known as the 1035 exchange] as long as the money is put directly into a new annuity.)

Tax-deferred compounding makes your money grow much faster than comparable taxable investments like CDs or money market funds. For instance, a guaranteed-return annuity with a 7% annual yield would double your money in about

Figure 5.1. The Power of Tax-Deferred Growth

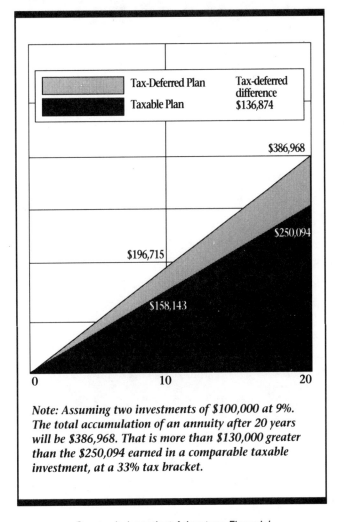

| | Tax-Deferred Plan | Tax-deferred difference $136,874 |
| | Taxable Plan | |

$386,968

$250,094

$196,715

$158,143

0   10   20

Note: Assuming two investments of $100,000 at 9%. The total accumulation of an annuity after 20 years will be $386,968. That is more than $130,000 greater than the $250,094 earned in a comparable taxable investment, at a 33% tax bracket.

Source: Independent Advantage Financial

10 years. On the other hand, taxable bank CDs paying 5% (which is only 3.35% after taxes, if you're in the 33% federal, state, and local tax bracket) would take over 21 years to double. See Table 5.1 for a comparison of annuity and CD returns.

In some cases, that means you could have twice as much money at retirement with an annuity than with a CD.

Annuities work in similar fashion to an IRA account. But, unlike an IRA account, there is no $2,000-per-year limit on contributions. You can also continue to invest in most annuities on an after-tax basis beyond age 70.

The minimum investment on most annuities is low, often as little as $2,000. And on most annuities, there is no upper limit.

Table 5.1. A Comparison of Annuity and CD Returns

End of Year	Projected Annuity Values (Deferred Tax)	Projected CD Values (After Tax)
1	$107,000	$103,350
2	114,490	106,812
3	112,504	110,390
4	131,079	114,088
5	140,255	117,910
6	150,073	121,860
7	160,578	125,942
8	171,818	130,161
9	183,845	134,522
10	196,715	139,028

Note: *Assumes $100,000 initial investment, 7% annual yield for the annuity, a 5% (3.35% after tax) yield on the CD and a 33% tax bracket. The actual tax savings at the end of year 5 will be $9,060.*
Note: as of November 1991.

FIXED ANNUITIES

Annuities are managed like a mutual fund. In other words, they have managers who invest your money for you. With a fixed annuity, the premiums are invested in fixed-rate vehicles, usually bonds or mortgages. You are guaranteed a fixed rate of return for a period of time, usually one to five years. Sometimes it can be a longer period of time.

After this period, your investments are rolled over for the next time period. The rate of return will change, based on the going rate of interest.

Most fixed annuities are guaranteed to pay a minimum interest rate; and no matter what happens to prevailing rates, your return will not fall below this "floor." This minimum guarantee is good for the life of the annuity. Because of its guaranteed rate of return, the fixed annuity is more conservative than the variable annuity.

But remember, with any fixed-rate investment, you may see inflation eat away the value of your annuity.

SAFETY TIP

Fixed vs. Variable Annuity:
Which Will Protect You Against A Failure?

With insurers like First Executive Life and Mutual Benefit Life going under during 1991, the question of the day is: If my insurer fails, will I lose my annuity investment?

It depends on the type of annuity: fixed or variable.

Most of the investments in a variable annuity are kept separate from the insurer's balance sheet. In other words, your investment return depends entirely on the performance of the investments in the portfolio—not the solvency of your insurer. Therefore, even if the insurer fails, the money in those accounts should remain unaffected.

If you own a fixed annuity, you could have problems should the insurer fail. A fixed annuity is backed by the insurer. If the company fails, any money you have in the annuity will likely be frozen while regulators look for a healthy insurer to bail them out. That is what happened with both First Executive and Mutual Life.

Investors holding variable annuities with First Executive and Mutual Life continue to earn tax-deferred interest or may withdraw funds at any time.

If you are concerned about your insurer's health (review the information in Chapter 8) and hold a fixed option, then consider these options:

1. Immediately switch your fixed option into its money market or bond fund now, before trouble occurs. (Be aware that most variables don't allow you to switch from a fixed option until you have owned it for one to three years. Or they may allow moving only 25% to 35% of the money per year.) Or . . .

2. You can transfer your entire annuity to another insurer via a "1035 exchange." If you transfer within the first six or seven years, expect to pay surrender charges of 1% to 7% of the amount of money removed.

Regardless of what you decide, do not simply pull your money out without considering the consequences. You must balance the possible surrender penalties and income tax liability on the funds withdrawn.

(If you transfer, it may be possible to defer taxes, but check with a professional tax advisor. The IRS rules are tricky on this issue.)

Also consider the possible loss of the tax-deferred investment opportunities that may occur when you put your money into an alternative investment.

VARIABLE ANNUITIES

A variable annuity is a riskier investment, with a greater downside, as well as upside, potential. The reason is that variable annuities are regarded as wealth-building instruments—they invest in stocks, bonds, real estate, money market funds, and mutual funds. Your rate of return is dependent on how well the investments fare. (As you saw in Chapter 3, mutual funds have done quite well.)

You can pay for your annuity in one of two ways:

1. You can put a lump sum into an annuity, in exactly the same way you would buy a CD or a time deposit.

2. You can make regular payments into the annuity in a way similar to making payments into an IRA or Keogh plan.

For most people, the whole point of an annuity is to accumulate money for their retirement years. So they take out a deferred annuity (which is the reason fixed annuities outsell variables by a huge margin).

However, if you are retiring and your company is about to give you a lump sum payment on your pension plan (that would be fully taxable when you receive it), you could roll the amount over directly into an annuity. Here, you would pay taxes on only the income you actually withdrew, and you could ask for an immediate annuity.

WHEN YOU REACH RETIREMENT AGE . . .

Once you reach the age when you require income on a regular basis, you have four choices from your annuity:

1. *Lump Sum:* You can opt to receive a lump sum, in which you take out all your funds at once.

2. *Period Certain:* The company pays you for a predetermined period; and should you die before the period is up, then your spouse would continue to receive payments.

3. *Straight Life:* The insurance company agrees to pay you a fixed monthly benefit for the rest of your life, no matter how long you live. This is calculated on how much money is in your account, plus how long the insurance company projects you are likely to live. If you can beat the odds, then you obviously stand to gain most by this option.

4. *Joint and Survivor:* This option promises a monthly check for as long as you or your beneficiary lives. Like option 3, if you beat the odds, then you stand to gain handsomely.

TAX NOTE

All withdrawals of interest earnings from an annuity are taxable. If you withdraw money before age 59½, you not only pay taxes on the interest, but you pay an extra IRS penalty of 10%.

THREE ADDITIONAL BENEFITS

1. *No probate.* There is no life insurance attached to an annuity. However, in the event of the death of the holder of the annuity, all proceeds are paid directly to the named beneficiary. This means that, in most states, you can totally avoid the delay, expenses and publicity of probate on your annuity, which can literally save you thousands of dollars.

2. *No hidden costs.* Annuity contracts are free of sales charges and front-end loads (however, some companies in a few states will charge a small state premium tax).

3. *No Social Security offset.* Earnings from an annuity during the accumulation phase do not offset your Social Security benefits as do bonds, CDs, and other investment income. Because you are not paying taxes on your annuity during the accumulation phase, it is not regarded as part of your income, even if you continue to accumulate beyond the age when you begin to receive Social Security.

CAUTION . . .

There are no front-end fees on annuities, but the salesperson's 4% to 7% commission is factored into the annuity's interest rate. Consequently, most annuities have an early withdrawal penalty (surrender charges), similar to those that banks impose on time deposits, or insurance companies impose on whole life insurance policies. The surrender charges are as high as 15% of your accumulated earnings for a withdrawal made in the first year of the contract and drop by about 1% each year until they disappear, typically in 7 to 10 years.

If you are under 59½, add the IRS 10% penalty on any income you may have accumulated in the account, and you will see that you have to be very sure that you:

1. Want to have an annuity, and . . .
2. Have the *right annuity for you,* before you enter a contract.

However, some companies offering annuities will give you a grace period after you have signed the contract (anywhere from 10 days to one full year, depending on the insurance company). If you have second thoughts, you can cancel the contract without subjecting yourself to a penalty.

And once you have made the decision and are comfortable with the annuity (and the insurance company behind it), you can sit back and watch the miracle of tax-deferred compounding build your retirement nest egg.

THREE WAYS TO BUY ANNUITIES

There are three methods to buying annuities:

1. *Mutual Funds.* A number of mutual funds now have annuities. One of the better funds is Templeton Investment Plus (Templeton Group of Funds, 700 Central Avenue, St. Petersburg, FL 33701; 1-800-237-0738), it invests in stocks, bonds and money market funds.

2. *Brokerage Houses.* Because annuities are tax-deferred investments, major brokerage houses now offer annuities.

3. *Insurance Agents.* If you plan to go this route, you should choose an independent agent who specializes in annuities and represents several different insurance companies. That way you get an objective view of several insurance companies, and the agent does not have a vested interest in selling you one company to the exclusion of all others. One company we highly recommend is:

Independent Advantage Financial and Insurance Services, Inc. (IAF), 330 Washington Blvd., 8th Floor, Marina Del Rey, CA 90292-5149; 1-800-829-2887 or (213) 821-1660.

Independent Advantage works with over 40 highly rated companies that offer the top-performing annuities on the market. They make sure every company they recommend ranks far above industry standards. The following is the basis of their insurance company screening process:

- An insurance company must have the top ratings by A.M. Best (A+ "Superior"). In addition, if the company is rated by Standard & Poor's, Moody's or Duff & Phelps, it must hold a rating in the top two categories.

- A company must be at least 40 years old (many of their recommended firms are over 100 years old).

- A company must have at least $1 billion in assets (several have over $4 billion).

- It must have less than 5% to 7% of assets in junk bonds and real estate.

- It must have a consistent growth rate over the last five years.

- It must have capital and surplus of 5% to 8%, depending on the size and business mix of the company.

HOW SAFE IS THE U.S. INSURANCE INDUSTRY?

As Senator Metzenbaum stated recently, "There is a crisis of confidence in the insurance industry today." Executive Life of California was seized by regulators and subsequently was paying only 70 cents on the dollar for annuities. Mutual Benefit was devastated by shaky real estate investments, causing a run on the bank (or in this case, a run on the insurance company).

Will there be more failures? Most likely, yes. Are all insurance companies in trouble? No, but you must be choosy.

Your biggest concern lies in the fact that insurance company investments, unlike bank deposits, are not federally insured against loss.

But this has a good side. Precisely because insurance companies are not federally insured, even the worst of the insurance companies have not been as lacking in good sense as many S&Ls. Historically, when an insurance company has reached insolvency, another much healthier insurance company has usually come along and purchased them.

All states have guaranteed funds or life and health insurance guaranty associations to help pay claims of financially insolvent insurance companies. According to the *Annuity and Life Insurance Shopper:*

"Coverage is for individual policyholders and their beneficiaries, and often extends to persons insured under group policies. Most associations limit their protection to policyholders who are residents of their own state. It does not matter where the policyowner's beneficiaries live. Other states protect all the policyholders of an insurance company domiciled in their state, extending coverage without regard to the state in which policyholders reside. Association laws also differ on amount of coverage. Typically, states protect life insurance death benefits to $300,000, cash values to $100,000, and $100,000 in present value of annuity benefits. Often there is an additional limit of $300,000 for all benefits combined, per policyholder."

Before you purchase an annuity (or insurance policy), review Chapter 8. Then call your state insurance commissioner (phone numbers are listed in Chapter 8) for the type and extent of coverage available in your state. Another source of information is:

National Organization of Life and Health Insurance Guaranty Associations (NOLHGA), 13873 Park Center Road, Suite 329, Herndon, VA 22071; (703) 481-5206.

GUIDELINES TO BUYING ANNUITIES TODAY

In addition to following Independent Advantage's screening methods listed above, follow these guidelines when choosing an annuity:

1. Buy annuities only from companies that get high grades from *multiple* rating agencies. Usually you will avoid any insurance company that has 5% to 7% or more of its portfolio in real estate and junk bonds (Table 5.2 lists the *current* largest holders of these bonds).

2. Diversify your deposits among several insurers.

3. Avoid those funds with higher yields than the industry average. If you shop yield only, you face trouble.

Table 5.2. Largest Junk Bond Holders

	% of Holdings
United Pacific Life Insurance Company	17.2%
Anchor National Life Insurance	15.8%
Kemper Investment Life Insurance	15.5%
Northwestern National Life	15.5%
Jackson National Life	11.0%
Prucho Life Insurance	10.2%

Source: Weiss Research

Some companies inflate their yields by playing games with the way they calculate them. Others advertise rates that have costly strings attached to them.

Chances are, if the yield is above average, the company is either sacrificing the quality of its investments or restricting your ability to get at your money. The most common deception today is the "bonus annuity" in which the insurer tacks on as much as 8% to its current interest rate, boosting the first-year yield to 15% or higher. But you will get the bonus on your accrued earnings *only* if you eventually annuitize and take the money in monthly installments over a period of at least 10 years.

4. Avoid tier-rated annuities. They offer two levels of interest rates—an above-average rate of, say 9%, but as with bonus rates, the accrued earnings in your account will reflect this accumulation rate only when you annuitize. A straight withdrawal will oftentimes end in rates as low as 6% for every year you've invested.

5. Watch out for safety claims. Although salesmen like to point out that an annuity's value is "guaranteed," that promise is only as strong as the insurer. To solicit investors who prefer the security of bank accounts, banks, and insurance companies, some companies have begun to offer so-called certificates of annuities. Don't be fooled by the name. No annuity—even one sold in a bank lobby—is federally insured.

To avoid being taken by a "loss leader" rate, compare the annuity's initial rates with its competitors. The bimonthly newsletter, *Annuity and Life Insurance Shopper* ($10 an issue; 1-800-872-6684), publishes the rates of more than 80 fixed annuities.

HARD-CURRENCY ANNUITIES

It is also possible to buy hard-currency annuities through European banks. For example: ABN-AMRO Bank (P.O. Box 90, 1000AB Amsterdam, Netherlands; Phone: 011-31-20-282-764, Fax: 011-31-20-239-940) can act as an intermediary for you to purchase hard-currency annuities.

Or contact ABN-AMRO Bank, Switzerland (Talstrasse 41, 8032 Zurich, Switzerland Phone: 011-411-211-5315; Fax: 011-411-212-1564).

Such contracts are made to measure, specifically tied to the client's wishes and personal needs. Obviously, their main business is in Dutch guilder annuities, but they can help you purchase annuities in other currencies as well.

SWISS FRANC ANNUITIES

Swiss Franc Single Premium Annuities and Swiss Franc Single Premium Endowments are particularly popular, because they off all the advantages of their U.S. counterparts, plus the benefits of Swiss privacy and the safety of a hard currency. The Single Premium Annuity also offers full liquidity. Other advantages include:

- *Higher interest rates than time deposits.* Swiss annuities usually pay a higher rate on Swiss francs than the average Swiss bank pays on a time deposit. While Swiss franc annuities pay lower nominal interest rates than U.S. annuities, there is a guaranteed interest rate floor of 3% set by the Swiss government. At the moment, you would receive approximately 5% to 6% on your annuity.

- *Higher real yields.* Historically, the combination of a strong Swiss franc and moderate interest rates has allowed Swiss annuities to vastly outperform U.S. annuities—despite historically higher interest rates available in the United States. For example, an investor who put $100,000 into a Swiss franc annuity in 1972 would have seen his savings rise to more than $800,000 today.

- *No IRS reporting requirement.* According to noted annuity expert Jean-Pierre Louvet, the ownership of a Swiss franc annuity is exempt from any reporting requirement, per se, on either your income tax Form 1040, or Treasury Form 90.22.2. The IRS does not regard them to be financial instruments in the legal sense.

  However, anyone who buys a Single Premium Annuity is expected by U.S. authorities to pay an excise tax of 1% of the initial investment amount. Treasury Form 720 should be used for this purpose.

  Be sure to reconfirm this tax information before taking any action. Tax laws and rulings change constantly, and if too many people take advantage of a loophole, you can be sure that the IRS will soon fill it.

- *No Swiss taxes.* The 35% withholding tax you are subject to on interest-bearing bank accounts in Switzerland does not apply to annuity payments.

- *Creditor protection.* Under Swiss law, if you name your spouse or children as beneficiaries to your annuity, it makes the policy immune from attachment by creditors, unlike funds deposited with a Swiss bank.

   Swiss law specifically states that even if a U.S. judgment or court order expressly orders the seizure of the policy, or inclusion in the estate in bankruptcy, such an insurance policy *may not* be seized in Switzerland or be included in the estate in bankruptcy.

- *Loan or pledge option.* The selected insurance company, upon request, grants a loan of up to 85% of the available cash against a Swiss annuity and will charge the going rate for such a loan. Yet, during the period of the loan, the annuity will continue to earn interest, which means you will get the loan for about 1% to 1.5% on the basis of current rates.

- *Termination of contract.* Unlike U.S. annuities, there is no minimum contract period and no penalty for early withdrawal of funds. You may cancel your contract at will.

- *Guaranteed capital security and growth in Swiss francs.*

- *No up-front fees.* All invested capital will start earning interest and dividends immediately.

- *No back-end fees upon redemption.*

- *Full liquidity at any time.* This is subject to a minimum handling fee during the first year only.

- *Legal protection against creditor lawsuits.*

- *A guaranteed life-income option.*

YIELD & SAFETY TIP

There is a new Swiss annuity product that has been developed called the "Single Premium Annuity Certificate."

This annuity has a clause where you can effectively take a loan against the entire amount of the annuity, and invest the resulting funds as you choose. The charge of a little more than 1% for this privilege compares favorably with trading on margin.

You can do anything you choose with the account and still be legally exempt from U.S. reporting requirements. That is, provided you follow the procedures advised when you take out your annuity contract. The procedures can be a bit complicated, but any expert on Swiss annuities can guide you through them.

For further details on Swiss franc annuities, contact any of the banks listed in Chapter 9. Or, contact Jean-Pierre Louvet, a very knowledgeable Swiss franc annuity consultant who writes *The Capital Preservation Strategist* (a monthly newsletter from England on European investments). His newsletter is published by New Classics Library, P.O. Box 1618, Gainesville, GA 30503; (404) 536-0309.

To contact Jean-Pierre directly, write or call: Globacor Ltd., 18 Kimbers Drive, Burnham, Green Lane, Berkshire, Great Britain SL1 8JE; Phone: 011-44-628-660-990 or 011-44-753-663-295, Fax: 011-44-753-663-167. Jean-Pierre's initial consultation is free.

In addition, three major companies that specialize in selling Swiss franc annuities to English-speaking investors are:

Annuity and Endowment Specialists, S.A., P.O. Box 170GY, 8033 Zurich, Switzerland.

Assurex, S.A., Postfach 18, 8311 Winterberg ZH, Switzerland.

Jurg M. Lattman, AG, Swiss Investment Counsellors, Germaniastrasse 55, 8033 Zurich, Switzerland.

RESOURCES

Annuity and Life Insurance Shopper, 98 Hoffman Road, Englishtown, NJ 07726; 1-800-872-6684. This bimonthly newsletter publishes the rates of more than 80 fixed annuities and the four rating services' ratings for several major insurance companies.

Insurance Investing, Editor: Doug Fabian, P.O. Box 2090, Huntington Beach, CA 92647; (714) 893-7332. This is the only independent informational source for insurance policyholders and insurance professionals. Doug is also editor of *Telephone Switch Newsletter* on mutual funds.

Life Insurance and Annuities From the Buyer's Point of View, American Institute for Economic Research, Great Barrington, MA 01230. The price is $9.

The Life Insurance Investor, Probus Publishing Company, 1925 N. Clybourn Street, Chicago, IL 60614; (312) 868-1100. This book is available for $27.50.

Andrew Westhem, Wealth Transfer Planning, 1925 Century Parkway East, Suite 2350, Los Angeles, CA 90067; 1-800-423-4891. Andrew Westhem is a very respectable and knowledgeable wealth transfer advisor.

— 6 —

Prudent Retirement and Estate Planning:

Taking Advantage of Tax Laws

"Cessation of work is not accompanied by cessation of expenses."

Cato the Elder

2nd Century B.C.

A mericans are living longer than ever before. That fact, in combination with modest inflation and a teetering Social Security system, means that you must set aside more and more of your wealth if you hope to live comfortably in retirement.

This chapter shows you ways to avoid taxes, build your wealth, and plan for retirement including:

- How to determine just how much money you will need to set aside *now* to ensure an adequate retirement income in the future,

- How to use tax-deferred compounding to build a larger retirement nest egg,
- Ten sources of tax-deferred income for retirement,
- A way to extend your retirement distribution by *four additional years,*
- How long-term care can wipe out your retirement, and methods to protect you and your spouse, and
- Strategies that allow you to pass more of your hard-earned wealth on to your children by avoiding costly estate taxes.

Until very recently, you only had to plan for about 10 years of retirement living. If you made it beyond 75 years of age, you considered yourself very lucky.

Today, that reality has changed. With the rapid advancement in medical technology, life expectancies have become longer than what we perhaps first expected (see Figure 6.1). At age 60, at least one spouse should reach 90. At age 70, at least one should reach 91. At age 80, one out of two should plan to live 13 years more. That means you have to plan for *30 years or more without earned income.* (See Table 6.1 for life expectancy projections.)

Currently, only 5% of all Americans over 65 are financially independent; 22% must still work and 28% depend on relatives to help them out. The rest live on welfare. This chapter is aimed at helping you become part of the 5%.

In the past, senior citizens expected to spend their golden years "growing old gracefully," which was a euphemism for giving up on life and staying home. Today, seniors join organizations like Elderhostel. That enables them to travel, take educational courses, and do all the things they did not have time to do when they were raising their families. *And this costs more money than staying home.*

Table 6.1. Life Expectancy Projections

Birth Year	L.E. at Birth	65 in Year	Male	Female
1900	47	1965	78	81
1920	54	1985	80	84
1940	63	2005	81	86
1950	68	2015	81	87
1980	74	2045	82	88
1990	75	2055	83	89

A man born in 1920 had a life expectancy of 54 years; but if he lived to be 65, his life expectancy increased to 80 years.

Source: NCHS, 1975, Middle Mortality projections

Figure 6.1. Rising Life Expectancy

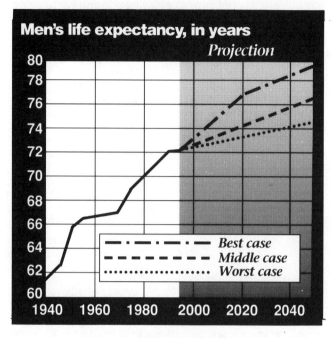

Source: Social Security Administration

As we all live longer and strive for an active life right until the end, our health costs will continue to rise. Medicare covers only half of your health care costs, so there also has to be a provision for health care in your retirement budget.

To make matters worse, statistics show that one in every two U.S. citizens will end up in a nursing home before they die. The average annual cost of a nursing home is $35,000.

In short, today's seniors need more money than ever before to maintain an active lifestyle.

And if that weren't enough, the consensus among economists is that the rate of inflation will run at a "bit more than 4% per year over the next few years"— that's if you believe the economists.

At an annual inflation rate of 6% (1990's figure), a $10 item will cost $21.60 in 10 years, $46.60 in 20 years and $100.60 in 30 years. Unless you are prepared to live very frugally, Social Security payments will not nearly cover your retirement living expenses. Figure 6.2 breaks down the income sources for people 65 and older with $20,000 in annual income.

In addition, there is the fear that the Social Security system won't even exist when you reach retirement. Also, employers today are moving away from defined benefit pension plans that guarantee a certain income after you retire. Instead they are moving to defined contribution plans, such as profit-sharing 401(k) plans. With these plans, your retirement benefits will depend on how much is

Figure 6.2.   Income Sources for People Age 65+ with $20,000+ Annual Income

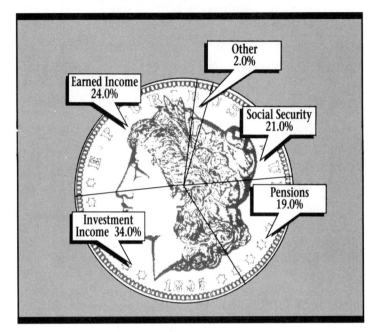

Source: Social Security Administration

contributed each year by you or your employer, *as well as on investment performance.*

THE POTENTIAL COLLAPSE OF THE SOCIAL SECURITY SYSTEM

For the economy, the problem of nonworking seniors didn't matter much in the 1970s and 1980s. The labor force was flooded with baby-boomers and with women seeking to expand their horizons or supplement their family income. But the 1990s will be another matter. The baby boom has been absorbed into the work force, and the percentage of women looking for work has stopped rising.

For the federal budget, the problem is critical.

Caring for the elderly has become the major preoccupation of the federal government. Payments to seniors already account for a third of federal outlays. But with the elderly population growing and health care costs rising, payments will soon soar to over 50% of outlays. By 2020, an estimated 53 million retirees will get federal benefits, up from 32 million today.

Today more than three workers pay Social Security taxes for every one beneficiary collecting checks. By 2035, that ratio will be less than 2 to 1.

Currently, the unfunded liability of the Social Security system is over $15 trillion. Despite these liabilities, the system is the second greatest generator of federal revenue—money that is shuffled to the general budget instead of paying retirement benefits, as intended.

We can't afford the Social Security system, and we can't afford to live without it. It's a time bomb waiting to go off. Even if the system were healthy, it would have a hard time coping with the bulge in retirees who will begin drawing Social Security at the end of this decade.

Therefore, if you have at least five years before you begin drawing Social Security, you should be making every effort to minimize your tax bills, and make contingency plans to survive retirement *without Social Security.*

Consider this: Your Social Security payments are not going into your retirement account, but instead are going to pay current bills. For every tax dollar you pay, including your Social Security payments, 54 cents is immediately spoken for to pay just the interest on the national debt!

According to the Grace Commission, of the remaining 46 cents, *25 cents goes to waste.* So for every dollar you now give to the U.S. government, you get back only 21 cents in services.

If government uses our tax dollars so inefficiently, we owe it to ourselves to structure our assets so as to minimize our taxes, and then to use those saved dollars to provide ourselves with services the government may no longer be able to provide for us.

However, while the Social Security system is still intact, you should carefully monitor your payments to see that the records are accurate and that you are being credited with all you are forced to pay.

ENSURING YOUR SOCIAL SECURITY RECORDS ARE CORRECT

Contact the Social Security Administration office and ask for a copy of your "Personal Earnings and Benefit Estimate Statement." This statement will explain your Social Security benefits and provide you with your earnings record and estimates of the benefits you qualify for, now and in the future.

According to Gwendolyn S. King, Commission of the Social Security Administration, ". . . this information is to be used as a planning tool. It is important that, as you plan your financial future, you keep in mind that Social Security is not designed to meet all your future financial needs. You need additional sources of income so that when you retire, you and your family can enjoy the financial security you have worked so hard to achieve."

To receive a copy of your "Personal Earnings and Benefit Estimate Statement" (Form SSA 7005, 9-91), call the Social Security Administration toll-free at 1-800-SSA-1213 or 1-800-772-1213. *This is a new number as of October 1, 1991,* so don't use their old listing. Service is available weekdays from 7 a.m. to 7 p.m. The best time to call is either early morning or late afternoon, Wednesday through Friday, after the first week of the month.

When you call for your statement, they will ask you for your Social Security number, previous year's earnings, estimated current year's earnings, and estimated future earnings until retirement.

Once you receive your statement, check that the information is correct—especially your earnings record. If your earnings record appears incorrect, call the above 800 number and challenge their figures. When you call, have your "statement" with any W-2 Forms, pay slips, tax returns or other proof of earnings available to support your claim.

POINTS TO REMEMBER ABOUT SOCIAL SECURITY

- You must have 40 Social Security credits to qualify for retirement benefits. (This is the same number of credits you need to qualify for Medicare at age 65.) In 1991, you would have earned one credit for each $540 of your covered wages or self-employment income. You can earn up to four Social Security credits a year.

- You can begin receiving benefits at age 62—provided you have enough credits to qualify. People who can retire now receive full, unreduced retirement benefits at age 65. However, starting in the year 2000, this full retirement age will be increased in monthly steps until it reaches age 67 in 2027.

- Social Security payments rise 3% for each year you delay collecting them.

- Until you reach age 70, for every $3 you earn over $8,880, the government will withhold $1 from your Social Security payment. If you can delay taking earnings until after age 70, you can receive full Social Security.

YIELD TIP

Increase Your Social Security Benefits Nearly 40%

By working an extra five to six years, you can impact your retirement life-style tremendously. Not only will you add extra years of contributions to your retirement plan, but you will reduce the pay-out by several years.

The result: You will increase the amount of pay-outs when you do retire and will cut medical costs by keeping full health benefits longer.

In addition, you can add part of your salary to savings during the extra time you work. For example: A 50-year-old executive and spouse have an income of $80,000. Under a typical retirement plan, they could maintain their lifestyle for only 19% of their retirement years if the executive retires at age 60—after working at the current job for 20 years. But if the executive retires at 66, they should never have to cut back on their lifestyle.

Based on a Social Security Earnings and Benefit Statement, a 42-year-old, with current annual earnings of $40,000 per year until retirement, would receive Social Security benefits of $935 at age 62, $1,295 at age 66 (nearly a 40% increase), and $1,745 at age 70.

HOW TO DETERMINE HOW MUCH YOU WILL NEED
FOR RETIREMENT

A simple formula you can follow to figure out how much you will need for your retirement years is:

1. Determine the *minimum monthly amount in current dollars* that you will need to live comfortably when you retire. Studies show that retirees need from 60% to 80% of preretirement, pretax income. Then add to that figure about 5% per year for every year you still have left in the work force. This will adjust, at least in part, for future inflation and consumer price increases. (Add a higher percentage if you feel inflation will be higher.)

2. Subtract half the amount you think you will get from Social Security from this total. That way, if Social Security does collapse, you will suffer, but not be destroyed.

3. This leaves you with the monthly amount you need to receive to live. Multiply that by 12 to get your annual requirement.

4. Multiply your yearly figure by 11 to calculate the amount of capital you need to build up to receive an approximate 9% steady income from a lump sum. That final figure is the amount you need to accumulate between now and your retirement.

(For your convenience, Figure 6.3 is a worksheet that will help you calculate your retirement needs).

HOW TO ACCUMULATE RETIREMENT WEALTH

You can earn even higher yields on your money if you either put your investments into some sort of sheltered form (such as an IRA or Keogh plan), or invest in the various bonds and securities that come with a built-in tax break (such as Municipals and Treasuries).

If you are a taxpayer in the 28% to 31% tax bracket (taxable income exceeding $34,000 for couples, or $20,350 for singles), you need to find a yield of 9% to 10% to make between 6% and 7% on your money after taxes. Whether you achieve that nontaxable status by buying tax-advantaged investments or by sheltering taxable investments, the results are the same. Remember, however, that *these figures do not consider the rate of inflation.*

Figure 6.4 shows how the magic of compound interest is even more magical if you can shelter your money from taxes as well.

TAKING ADVANTAGE OF DISCOUNTS

Many retirees are eligible for senior-citizen discounts on certain goods and services, and some of these discounts are obtainable at 50 or 55 years of age, even before you retire. By taking advantage of these discounts as early as possible, you not only save valuable dollars, but can invest these savings for retirement.

Figure 6.3. How to Figure How Much You Will Need for Retirement

How to Figure How Much You Will Need for Retirement

	Example Figures	Your
A - Enter your current pre-tax monthly income.	$4,000	$ _____
B - Estimated retirement income (60% - 80%).	.60 (i)	_____
C - Estimated retirement income needs (A times B).	$2,400	$ _____
D - Years remaining until retirement.	10	_____
E - Estimated annual inflation rate.	.05	_____
F - Inflation adjustment factor (E times D).	.50	_____
G - Monthly retirement income adjusted for inflation. [C times (1.00 plus F)]	$3,600	$ _____
H - Enter 50% of the amount you will receive from Social Security.	$500	$ _____
I - Net monthly retirement amount (G minus H).	$3,100	$ _____
J - Annual retirement requirement (I times 12).	$37,200	$ _____
K - Factor to determine the amount of capital you need to build to receive an approximate 9% steady income from a lump sum.	11	11
L - Amount you need to accumulate between now and retirement (K times J).	$409,200	$ _____

(i) Studies show that most retirees can live comfortably on 60% to 80% of their pre-retirement income.

The main areas for discounts include travel expenses (airlines, trains, rental cars, and hotel rooms) and restaurant meals.

You also can become eligible for certain tax breaks (such as on the sale of real estate) in your 50s. With baby-boomers reaching middle years, age is being viewed differently. You are no longer "over the hill" at 50.

To find out what discounts are available to people over 50, contact the American Association of Retired Persons (AARP), 1909 K Street NW, Washington, DC 20049. For a few dollars a year, this organization will supply you with useful information about discounts, government benefits, Social Security, and so forth. It is well worth the price of membership.

**Figure 6.4.   Compounding Interest PLUS
Regular Contributions Can
Yield Amazing Results**

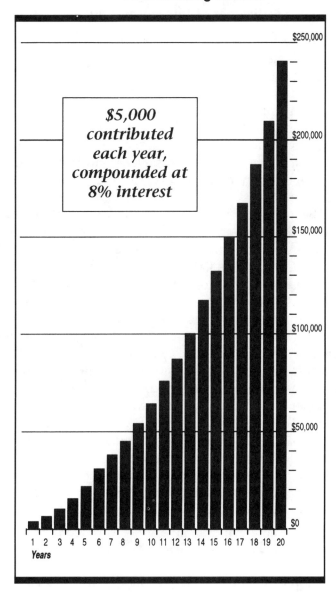

TEN SOURCES OF TAX-DEFERRED INCOME FOR RETIREMENT

1. *Individual Retirement Accounts (IRAs):* If both you and your working spouse do not participate in a company pension or profit-sharing plan, you can each deduct up to $2,000 a year in annual contributions to an IRA. If you are married and only one spouse is working, then you can deduct up to $2,250 per year. If you are also a participant in an employee-

> ## YIELD TIP
>
> ### Extend Your Retirement Distribution Four Additional Years
>
> According to Robert C. Carlson, editor of *Tax Avoidance Digest* (824 E. Baltimore St., Baltimore, MD 21202; 1-800-223-1982, Ext. 418): "Many retirees pay thousands of dollars in unnecessary taxes. By choosing the wrong way to report lump sum retirement plan distributions on their tax return, retirees pay more taxes than are legally required and increase the risk that they will outlive their financial resources."
>
> When you retire and take a lump-sum retirement distribution, you can do one of these things: You can roll it over to an IRA, or you can keep it outside an IRA and report it on your tax return, using either five-year or 10-year averaging.
>
> With an IRA rollover, there is no immediate tax, but the money is fully taxed as it is withdrawn from the IRA. The averaging methods incur a substantial tax now as well as taxes on the annual income.
>
> According to Carlson, the IRA rollover is better for many retirees. "The earnings on the lump sum accumulate tax-deferred as long as the money remains in the IRA. Many people overlook the power of tax-deferred compounding. If a retiree does not need to spend a large portion of the lump sum soon and will be taking annual withdrawals from the IRA, the IRA rollover produces the best results. My projections show that a rollover will make your assets last 4 or more years longer than an averaging method without reducing your standard of living." (See Figure 6.6.)
>
> For additional information, we suggest that you order the *Retirement Tax Guide* from R. C. Carlson Advisors, P.O. Box 4954, Falls Church, VA 22044; (703) 941-2032. Besides acting as editor of *Tax Avoidance Digest,* Carlson operates R.C. Carlson Advisors, which provides total financial planning, special situation planning, and tax consulting. They work on a *fee-only* basis, so you can get recommendations that are objective and independent.

sponsored retirement plan, you are not entitled to the full $2,000 a year. Check with your accountant. Table 6.2 shows many of the advantages of an IRA.

You cannot put the following investments into an IRA: life insurance, art objects, antiques, gold or silver coins (except gold and silver bullion coins minted in the United States), stamps, and other collectibles. If you invest in any of these, the IRS regards the investment as a withdrawal from your IRA and not only charges you tax, but a penalty as well. (See Figure 6.5.)

2. *401(k) Plans:* Also known as a Cash or Deferred Arrangement (CODA), a 401(k) plan is an employee sponsored company employee benefit plan.

Figure 6.5. Investing in a Tax-Deferred IRA and a Fully Taxable Investment*

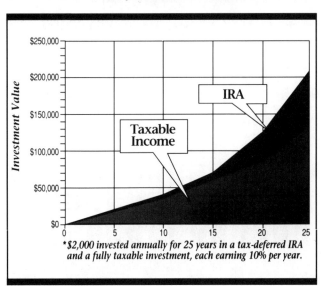

*$2,000 invested annually for 25 years in a tax-deferred IRA and a fully taxable investment, each earning 10% per year.

You instruct your company to deduct an agreed amount from your check each payday and to deposit that money into a 401(k) account that bears your name.

A 401(k) plan differs from an IRA in the way the IRS treats this money. Instead of deducting your 401(k) plan contribution on your Form 1040, it is treated as deferred income, which means it simply isn't listed on your 1040. However, the money you put into your 401(k) is not exempt from Social Security payments.

So how much can you contribute? As the employee, you may set aside no more than $7,979 in pretax dollars. Your employer can act as a partner with you; and you *and* your company, as joint partners, may contribute

Table 6.2. IRAs Still Offer Advantages

Years to Retirement	Non-deductible IRA 8%	CD 8%	Municipal Bond 6%
10	$ 26,461	$26,066	$ 26,362
15	47,499	45,710	46,552
20	77,097	71,701	73,571
25	119,273	106,091	109,729
30	179,928	151,594	158,116

Figure 6.6.   Lump Sum Comparison

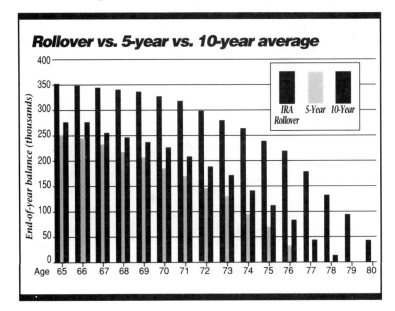

Source: R. C. Carlson Advisors

up to $30,000 or 25% of your compensation to a 401(k) in your name. The law places few limitations on the types of investments you can make with the money in your account, but they have to be confined to those that your company makes available to you.

If you work for a college, university or other public institution, you cannot participate in a 401(k) plan. Instead, you contribute to what is known as a 403(b) plan that is very similar.

3. *Keogh Plans:* If you are self-employed, you can still shelter income from taxes in a Keogh plan, even if you are also covered by another employer's retirement plan.

    Keogh plans come in two types: 1) defined-contribution plans, and 2) defined-benefit plans. With a defined-contribution plan, you decide in advance how much you will contribute each year. With a defined-benefit plan, you make annual contributions large enough to guarantee a specified income per year upon retirement.

4. *Simplified Employee Pension Plans (SEPs):* This works like a Keogh, except it is simpler. To set up a SEP, simply fill out a form that is available at most financial institutions. Once you have completed the form, you may contribute 15% of your earnings up to a maximum of $4,500.

5. *Life Insurance:* Interest you earn from a life insurance policy is tax-deferred until you cash in the policy. If you bought your policy before June 21, 1988 (unless your policy is term life insurance), you also can borrow against your policy. The amount you are required to pay the

insurance company, as loan interest, is often less than you would pay in taxes on the same amount. *The amount that you borrow is tax-free.*
Certain types of whole life insurance can help you build significant assets for retirement on a tax-favored basis. But the rules governing the tax-favored status are fairly complicated. We suggest you discuss this with your accountant, financial planner, or even your broker (many brokerage firms now offer various forms of life insurance).

6. *Health and Accident Insurance:* Provided you paid for your own accident or health insurance (your employer did not pay it for you), any benefits you get from it are tax-free to you. However, if your employer has paid your premiums, benefits may be regarded as taxable compensation.

7. *Tax-Deferred Annuities:* Also known as single-premium deferred annuities, these plans allow you to invest money with an insurance company (either in a lump sum or on a regular-payment basis) with tax-free interest until you withdraw it.

8. *Real Estate:* Homeowners over 55 get a one-time tax break when they sell their principal residence. The first $125,000 in capital gains that you get from the sale is tax-free.
So if you are over 55 and living in a house that is now too large for just you and your spouse, and if you have owned it long enough to have a large capital gain (in spite of falling market values), you might consider selling now and moving into much smaller and more convenient property. (See Chapter 11 for more on this.)

9. *Reverse Mortgage:* An excellent way to provide yourself retirement income is through the conversion of your home's equity with a reverse mortgage. This FHA-backed loan is designed primarily for homeowners 62 and older. It pays a homeowner a fixed monthly income amount and defers repayment of the principal and interest until the house is sold, usually after the owner dies. (For additional information see Chapter 11.)

10. *Tax-Exempt Municipal Bonds:* These can be a good source of tax-free income for retirement or for current use. (See Chapter 7 for a full discussion of municipal bonds.)

BEWARE OF THE CD TRAP

Many retirees make the mistake of relying too heavily on short-term, fixed-rate cash investments like CDs and money market funds for their retirement income.

Richard Band, editor of *Profitable Investing* (Phillips Publishing, 7811 Montrose Road, Potomac, MD 20854; 1-800-777-5005) says, "Today's low interest rates may be good for the economy, but they're not good for everybody—certainly not retirees. Typically, a high-yielding bank CD they owned has just matured. It was paying 9% or more, and they were counting on that level of interest for living expenses. Without it, they can't make ends meet. Welcome to what I call the 'CD trap.' When yields slide, these people find their lifestyles severely crimped."

What are the alternatives? One possibility is utilities.

Utilities are safe and pay a fixed rate of interest. Utilities can even raise their dividends, and do so on a regular basis. Over the past 10 years, $10,000 invested in Treasury bonds would have grown, with compounding, to $32,800. But over the same time, a $10,000 utility index would have grown to $56,100.

For a recession-proof investment, you can't own a better one. They enjoy a government-protected monopoly, and their customers can't get by without buying their products. Besides, the new Clean Air legislation almost guarantees new demand for utilities that burn clean fuels and do not threaten the environment. With a sluggish economy and lower interest rates, utilities will thrive. Since utilities are heavy borrowers for construction and expansion projects, lower interest rates reduce their costs of borrowing and the savings flow right through to their bottom line.

Richard Band's recommendations are:

Utility Stocks: Ameritech NYSE (AIT), BellSouth NYSE (BLS), Duke Power NYSE (DUK), Indiana Energy NYSE (IEI).

Mutual Funds: Fidelity Utilities Income, 1-800-544-8888 (safest, most diversified utility fund); Flag Telephone Investors, 1-800-767-3524; Rushmore American Gas Index, 1-800-621-7874.

According to Band, " . . . In the next 18 months the typical utility yielding 7% will increase about 25% to 35% (not even counting dividends); others with 4% annual dividend gains will advance 49% and a few could leap 50% to 100%."

ESTATE PLANNING

None of us likes to think about our own death. Yet, by planning our estate carefully, we can continue our control of our assets "beyond the grave" and ensure a higher standard of living for our loved ones.

Five ways to ensure that your estate passes smoothly to your heirs are:

1. *A Living Trust or Testamentary Bypass Trust* splits a couple's estate so that each spouse can take full advantage of their $600,00 estate tax exemption ($1,200,00 per couple).

2. All life insurance owned individually is subject to estate tax, which means that up to 80% of the death benefit could be subject to estate taxes. All life insurance benefits other than those needed for immediate family economic survival should be owned by a *Tax-Free Inheritance Trust.* Many people have a substantial sum in qualified retirement plans (IRA, 401(k) and pensions) that are taxed twice at death. Therefore, at least a portion of these funds should be transferred to a Tax-Free Inheritance Trust.

3. Each of us can give up to $10,000 per year to as many people as we wish. A

mother and father with two children and three grandchildren, for example, can give $100,000 a year. If this *gift is given through a trust,* then it can grow, tax-free, until death.

4. *A Family Limited Partnership* can be established, with the husband or wife as general partner and the wife or husband and children as limited partners. This limited partnership makes it possible to eliminate estate tax without giving up control of your assets.

5. *Family Charitable Foundations* have long been a strategy used by the very wealthy (Forbeses, Rockefellers, Mellons, etc.) to perpetuate income for their heirs indefinitely while also serving mankind. This strategy should be considered only if your total estate exceeds $10 million.

WHERE TO LIVE IN YOUR RETIREMENT YEARS

Another important consideration for your retirement is where to live. Some states offer excellent income tax rates (or no tax at all), while others will take big bites out of your retirement income. Table 6.3 shows how the per capita collections of taxes varied in 1990.

Besides these taxes, you should check the property taxes as well.

NURSING HOME CARE

Quite possibly the most frightening aspect of facing your retirement years is the prospect that you (or your spouse) will require nursing home (long-term) care. If you have not thought about this possibility, you should. It could very likely wipe out your entire retirement income, leaving you impoverished for your (or your spouse's) remaining years.

The likelihood that you or your spouse will enter a nursing home before you die is one in two. In 1991, more than 6 million men and women over the age of 65 needed long-term care. By the year 2000, over 7.5 million older Americans will need long-term care.

What does long-term care cost? As a national average, one year in a nursing home now costs between $25,000 and $30,000. In some areas it is as much as $50,000. The average stay is 2.5 years, which can wipe out your retirement savings rapidly.

Many people think that their savings or Medicare, the federal health insurance program for older people, will pay the cost of nursing home and at-home care. But, Medicare pays very little of the extended day-in and day-out care that many older people need.

Slightly more than half of all nursing home costs are paid out-of-pocket by individuals and their families. Only about 2% are paid by Medicare. Many people who begin paying for nursing home care out of their own pockets find that their savings are not enough to cover lengthy stays. If they become impoverished after entering a nursing home, they turn to Medicaid to pay the bills. The problem lies

Table 6.3. How Individual Taxes Vary

State	Sales tax	Individual income	Gas tax	Tags	Total tax	State	Sales tax	Individual income	Gas tax	Tags	Total tax
Alabama	$257	$278	$73	$31	$945	Nebraska	$322	$314	$133	$36	$959
Alaska	0	0	75	37	2,811	Nevada	667	0	93	56	1,317
Arizona	523	290	91	63	1,194	New Hampshire	0	37	73	46	537
Arkansas	357	314	93	33	962	New Jersey	426	382	54	44	1,350
California	458	565	46	36	1,459	New Mexico	552	238	109	67	1,329
Colorado	251	407	99	33	932	New York	334	850	30	30	1,591
Connecticut	743	186	94	53	1,603	North Carolina	267	511	120	34	1,186
Delaware	0	685	95	35	1,696	North Dakota	362	165	105	60	1,060
Florida	633	0	60	37	1,027	Ohio	331	380	90	36	1,054
Georgia	407	443	68	12	1,093	Oklahoma	268	318	105	85	1,105
Hawaii	1,062	627	48	18	2,107	Oregon	0	643	83	76	980
Idaho	381	400	107	56	1,131	Pennsylvania	356	271	63	36	1,113
Illinois	357	375	80	54	1,128	Rhode Island	396	425	73	40	1,229
Indiana	460	377	102	32	1,101	South Carolina	415	396	103	22	1,128
Iowa	340	458	120	78	1,193	South Dakota	359	0	115	29	719
Kansas	352	346	91	39	1,077	Tennessee	481	21	129	31	870
Kentucky	295	328	98	40	1,156	Texas	449	0	89	42	866
Louisiana	299	175	95	17	968	Utah	410	375	77	24	1,026
Maine	415	473	112	39	1,271	Vermont	242	446	95	66	1,183
Maryland	329	599	94	31	1,349	Virginia	219	498	101	40	1,067
Massachusetts	325	816	50	42	1,557	Washington	919	0	99	36	1,525
Michigan	343	422	80	52	1,220	West Virginia	426	288	116	41	1,243
Minnesota	427	658	105	73	1,559	Wisconsin	406	537	108	33	1,341
Mississippi	423	167	120	24	931	Wyoming	358	0	83	93	1,348
Missouri	371	350	69	39	965						
Montana	0	350	140	46	1,073	U.S.	402	387	78	40	1,211

in what happens to the other spouse. Since no aid (except for private long-term-care insurance) is available until savings have been depleted, the spouse living outside the nursing home is faced with tremendous financial problems.

If you have health insurance and think that will pick up the slack on nursing home costs, you could be wrong. The average person doesn't go directly from the hospital to a nursing home (in which your insurance policy would help pay), but from your home to the nursing home.

So what is the answer? You may want to consider long-term-care insurance.

Long-term-care insurance is similar to other insurances in that it allows people to pay a known and affordable premium that offsets the risk of much larger out-of-pocket expenses. More than 130 companies now offer coverage. Policies cost between $480 and $3,800 per year.

But be careful. There are some salespeople who misrepresent the benefits provided by their policies. Before you consider any long-term-care insurance, contact:

Health Insurance Association of America, 1025 Connecticut Avenue NW, Washington, DC 20036; (202) 223-7780. Ask for their free "Consumer Guide to Long-Term-Care Insurance." Also ask for their recommended list of companies that sell long-term-care insurance.

AND FINALLY . . .

All retirement and estate planning should begin when you are at the peak of your working life. This means that when you are around 55, you should have the rest of your financial life planned.

None of us know when we will get sick, or how soon we will become too frail to continue with a particular lifestyle. All contingencies need to be planned for ahead of time. This isn't morbidity; this is the way we control our lives to the end.

Do you have strong feelings about not being kept alive for months while in a coma? Draw up a Living Will. Do you have strong feelings about the form of burial you want? Leave explicit instructions. The list goes on.

If you plan for all eventualities, not only will you lead a happy, full and prosperous life until the end, but you will not leave a financial burden to your heirs.

The purpose of this chapter has been to give you a very general overview of the different options, particularly (but not exclusively) in the area of cash investments, that are available to help make your retirement more comfortable. For the specifics of your own retirement and estate planning, we urge you to seek professional advice suited to your particular needs.

There are several free booklets available on this subject. In particular, Merrill Lynch, Pierce, Fenner & Smith publishes a superb series, *Ensuring an Independent Lifestyle: Retirement Financing Strategies; Making Your Gift Count: Innovative Trends in Charitable Giving; 43 Tax-Saving Ideas for Investors,* and *How to Cut Your Business Tax Bill.* You can obtain them by calling 1-800-637-7455.

RESOURCES

The American Association of Retired Persons (AARP), 1909 K Street NW, Washington, DC 20049. They have published a booklet called "Information on Medicare and Health Insurance for Older People," that is available free of charge.

Department of Health and Human Services, Health Care Financing Administration, Baltimore, MD 21207; 1-800-888-1998. For more information on Medicare, ask them to send you the following booklets:

> *A Brief Explanation of Medicare*
> *Your Medicare Handbook*
> *Medicare/Medicaid—Which is Which*
> *How to Fill Out a Medicare Claim Form*

Elderhostel, 80 Boylston Street, Suite 400, Boston, MA 02116; (617) 426-7788.

Health Insurance Association of America, 1025 Connecticut Avenue NW, Washington, DC 20036; (202) 223-7780. They offer a free *Consumer Guide to Long-Term-Care Insurance.* Also ask for their list of companies that sell long-term-care insurance.

Tom Hill, Merrill Lynch, Pierce, Fenner & Smith, 14th Floor, Liberty Center, Pittsburgh, PA 15222-3720; 1-800-937-0761. Tom Hill is an ideal broker to deal with your ultra-conservative retirement assets.

Lynch Municipal Bond Advisory, Editor: James F. Lynch, P.O. Box 1086, Lenox Hill Station, New York, NY 10021; (212) 249-9595.

Muni Bond Fund Report, Editor: Ralph Norton, Greystone Media Services, Inc., P.O. Box 2179, Huntington Beach, CA 92647; (617) 721-4511.

Dr. Gary North, P.O. Box 7999, Tyler, TX 75711; 1-800-527-8608. Dr. North has written and lectured extensively on the problems in the Social Security system. He has also published several books on the subject.

Profitable Investing, Editor: Richard Band, Phillips Publishing, 7811 Montrose Road, Potomac, MD 20854; 1-800-777-5005.

Social Security Administration Office. For a copy of your "Personal Earnings and Benefit Estimate Statement," call 1-800-772-1213. To correct your records, call 1-800-537-7005.

Andrew Westhem, Western Capital Financial Group, Wealth Transfer Division, 1925 Century Park East, Suite 2350, Los Angeles, CA 90067; 1-800-423-4891. Mr. Westhem is an estate advisor who offers a service, through insurance policies, where you can provide enough money for your heirs to pay any estate taxes that come due.

7

Keeping More of What You Earn: Saving Taxes Now

"It is inseparably essential to the freedom of a people that no taxes be imposed on them but with their own consent, given personally or by their representatives."

JOHN DICKINSON, Resolutions of the Stamp Act Congress, October 19, 1765

C hapter 6 showed you some of the tax-advantaged methods to build up your wealth for retirement and beyond. In this chapter we will concentrate on ways you can cut your taxes now, and we'll show you money-saving tips that will help you to get more value for your dollar.

There are many ways to cut your taxes without raising a "red flag" to the IRS. This chapter gives you simple, straightforward ways you can increase your yields by saving taxes or penalties, including:

- Thirteen ways to cut your taxes,
- How tax-exempt investments provide higher yields, and a formula to help you compute the taxable equivalent yields,

- Specific tax-advantaged money market, municipal bond, and mutual fund recommendations,
- A utility revenue bond that yields a taxable equivalent yield of 10.14%,
- A bond fund that yields a taxable equivalent of 13%,
- Which municipal bonds you should hold if the city defaults, and
- *Safety* and *yield* tips on several tax-advantaged investment instruments.

As stated in Chapter 7, our goal is to provide *general* tax strategies. We can't offer specific tax advice appropriate for your individual situation. You should, therefore, discuss any tips or strategies with your accountant before taking action.

While there are many ways you can legally save on taxes, several of these methods are *red flag loopholes*. If you use them, there may be a greater chance that the IRS computer will tag your return for an audit. While you may have done absolutely nothing illegal, you have to weigh the emotional and financial expense involved with being audited, against the amount of your potential tax savings.

We've all heard horror stories about the IRS. Although many of its methods have been considered questionable, it makes no sense to challenge the IRS, unless you find such run-ins good for your adrenalin.

This chapter, therefore, will not include the more creative ways to save on taxes. It will list simple, straightforward ways in which you can increase your yields in 13 investment areas by saving taxes. They are:

1. Investment expenses
2. Annuities
3. Certificates of deposit
4. Child's unearned income
5. Corporate bonds
6. EE Savings Bonds
7. Failed bank assets
8. Foreign bank accounts
9. Money market accounts
10. Municipal bonds
11. Mutual funds
12. Real Estate
13. U.S. Treasury issues

Investment Expenses

Investment expenses are tax-deductible under Sections 67 and 212 of the Internal Revenue Code, as long as all miscellaneous itemized deductions exceed

2% of adjusted gross income. Thus, if the accumulated gross amount of your miscellaneous deductions is already at least 2% of your income, any further investment-related expenditures would be *100% tax-deductible.*

In addition, such expenditures are 100% deductible as business expenses by most corporations under Section 162 of the Code.

Annuities

Payments from annuities have no tax advantages. The tax advantages come from:

1. The fact that you can exchange one annuity or life insurance policy for another (roll it over) with no tax being due—provided the policyholder remains the same. This allows you to maintain a higher guaranteed rate of return.

2. The fact that you can borrow against your annuity (in most cases) and have tax-free use of the money before the due date. If you use the money for investment, you can probably deduct the interest you pay on this loan as well.

However, the IRS does impose many complicated rules on annuities. If you plan to do something too creative with your policy or endowment, it could very easily be a "red flag" issue. Check with your accountant before you act.

Certificates of Deposit

If you buy a CD of one year or less, you are allowed to defer the interest on that CD until it is actually paid. By purchasing a CD in the latter half of the year (with a maturity in the following year), you can defer income in a year when your income may be higher. For longer-term CDs, you have to report the interest yearly, whether you actually receive it in a spendable form or not.

Your Child's Unearned Income

It usually makes little tax sense to open an account for your child until he or she is 14 years of age. Before that age, the child's income could be taxed at the parents' rate, if that rate is higher.

The IRS allows your children to accumulate income to pay for college or other future goals. This enables you to transfer up to $10,000 each year per parent per child (i.e., you and your spouse can transfer $20,000 a year per child) and have that amount taxed at the (presumably lower) child's rate. The transfer is also tax free.

Corporate Bonds

If your state levies little, or no, income tax on unearned income, your net interest rate on corporate debt securities may be higher than U.S. Treasury bonds. Buy corporates only of the highest quality. There are only 12 public U.S. companies that have a AAA rating from Standard & Poor's. They are:

1. Amoco,
2. Bristol-Myers, Squibb,
3. Carnation,
4. Eli Lilly,
5. Emerson Electric,
6. Exxon,
7. General Electric,
8. IBM,
9. Johnson & Johnson,
10. Kellogg,
11. Minnesota Mining & Manufacturing, and
12. Shell Oil

EE Savings Bonds

With EE savings bonds you have two options:

1. You can pay the tax on the interest in the year in which it accrues—even if you don't receive it. Or . . .
2. You can pay it when you cash out the bonds.

EE savings bonds are excluded from state and local taxes.

Failed Bank Assets

If your bank, savings and loan, or other financial institution fails (and your money is frozen), you do not pay taxes on the income until you receive it in a spendable form—even if you have interest payments for that year sitting in the account.

Foreign Bank Accounts

As a U.S. citizen or resident, you are required to pay taxes on all your income worldwide—even when it is in an "anonymous" trust. Besides that, many foreign governments withhold tax at the source.

Before you make any investment abroad, check what the local tax consequences will be and whether it is possible to structure your foreign investment so that you pay no foreign taxes. This is often possible by using special laws for foreigners.

If you do end up paying foreign taxes, the IRS allows you to deduct those taxes against your U.S. tax. However, calculating the foreign tax credit requires

---

YIELD TIP

Tax-Exempt Investments May Provide You With Higher Yields

If you are in a higher tax bracket, tax-free money market or mutual funds may provide you higher net income than a comparable taxable investment. For example, if your federal income tax rate is 31%, you would have to earn 7.25% from a taxable investment to match the income from a tax-free investment yielding 5%.

To figure out your income bracket, review the following:

	28%	**31%**
Joint Return	$34,001–82,150	$82,151 and above
Single Return	$20,351–49,300	$49,301 and above

To match a tax free yield of:	A taxable investment would have to pay:	
4%	5.56%	5.80%
5%	6.94%	7.25%
6%	8.33%	8.70%
7%	9.72%	10.14%

NOTE: To compute the exact taxable equivalent yield, use the worksheet at the end of the chapter.

---

the assistance of a professional tax preparer. Thus, it is a lot less expensive to avoid the foreign tax in the first place.

NOTE: The 1986 Tax Reform Act requires that you report the existence of a foreign account on your tax return if the total value of all accounts exceeds $10,000. Investments such as insurance policies, annuities, real estate, or precious metals not held by a bank, are exempt from reporting.

Once you report the existence of a foreign bank account, you will then be required to complete the Treasury Form TD F 90-22.1, which asks for the location and name of your bank, with the identification numbers of your account.

Money Market Accounts

Carefully consider tax-advantaged money market funds—depending on where you live. The benefits can be considerable. As William Donoghue says, *"In high-tax states, T-bills are actually out-yielding all the exotic funds."* See Table 7.1.

Table 7.1. Money Market Funds Five-Year Highest Yields

Tax Exempt	Toll Free Number	Initial Investment	5-Year Annual Return
Benham Nat'l Tax-Free Trust	1-800-472-3389	$ 1,000	5.02%
Dreyfus Connecticut Municipal	1-800-782-6620	$ 2,500	5.08% (since 07/90)
Dreyfus Michigan Municipal	1-800-782-6620	$ 2,500	5.37% (since 07/90)
Dreyfus New Jersey Municipal	1-800-782-6620	$ 2,500	5.84% (since 06/88)
Dreyfus Pennsylvania Municipal	1-800-782-6620	$ 2,500	5.30% (since 07/90)
Fidelity Tax-Exempt	1-800-544-8888	$ 5,000	5.02%
Scudder Tax-Free	1-800-225-2470	$ 1,000	4.81%
Strong Municipal	1-800-368-3863	$ 2,500	5.42% (since 10/86)
T. Rowe Price Tax-Exempt	1-800-638-5660	$ 2,500	4.93%
USSA Tax Exempt	1-800-531-8181	$ 3,000	5.38%
Vanguard California Tax-Free	1-800-662-7447	$ 3,000	5.34% (since 06/87)
Vanguard Muni Bond	1-800-662-7447	$ 3,000	5.27%
Vanguard Muni Bond Short Term	1-800-662-7447	$ 3,000	5.95%
Vanguard New Jersey Tax-Free	1-800-662-7447	$ 3,000	5.61% (since 02/88)
Vanguard Ohio Tax-Free	1-800-662-7447	$ 3,000	5.33% (since 06/90)
Vanguard Pennsylvania Tax-Free	1-800-662-7447	$ 3,000	5.79% (since 06/88)
U.S. Government (Tax-free in most states)			
Benham Government Agency	1-800-472-3389	$ 1,000	7.85% (since 12/89)
Capital Preservation Fund	1-800-321-8321	$ 1,000	6.84%
Dreyfus 100% U.S. Treasury	1-800-782-6620	$ 2,500	7.32% (since 03/87)
Fidelity Spartan U.S. Treasury	1-800-544-8888	$20,000	7.55% (since 01/88)

Money Market Recommendations: Some safe, high-yielding money market funds you should look into are:

Benham Government Agency Fund, 1665 Charleston Road, Mountain View, CA 94043; 1-800-472-3389. Minimum investment is $1,000. The Benham fund invests primarily in securities issued by agencies of the U.S. government and U.S. Treasury paper. Because most agency securities are on step removed from the direct backing of short-term Treasury securities, they pay a higher return than investments in T-bills. And because the state tax exemption of federal government securities is "passed through" to investors (in over 38 states), there is no state income tax on earnings from this fund in these states.

Fidelity U.S. Treasury Agency Fund, Fidelity Investments, 82 Devonshire Street, Boston, MA 02109; 1-800-544-8888. Minimum investment is $20,000.

Dreyfus U.S. Treasury Money Market Account LP, P.O. Box 6527, Providence, RI 02940; 1-800-782-6620, Ext. 8079. The minimum investment is $2,500. The Dreyfus fund invests exclusively in U.S. Treasury securities. This fund can provide income free of state and local taxes in 49 states.

The top-performing tax-free money market funds recommended by mutual fund expert William Donoghue are:

Calvert Tax-Free Reserves Money Market Fund, 4450 Montgomery Avenue, 1000N, Bethesda, MD 20814; 1-800-368-2748. Minimum investment $2,000. No load or 12b-1 fees. Five-year average return 5.44%.

Strong Municipal Fund, 1-800-368-3863. $2,500 minimum initial investment. No sales or 12b-1 fees. Average return since inception (10/86), 5.42%.

Fidelity Spartan Municipal Fund, 82 Devonshire Street, Boston, MA 02109; 1-800-544-8888. Initial investment is $2,500. No sales charges, but includes 12b-1 fees.

Evergreen Tax-Exempt Money Market Fund, Evergreen Funds, 2500 Westchester Avenue, Purchase, NY 10577; 1-800-235-0064. $2,000 initial investment. No sales or 12b-1 fees. Fund was started in November 1988; annual return for 1989 and 1990 was 6.39% and 6.12%, respectively.

Municipal Bonds

Municipal bonds (munis) are free from federal income taxes and, except for Illinois, Iowa, Kansas, Nebraska, Oklahoma, Pennsylvania, and Wisconsin, munis are exempt from state taxes within the state where they are issued. If you live in a high-tax state, then it is especially beneficial for you to buy munis for the state in which you live.

Even if you live in a low- or no-tax state, munis may still make more sense than Treasuries (which are not exempt from federal taxes).

Some states do not levy taxes on ANY munis, even if they are issued outside their state. These states are Alaska, Florida, Indiana, Kentucky, Nevada, New Hampshire, New Mexico, North Dakota, Texas, Utah, Washington, Wyoming, and the District of Columbia.

If you invest in a bond fund that holds bonds from several states, the fund will send you a breakdown. It is then up to you to work out which portion you will owe taxes. Tables 7.2 and 7.3 show the current state-by-state tax laws and how much your tax-free income is worth in taxable income by state.

For maximum savings, look for bonds that are advertised as double-tax-free (exempt from federal and state taxes) or triple-tax-free (exempt from federal, state and local taxes). See Table 7.4 for a listing of state specific munis.

Is Safety An Issue? The attempted bankruptcy of Bridgeport Connecticut and the poor condition of several state, county, and city governments has alerted bond investors that municipal bonds may not be as safe as they once thought.

Table 7.2. Comparative State Taxes

	State income tax on taxable income		State income tax on taxable income
Alabama	2%–5%	Montana	2%–11%
Alaska	None	Nebraska	2.37%–6.92%
Arizona	3.8%–7%	Nevada	None
Arkansas	1%–7%	New Hampshire	5%
California	1%–11%	New Jersey	2%–7%
Colorado[1]	5%	New Mexico	1.8%–8.5%
Connecticut	4.5%	New York	4%–7.875%
Delaware	3.2%–7.7%	N. Carolina	6%–7.75%
Dist. Colum.	6%–9.5%	N. Dakota	2.67%–12%
Florida	None	Ohio	0.743%–6.9%
Georgia	1%–6%	Oklahoma	0.5%–7%
Hawaii	2%–10%	Oregon	5%–9%
Idaho	2%–8.2%	Penn.	2.1%–3.1%
Illinois	3%	Rhode Island[3]	27.5%
Indiana[2]	3.4%	S. Carolina	2.5%–7%
Iowa	0.4%–9.98%	South Dakota	None
Kansas	3.65%–5.15%	Tennessee	6%
Kentucky	2%–6%	Texas	None
Louisiana	2%–6%	Utah	2.55%–7.2%
Maine	2.1%–9.89%	Vermont[4]	25%
Maryland	2%–5%	Virginia	2%–5.75%
Massachusetts	6.25%	Washington	None
Michigan	4.6%	West Virginia	3%–6.5%
Minnesota	6%–8.5%	Wisconsin	4.9%–6.93%
Mississippi	3%–8.5%	Wyoming	None
Missouri	1.5%–6%		

[1]Of federal taxable income. [2]Of adjusted gross income. [3]Of modified federal tax. [4]Of federal income tax.

Source: Commerce Clearing House

Through the first six months of 1991, $2.2 billion munis have defaulted, mostly at the city and county level. Revenue bonds, issues whose interest is paid by dedicated revenue streams such as highway tolls, dominate the defaults.

Important Bond Definitions: *General Obligation Bonds* are guaranteed by

Table 7.3. Comparative Ranking of State Income Taxes[1]

TEN HIGHEST

State	Rate	State	Rate
Massachusetts	12.0%	Georgia	6.0%
North Dakota	12.0%	Kentucky	6.0%
Vermont	11.22%[2]	Louisiana	6.0%
California	11.0%	Missouri	6.0%
Montana	11.0%	Tennessee	6.0%[3]
Hawaii	10.0%	Kansas	5.95%
Iowa	9.98%	Virginia	5.75%
Maine	9.89%	Alabama	5.0%
Rhode Island	9.075%[2]	Colorado	5.0%
Oregon	9.0%	Maryland	5.0%
Minnesota	8.5%	Mississippi	5.0%
New Mexico	8.5%	New Hampshire	5.0%[3]
Idaho	8.2%	Michigan	4.6%
New York	7.875%	Connecticut	4.5%
North Carolina	7.75%		
Delaware	7.7%	**TEN LOWEST**	
Utah	7.2%	Indiana	3.4%
Arizona	7.0%	Pennsylvania	3.1%
Arkansas	7.0%	Illinois	3.0%
New Jersey	7.0%	Alaska	0.0%
Oklahoma	7.0%	Florida	0.0%
South Carolina	7.0%	Nevada	0.0%
Wisconsin	6.93%	South Dakota	0.0%
Nebraska	6.92%	Texas	0.0%
Ohio	6.9%	Washington	0.0%
West Virginia	6.5%	Wyoming	0.0%

[1]Percentages show top rate in each state.

[2]Percentage is based on federal income tax liability.

[3]Unearned income only.

Source: Fortune

the issuing municipality. These are among the safest bonds, as the state is obligated to go as far as raising taxes to pay you.

Revenue Bonds are backed only by the income from the project they are set up to finance. If the project fails, you lose the investment.

Insured Bonds offer protection in case of default. Bonds backed by a major

Table 7.4. State-Specific Municipal Bond Funds

Benham California Intermediate	800/472-3389
Benham California Long-Term	800/472-3389
California Tax Free Income	800/225-8778
Dreyfus California Tax Exempt	800/782-6620
Dreyfus Massachusetts Tax Exempt	800/782-6620
Dreyfus New York Tax Exempt	800/782-6620
Fidelity California High Yield	800/544-8888
Fidelity Massfree Muni	800/544-8888
Fidelity Michigan Tax-Free	800/544-8888
Fidelity Minnesota Tax-Free	800/544-8888
Fidelity New York High Yield	800/544-8888
Fidelity New York Insured	800/544-8888
Fidelity Ohio Tax-Free	800/544-8888
Fidelity Texas Tax-Free	800/544-8888
Kentucky Tax-Free Income	800/432-9518
New York Muni	800/528-6050
Pacific Horizons California	800/645-3515
Park Avenue N.Y. Intermediate	800/848-4350
Safeco California Tax-Free Income	800/426-6730
Scudder California Tax-Free	800/225-2470
Scudder New York Tax-Free	800/225-2470
T. Rowe Price California Tax-Free	800/638-5660
United Municipal Indiana	800/862-7283
Vanguard California Insured	800/662-7447
Vanguard New York Insured	800/662-7447
Vanguard Pennsylvania Insured	800/662-7447

insurer usually earn the highest rating, AAA, based on the strength of the insuring company. The market considers these bonds less secure than bonds that earn the AAA ratings on their own merits, so the yields on insured bonds are higher than those of pure AAA issues. On insured bonds, the insurance premium is paid by the issuer.

State and local governments now face their worst financial crisis in decades. So why would you consider pumping more money into munis? Because hard-pressed states are hiking income taxes by $2.5 billion in fiscal 1991. Eleven

---

YIELD TIP

New York City has recently issued 20- and 30-year tax-exempt bonds. New York still has an A rating from Standard & Poor's. To top the tax-free yield of 20- and 30-year 8.55% NYC bonds, a city resident would have to find a taxable investment yielding more than 12%. This compares well with the yields on corporate junk bonds, with a *lot less risk.*

Bonds sold by states, such as Tennessee, with low debt levels are also good bets. And "essential service" revenue bonds, such as water, sewer and electric bonds, provide a relative degree of stability in recessionary times. A 10-year San Antonio Electric & Gas revenue bond currently yields around 7% (10.14% taxable equivalent for a 31% tax bracket).

---

states are proposing income-tax increases in their 1992 budgets. That is a very good reason to invest in munis.

Municipal Bonds You Should Hold if the City Defaults: It is important to note that some municipal bonds are insured and some are not. The best-rated and insured bonds will pay less interest than the riskier ones. So if you buy them primarily for tax reasons, buy only bonds that have earned an uninsured rating of A or better.

But there may be other dangers.

Illiquidity, or the risk that you won't be able to sell your holdings quickly without stiff losses, is another important consideration. In 1987, a 1.5% jump in interest rates intensified the seasonal surge in redemption by shareholders raising cash to pay taxes. The result: Investors pulled more than $3 billion out of munis, and share prices dropped 5% in just five days.

SAFETY TIP

With a sales tax tied to the bond, you never know what kind of income you will have for the city. With bonds tied to income tax, you will have a chance at predicting the amount.

Conservative investors should be looking at AA-rated and better. Pre-refunded bonds backed by Treasury securities almost guarantee you will get your money back. They are the Cadillac of all muni bonds. Diversify outside your state, as well, for safety.

With local governments looking more shaky as the sluggish economy continues, more than $19 billion of muni bonds had been downgraded by Moody's through June 3, 1991. This downgrade could cause a liquidity squeeze, as well, if investors begin pulling their funds from these bonds.

If you have less than $100,000 to invest, you should consider buying through a municipal bond fund. A fund can afford to spread the risk through diversification.

To minimize your liquidity risk, even with a bond fund, focus on funds with high cash reserves (5% of assets or more). High reserves can help fund managers meet redemptions without dumping bonds. You can discover a fund's cash level by calling the fund.

Also stick with highly diversified muni funds that own bonds with maturities of less than 10 years. These funds will have yields of 0.5% to 1% less than their long-term counterparts, but they will be more liquid. Table 7.5 lists the top five insured municipal funds.

Municipal Bond Funds: Mutual funds that buy only municipal bonds are free of federal and state taxes if the bonds held by the fund are issued in the state of the purchaser's residence.

However, check the fees charged by the fund before you buy. The average fee is about 0.78% of the fund's assets. Also, the final profit you make will depend on how the municipal bond fund is structured. Table 7.6 outlines your various op-

Table 7.5. Five Top Insured Municipal Funds

Insured Muni Fund	Total Return Year to date*	Assets In millions	Annual Expenses	Sales Load	Current Yield
Alliance Municipal Income Insured National 800-227-4618	10.13%	$123	0.92%	4.50%	6.01%
Vanguard Municipal-Insured Long-Term 800-662-7447	9.74%	$1,329	0.25%	None	6.38%
Merrill Insured Municipal A 800-637-3863	9.45%	$2,400	0.46%	4.00%	6.14%
Nuveen Insured Tax-Free National 800-351-4100	9.36%	$186	0.83%	4.75%	5.89%
Franklin Insured Tax-Free Income 800-342-5236	4.52%	$850	0.54%	4.00%	6.37%

*Through 12/16/92

Source: Communique Marketing & Associates, Inc.

tions and illustrates that you can make more money by investing in individual bonds (although at some higher degree of risk).

In addition, you may want to compare annual returns. Remember, the higher the yield, most likely the higher the risk. To help you compare specific municipal bond funds, Table 7.7 provides Lipper's Municipal Bond Indexes that show the average annual returns for all municipal bond funds. For example, if you find a short term fund that exceeds a five-year annual return of 4.89%, be careful. The risk may be higher than you wish to take.

The Top Municipal Bond Funds: The following are among the top municipal bond funds in terms of yield and safety:

Dreyfus Intermediate Tax-Exempt Bond Fund, P.O. Box 3498, Camden, NJ 08101; 1-800-782-6620. Invests in tax-exempt bonds with intermediate maturity. $2,500 initial investment. Average return: Five-year, 7.3%; since 08/83, 8.84%.

IDS Insured Tax-Exempt Fund, IDS Tower 10, Minneapolis, MN 55440; 1-800-437-4332. Invests primarily in municipal securities that have insured the principal and interest.

IDS Tax-Exempt Bond Fund, IDS Tower 10, Minneapolis, MN 55440; 1-800-437-4332. Invests mainly in bonds and notes of state or local government units, with at least 75% in the four highest rated, lowest risk bond categories. Average return: Five-year, 6.57%, 10-year, 10.76%.

Table 7.6. Six Options for Municipal Bonds

Type of Investment	Fee to Buy	Annual Expenses	Fee to Sell	Value of $10,000 Investment After Past 5 Years
No-Load Fund	None	0.8%–1% of Assets	None	$14,760
Front-End Load Fund	2%–5%	0.8%–1.75%	None	$14,060[1]
Back-End Load Fund	None	0.8%–1.75%	5%[2]	$14,290
Unit Trust	2%–5%	0.1%–0.2%	None	$14,830
Closed-End Fund	1%–6%	0.8%–1%	1%–3%	N/A
Individual Bonds	3%	None	None[3]	$15,459

[1]Return for front-end-load funds assumes a 4.75% initial sales charge.

[2]Sales fees on back-end-load funds generally decline from 5% of redemptions in the first year to zero after five years.

[3]No outright fees, but bond trading costs reduce the value of your portfolio by up to 3%.

Note: This table gives the costs of investing $10,000 in municipal bonds with maturities of six to ten years. Returns represent totals for the five years previous to September 1, 1990, and are net of commissions and expenses. Since no closed-end funds invest exclusively in intermediate-term munis, the information supplied is for long-term funds.

Source: Lipper Analytical Services, Clayton Brown, Municipal Market Data

**Table 7.7. Comparative Municipal Indexes:
Average Annual Returns**

	5 Year	10 Year
Lipper Short-Term Tax-Exempt Bond Average	4.89%	5.28%
Lipper Intermediate Average	6.60	7.92
Lipper General Bond Average	7.71	11.06
Lipper High-Yield Average	7.62	10.87

*Convert annual returns to the taxable equivalent yield based on your tax
bracket, using the formula in Table 7.8*

IDS High Yield Tax-Exempt Fund, IDS Tower 10, Minneapolis, MN 55440;
1-800-437-4332. Invests primarily in medium- and lower-quality municipal bonds
and notes with high yields. Average return: Five-year, 7.07%, 10-year, 11.21%.

IDS funds have initial investments of $2,000 and include a 5% sales charge.

Fidelity Limited-Term Munis, 82 Devonshire Street, Boston, MA 02109;
1-800-544-8888. Invests primarily in high- and upper-medium-quality municipal
obligations with an average portfolio maturity of 12 years or less. Average return: Five-year, 7.24%; 10-year, 9.88%. No sales charge, no 12b-1.

Fidelity Municipal Bond Portfolio, 82 Devonshire Street, Boston, MA 02109;
1-800-544-8888. Invests in high- to upper-medium-quality municipal bonds with
no restriction to maturity. Average maturity exceeds 20 years.

Fidelity funds have initial investments of $2,500 and no sales charges. They
do have 12b-1 fees.

Scudder Tax-Free Target-1996, P.O. Box 2291, Boston, MA 02107;
1-800-225-2470. This fund invests primarily in high-quality municipal securities
providing higher tax-free income than generally available from tax-free money
market funds—maturing not later than the second Friday in December 1996. (A
1993 fund is available as well, but on average, has lower yields.) $1,000 initial
investment and it is a "pure no-load" fund. Average return: Five-year, 6.92%;
since inception, 7.99%.

Benham's National Tax-Free Trust Fund, Benham Capital Management
Group, 1665 Charleston Road, Mountain View, CA 94043; 1-800-472-3389. Invests primarily in higher-quality municipals. Two funds are available: Intermediate-Term that invests in maturities of two to 10 years, and Long-Term that
invests in maturities of 10 years or longer. Initial investment is $1,000 and there
are no sales or 12b-1 fees. Average return for the Intermediate-Term: Five-year,
6.96%; 10-year, 7.51%. For the Long-Term portfolio: Five-year, 6.40%; 10-year,
9.59%.

Vanguard Muni Bond Intermediate, P.O. Box 2600, Valley Forge, PA 19482;

YIELD TIP

Earn a Taxable Equivalent of 13%

Alex Green and Michael Spartz of International Assets recommend the following high-yielding bonds:

Summit Tax-Exempt Bond Fund. Summit is a limited partnership traded on the NYSE, that invests in first mortgages issued by state and local governments. At its current price of $10 a share, the fund is yielding 9% tax-free (after-tax equivalent is 13% for investors in a 31% tax bracket) and makes distributions quarterly. Mortgages are all in senior positions. In other words, no properties are mortgaged at more than 85% of their appraised value, and the occupancy rate on the commercial properties is currently averaging 95%. In addition, the fund is trading at almost a 40% discount to its NAV. Aggressive income investors seeking high tax-free income should give Summit serious consideration.

For more information on this and other taxable and tax-exempt bonds, contact Alex Green or Michael Spartz at International Assets, 201 West Canton Avenue, Suite 100, Winter Park, FL 32789; (407) 629-1400, Fax: (407) 629-2470.

1-800-662-7447. Vanguard has seven portfolios offering tax-free income that is payable monthly. Specifically, the Intermediate Fund invests in high-quality munis with an average maturity of seven to 12 years. Initial investment is $3,000. No load or 12b-1 fees. Average return: Five-year, 8.44%; 10-year, 10.20%.

The Top Double and Triple Tax Exempt Funds*: The top-performing double and triple tax-exempt no-load (no sales charges) bond funds for people in high-tax states are:

Benham California Tax-Free Funds, 1665 Charleston Road, Mountain View, CA 94043; 1-800-472-3389. Benham has two California Tax-Free funds that have performed well:

Intermediate-Term

Long-Term

See Table 7.8.

Dreyfus Tax-Exempt Bond Funds, P.O. Box 3498, Camden, NJ 08101; 1-800-782-6620. Dreyfus' top state funds are in California, Massachusetts, New Jersey and New York. Initial investment is $2,500. Some funds include 12b-1 fees. Average five-year returns range from 6.62% (MA) to 7.04% (NY). Since inception, the average returns range from 7.39% (MA) to 9.70% (NY).

---

*Double and triple tax-exempt bond funds are exempt from federal, state and/or local taxes.

Table 7.8. Performance of Benham's California
Tax-Free Funds

	Average Five-Year	Annual Returns Since Inception
Intermediate-Term	6.27%	7.07% (since 11/83)
Long-Term	7.04%	8.81% (since 11/83)

$1,000 initial investment. No 12b-1 fees.

Fidelity Tax-Free Portfolios, 82 Devonshire Street, Boston, MA 02109; 1-800-544-8888. Fidelity's top state funds are in California, Connecticut, Massachusetts, Michigan, Minnesota, New Jersey, New York, and Ohio. Average five-year returns range from 7.21% (NY) to 7.95% (CA). Since inception, the average returns run from 8.62% (CA) to 10.38% (NY). Initial investment is $2,500. They have 12b-1 fees.

Vanguard Insured Long-Term Funds, P.O. Box 2600, Valley Forge, PA 19482; 1-800-662-7447. Vanguard offers single-state and municipal funds for California, New Jersey, New York, Ohio, and Pennsylvania as well. Minimum $3,000. No 12b-1 fees. Average annual return since inception ranges from 2.70% (CA, since 12/90) to 10.27% (OH).

Final Point: While you may get the benefits of both federal and state tax savings, if you invest in a single state bond fund and you live in that state, there is a higher risk factor involved. If your state plunges into a recession (e.g., Massachusetts), then those bonds could plummet. And remember:

"What doth it profit a man to gain his tax advantage and lose his principal?"

Build Your Own Portfolio: If you would rather forgo a fund and build your own portfolio of municipal bonds, you should consult an expert in the field.

One of the brightest specialists in municipal bonds in John Bintz, Vice President of Institutional Sales at Hutchinson, Shokey, Erley & Company (135 South La Salle, Suite 1230, Chicago, IL 60603; (312) 443-1550, Fax: (312) 443-7225). He deals primarily with institutions, but has offered to help any *Cash Book* readers establish personal portfolios of municipal bonds.

Mutual Funds

To understand the tax consequences of mutual funds, you must first understand that mutual funds are considered "regulated investment companies." That means the fund can avoid paying taxes on their investment income and capital gains by passing most of it to their shareholders—who are subsequently taxed on those distributions.

Mutual fund distributions fall into two classifications:

1. *Capital Gains Distributions:* The amount by which long-term gains exceed its long-term losses.
2. *Dividend Income:* Dividend and interest earnings, less management fees and other operating expenses, plus the excess of a fund's short-term securities' gains over short-term losses (securities owned one year or less).

Capital gains and income distributions received by fund shareholders are taxed at your particular tax bracket (i.e., 28% to 33%). (For IRA and Keogh plans, you do not have to declare these distributions.)

Avoid Double Taxation: If you redeem (sell) or exchange fund shares at a loss, you can report that loss on your Form 1040. If you sell at a profit, then you have to report those gains as well. But frequently when investors redeem mutual fund shares, they pay too much. For example:

When you sell shares, you must add the amount of reinvested distributions to your original cost when determining a capital gain or loss. That is, let's say you invested $10,000 in a mutual fund and received $2,000 in distributions (in which taxes were incurred at the time of distribution). The distributions were reinvested as they were received. Now, you want to redeem the shares for $15,000. The total cost for capital gains purposes is the initial $10,000 plus the $2,000, or $12,000. (Remember, tax has already been paid on the $2,000 distribution.) Thus the taxable gain from the $15,000 sale is only $3,000 instead of $5,000.

Many investors fails to make this critical adjustment and end up paying double the income tax. Be sure to keep your Form 1099-DIVs in a special file for the mutual fund. That will save you time and tax dollars later when you sell.

Redemption of Shares: If you are like most mutual fund investors, you probably purchased shares more than once at different prices. This is referred to as dollar-cost-averaging—a very important benefit of mutual fund investing. But what if you wish to sell a portion of your shares, how to you figure the tax consequences?

Fortunately the current tax laws allow you tremendous flexibility in choosing which shares are to be sold and the subsequent capital gain or loss. For example, you purchase:

100 shares at	$8 =	$800
200 shares at	$12 =	$2,400
100 shares at	$9 =	$900

400	$41,000 or an average cost of $10.25

Let's assume you sell 100 shares of your 400-share portfolio for $10 a share. What is the capital gain or loss?

You have several methods to figure this:

- *First-In, First-Out Method:* Sell 100 shares at $8, showing a $2-per-share gain.
- *Cost-Average Method:* Sell 100 shares at $10.25 with a 25-cents-per-share loss.
- *Dual Average Cost Method:* Group all the shares owned before a sale into those owned long enough to qualify for long-term capital gain or loss treatment, and those that qualify for short-term treatment. Then the average cost per share for each group is calculated. When lower tax rates favor long-term gains versus short-term gains, you should elect to sell shares from the long-term group. For a loss, you would sell shares from the short-term group for the most advantageous tax treatment.
- *Specific Share Method:* The most flexible and favorable method in the majority of cases is to identify specific shares in your portfolio to sell. In the preceding example, 100 shares purchased at $12 would be sold at a $2 per share capital loss.

NOTE: Congress has been reviewing these methods, so check with your tax advisor before you sell. The Mutual Fund Simplification Bill before Congress was originally designed to ease the tax burden on mutual funds. However, the Treasury Department's version of the bill recommends the concept of the average-cost basis calculation, but only if the three other choices for determining tax basis are repealed. This would eliminate the more advantageous "special identification" method.

Distribution Tax Problem: If you buy a fund today, and the fund pays a distribution tomorrow, you will owe tax on the amount of distribution. Since the capital gains and ordinary income may have been earned before your purchase, this may seem unfair. Nevertheless, as we mentioned earlier, as a "regulated investment company," the fund must pass the bulk of the profits along to the shareholders. And someone, the shareholders, must pay the tax on those profits.

Here is a way you can avoid the distribution. Most funds make distributions at the same time each year and will announce them in advance. So just before buying shares of any fund, call the fund and ask if the distribution will be made soon. If a distribution is scheduled, delay your purchase until the day after the distribution, to avoid its tax impact.

When selling shares of a fund, contact the fund to find out if a distribution is scheduled shortly. If so, sell the shares before the distribution, to avoid its tax liability.

Fund Expenses: Custodial fees incurred in connection with mutual fund investments, including maintenance fees paid on tax-deferred IRA and Keogh plans, are deductible from ordinary income by taxpayers who itemize. Follow the 2% rule discussed earlier.

Sales charges or loads should be added to the cost of the shares, which subsequently reduces the amount of capital gain (or increases the capital loss) when the shares are sold. Additionally, redemption fees paid to a fund at the time shares are sold are deducted from the sale proceeds.

Real Estate Mortgage Interest

As long as you incurred the debt on your real estate before October 13, 1987, your mortgage interest payments are 100% deductible. If you acquired the debt after that date, some restrictions apply.

Home Equity Loans: Home equity loans cannot only save you taxes, but save you money as well. If you have several small debts, such as credit card debts (where you are paying excessively high rates of interest), it makes sense to consolidate them into a home equity loan.

Besides, interest paid on these debts is no longer tax-deductible per the Tax Reform Act of 1986. That way you can pay off the higher-interest debt, plus be able to deduct your equity loan interest payments as well—up to $100,000.

See Chapter 11 for additional information.

Rental Real Estate: Provided you own at least a 10% stake in a rental property and you participate in setting rents, approving tenants, and so forth, you can take rental real estate deductions—even if you use a rental agent to find your tenants. Your real estate property is then regarded as a business, and you can deduct depreciation, utility bills, repair and other expenses—but only against the rental income. If your potential deductions exceed the income on the property, you cannot use them against other businesses you own.

You can, however, carry them forward and deduct any remaining expenses when you sell your property.

If you own rental property, you can deduct:

1. Operating costs,
2. Mortgage interest payments, and
3. Any other expenses *directly related* to your rental income business. You can deduct these expenses just as you would if you were running any other sort of business. It also may be possible to claim depreciation—talk to your accountant.

Vacation Homes: If your second home is used entirely by you and your family, then you can write off your mortgage interest and property taxes. But you cannot deduct other expenses such as repairs.

You can also rent this home out for fewer than 15 days a year with the rental fees being tax-free to you. You may regard it as a rental property for tax purposes if you don't use it yourself for more than 14 days a year, or for more than 10% of the days it is rented at a fair market value.

A Potential Property Tax Break: Since your home or investment real estate was mostly likely assessed when real estate values were higher, now that values have dropped, you may be paying too much tax. It is very possible you can get a new, more realistic assessment on your home to bring your property taxes into line with today's values.

Second, your assessment may be incorrectly figured. According to Property Valuation Consultants, Joliet, Illinois, approximately 40% of all property tax valuations are incorrect—and in most cases the errors favor the tax collector. Errors can include everything from listing maintenance or repairs as a capital improvement, or incorrectly figuring your home's square footage, to failure to discount features that detract from your property (such as living next to a freeway, flood plain, and so on).

To verify that your property assessment is correct (and not overvalued):

1. Ask your assessor for the latest assessment and "sales ratio" study. This study shows how assessments compare to sales prices in the area. If the ratio is 65%, it means that homes in your area are assessed at 65% of their selling prices. Thus, if your assessment is 75%, you're probably over-assessed.

2. Check your property assessment for other errors.

To appeal your assessment, you must appeal to the assessor. Remember that when you are dealing with your assessor, you are dealing with a tax officer; so don't antagonize him or her. Be friendly, be informal.

U.S. Treasury Issues

Any U.S.-government-related security is exempt from tax at the state level, no matter in which state you might live. It is, however, taxable at the federal level. So if you live in a low-tax or tax-free state, such as Texas or Florida, you are better off with good-quality municipals than Treasuries. You also have the advantage of being able to buy a multistate municipal bond fund without tax penalties.

If you buy a T-bill, you can defer the interest you earn to the following tax year by buying a bill that comes due in that year.

A FINAL NOTE

In these days of tighter money, we all should be much more conscious of our expenses and our balance sheets.

If you do not usually check your credit card bills or your banks statements, now is the time to start. Keep track of your outgo and income carefully. It is amazing how often we can maintain the same standard of living by monitoring our expenses more closely. And you'll be amazed how many overcharges and improper charges you will find on your monthly statements.

Most important: Many of us, particularly those who run our own businesses, are very sloppy about keeping every receipt and adequate records. Unless you make a habit of recording everything you spend that might be deductible, the changes are you are losing track of many legitimate tax deductions.

Table 7.9. How to Determine a Taxable Equivalent Yield

	Example	Your Figures
A-Tax-Free Yield	7%	_____%
	1.00	1.00
B-Tax Bracket *[Convert percentage to decimal (28% to .28)]*	.28	_____
C-Equals *(1.00-B)*	.72	_____
Taxable Equivalent Yield *(A + C)*	9.72%	_____

If you keep records of every mile you use your car, every parking receipt, and every publication you subscribe to for business purposes, you'll be amazed how these expenses mount up. A 60-cent newspaper every day for one year is a $213 tax deduction. No legitimate expense should be dismissed as not worth recording.

Finally, when trying to get taxes reduced, when you are called for an audit, or when you need to deal with a bank or credit card company who has made an error in your account, remember that *the bottom line is the increase of your bottom line.* Don't antagonize the other person. The object of the confrontation is to gain an outcome in your favor.

The wrong attitude can mean the difference between a quick settlement in your favor or being harassed for months, being forced to produce records for every cent you spent, and then losing the case after all. It just isn't worth it.

If you want to work the system, do it through the organizations we list in Appendix B. Don't try to do it in an assessor's office or during an IRS audit. You will lose any advantage you might have gone in with; and worse, you will change nothing.

RESOURCES

John C. Bintz; Hutchinson, Shokey, Erley & Company; 135 S. La Salle Street, Suite 1230, Chicago, IL 60603; (312) 443-1550. John Bintz is a very knowledgeable municipal bond broker.

Ernst & Young Financial Planning Reporter, William Brennan, Editor, P.O. Box 33337, Washington, DC 20033.

Mutual Fund Education Alliance, 1900 Erie Street, Suite 120, Kansas City, MO 64116; (816) 471-1454. Publishers of the *Investor's Guide To Low-Cost Mutual Funds.* See Chapter 3 for additional information.

Mutual Fund Forecaster, Norman Fosback, Editor, Institute for Econometric Research, 3471 N. Federal Highway, Fort Lauderdale, FL 33306;

1-800-327-6720. *Mutual Fund Forecaster* provides excellent information on mutual funds and has special reports available on the tax consequences of such funds.

Tax Avoidance Digest, Robert C. Carlson, C.P.A., Editor, 824 East Baltimore Street, Baltimore, MD 21202; 1-800-223-1982, Ext. 418. Robert Carlson writes an excellent newsletter that can provide you hundreds of ways to save on your taxes, including "green flags" that will tell the IRS to let your return through without hassle. He also has several excellent reports available to subscribers, including *Retirement Tax Guide* and *How To Slash Your Mutual Fund Taxes.*

8

How Safe Is Your Bank, Brokerage House, and Insurance Company?

"Banking establishments are more dangerous
than standing armies."

THOMAS JEFFERSON

There has been an unprecedented number of bank, S&L, and insurance company failures in recent years, and the continuing weak recovery (or continued recession) promises to worsen these problems. It is *vitally important* for you to know how safe your financial institution is. This chapter shows you how, including:

- Three foolproof self-help tests for determining the safety of your bank,
- How to find the strongest banks and S&Ls in your state and the United States,
- How to rate the health of your insurance company, and
- The first rating service to rate the safety of brokerage houses.

A decade of unwise loans to Third World countries, corporate buyout deals, excessive credit, and most importantly, speculative commercial real estate ventures has placed the banks, S&Ls and insurance companies in a dangerous position.

FINDING SAFETY IN AN UNSAFE WORLD

It is no longer enough to buy the right stock, bond or other financial instrument to make a profit and preserve your capital. Today, one has to weigh carefully the reliability of the financial institution as well.

The highest yield makes little sense if the institution that holds your money goes under—and goes under when the government's safety net may have been stretched beyond the breaking point by previous failures!

In truth, there has never been more cause for worry in this regard since the Great Depression. As *The Bank Credit Analyst,* one of the nation's most conservative and widely respected financial publications, recently warned:

"Confidence in the U.S. financial system continues to deteriorate, and the odds of a full-fledged crisis are mounting daily. Federal Reserve intervention has done little to stem the flight of money from several large banks in deep trouble. The preconditions are in place for a run on several banks simultaneously for the first time since the 1930s. The authorities seem powerless, and in fact government policies have been exacerbating the crisis . . ."

Americans are very jittery about the health and integrity of the nation's financial institutions. A recent *Wall Street Journal* poll of 1,510 adults showed that 62% said they were concerned about the banking system's soundness, and 11% have withdrawn money because of safety reasons. About 46% of the adults polled believe the nation's insurers are "just somewhat sound" or "not at all sound." About 8% say they have moved their insurance policies or cashed them in specifically because of their worries.

If you are not concerned, you should be.

Today's crisis can be compared on many levels with the fall of the Roman Empire. When the city of Rome fell to the barbarians, the economic infrastructure of the entire civilized world was unable to sustain itself. Without guidance from the central government, it didn't know how.

Conditions exist today that could trigger not only an international flight from the dollar, but a breakdown of the infrastructure of the international banking system. If any one large U.S. bank failed, the results could be similar to the Roman Empire occurrence. The U.S. dollar is as much a monetary dictatorship in the world today as the Roman Forum was in 400 A.D.

THE BRITISH EXPERIENCE

England was faced with similar, though much less severe, situations in the early 1970s when the British pound was plummeting on overseas markets.

Prior to this time, Arab oil money had been mainly in pounds, not dollars. The Arabs threatened to pull all money out of London unless some guarantees were offered. So Britain guaranteed their exchange rate, while forcing ordinary British citizens to buy any foreign currencies they needed through a closed, limited currency exchange. This meant that the internal exchange rate (the dollar premium market, as it was called) was much higher than the external rate.

As a result, no British subject who wanted to move permanently out of England could take all his or her assets with them. They could either exchange assets at the unrealistic exchange rate, or leave them in England for at least five years before being allowed to exchange at the going international rate.

However, the pound continued to plummet for much of the 1970s. The upshot was that those who took the losses up front and did not leave their money in England, lost less than those who left their money in England for the required five years.

WATCH OUT FOR EXCHANGE CONTROLS

If things get too tight, the United States could go the same route as Britain did in the 1970s. So if you are considering diversifying outside the United States for safety and privacy, this is the time to do it.

Desperate times require desperate measures. The Treasury will do whatever is necessary to stop foreigners from pulling the rug (and the money) out from under the U.S. banking system. Very soon, it may no longer be possible to transfer funds outside U.S. borders. This fact is becoming more visible as the U.S. government cracks down on drug lords and money launderers. Remember, the same laws that restrict unlawful transactions also restrict your lawful transactions and privacy. Chapter 9 will show you how you can safely transfer funds overseas.

SHOPPING FOR SAFETY AT HOME

At home in the United States, it is more important than ever to seek out those banks, brokerage houses, and insurance companies that have responsible management policies.

In the past, diversification simply meant putting your money in several different investment vehicles. Today—with many banks, brokerage houses, and insurance companies all teetering on the edge—diversification means spreading your investments among several top banks and brokerage houses, and checking out your insurance company very, very carefully.

And while prognostication was once confined to projecting the future performances of your securities, it now involves projecting the future performance of the financial house that holds those securities!

An additional benefit: When you take the time and effort to check out the condition of your financial institution, you are performing a public service. By doing business only with financial institutions that are acting responsibly, you help to promote sound management policies throughout the system.

BANKS AND SAVINGS & LOANS: PRESERVING THE SAFETY OF YOUR DEPOSIT ACCOUNTS

As mentioned earlier, the key to surviving the turbulent 1990s is to diversity where you put your assets. To build a sound financial foundation for your investments, you should:

1. *Conduct a nationwide check of banking institutions* that offer the kind of services you require. You can do this yourself or use the services of an independent company that specializes in rating bank safety.
   To verify the condition of your bank, S&L or credit union, we recommend that you contact:
   Weiss Research, Inc.. P.O. Box 2923, West Palm Beach, FL 33402; 1-800-289-9222. Weiss Research can provide you, over the phone, with the safety rating of your bank or S&L, along with an explanation of what the rating means. This allows you to get the rating you need immediately, without waiting for the return mail. They charge $15 per institution and will accept credit cards for payment. You can also obtain a one-page *Personal Safety Brief* for $25 per institution (three reports for $55); or the *Personal Safety Report,* an in-depth report, for $45 (three for $95).
   VeriBanc Inc., P.O. Box 461, Wakefield, MA 01880; 1-800-442-2657.
   VeriBanc will verify for you, in plain English, the condition of your bank, S&L, or credit union. They charge $10 for the first institution and $3 for each additional institution—which can be charged to your credit card. By calling their toll-free number, you will receive an *immediate* verbal report, as well as a printed report through the mail.

2. *Be very suspicious of any bank that is paying above-average (market) interest rates.* Even if the bank has a good rating right now, there is likely some reason it needs to attract deposits that badly. There may be exceptions to the rule, but double-check any apparently sound bank that is offering high rates.

3. *Compile a list of the top 10 banking institutions* that offer the financial products you require.

4. From that list, *take the top four* institutions (more if your assets are large) and *distribute your assets* that are designated for banks among these institutions.
   For example, if you wish to put $100,000 into a CD, we suggest that you split your funds into smaller deposits (e.g., $25,000 for each account) in four different banks. You can diversify even further by putting each time deposit at a different maturity—the longest with the safest bank, and the shortest with the least safe.

WHAT ABOUT FDIC INSURANCE?

According to the FDIC, there are 975 problem banks in the United States today. This list is kept secret by federal regulators. (Later in this chapter we will present you with a self-test that you can use on your institution. Actually, it is more effective than having the FDIC's problem bank list in your pocket.)

Of the 2,400 federally insured S&Ls, only 1,260 are in somewhat good shape; and 486 are insolvent (or near insolvency). Hundreds more are operating on minimum capital margins. Therefore, it is essential that you thoroughly check out any financial institution with which you wish to do business.

Prior to leaving his post as head of the FDIC, William Seidman stated that there was not enough money in the FDIC fund to cover the anticipated number of bank failures for 1991. He also make it clear that the banking crisis would not be resolved until the entire U.S. banking structure was changed. (See Figure 8.1.)

In January 1991, the FDIC said the insurance fund's assets at the end of 1992 could range from $3.6 billion in the black to $4.6 billion in the red. In October,

Figure 8.1.   The Evaporating Bank-Rescue Fund

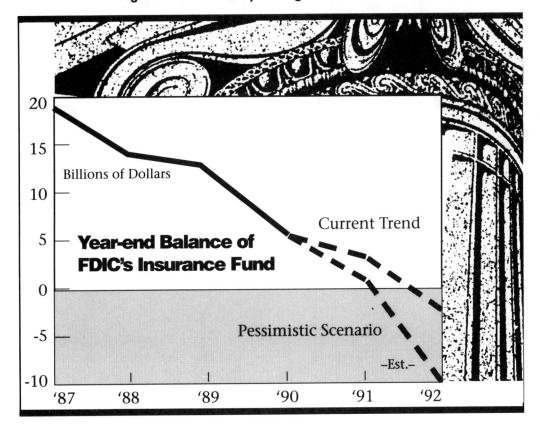

Data: Federal Deposit Insurance Corp.

the FDIC said that the balance could range from a $3 billion deficit (if things went well) to $11 billion in the hole.

For obvious reasons, the FDIC is already asking for more money. The latest forecast is that 400 institutions, with $200 billion in assets, will fail in 1992. And that doesn't include interest, which could add an additional $40 billion by 2006.

SAFETY TIP

Federal Deposit Insurance Corporation

The Federal Deposit Insurance Corporation (FDIC) insures most bank and savings and loan accounts up to $100,000. However, if you have several accounts within the same bank, you may not be covered.

For example, if you have two accounts that add up to $150,000, only $100,000 of your money is covered. The balance ($50,000) is not. The FDIC will group together savings and checking accounts. Joint and retirement accounts are not lumped with individual accounts, but they are still covered by the $100,000 limitation.

Our suggestion is to move any amount over $100,000 to other banks; otherwise you could lose your money if the bank fails.

For additional information write to: FDIC Consumer Affairs, 550 17th Street NW, Washington, DC 20429.

If the real estate doldrums continue or, worse yet, the economy sinks back into a recession, no bank will be safe. And if the FDIC runs out of money, then no bank account is safe. (See Figure 8.2.)

Therefore, to keep your options open, find out what the penalty is for early withdrawal *before* you open an account; and be fully prepared to pay that penalty should you need to switch banks quickly. (And, as mentioned in a previous chapter, you can buy your CD through a brokerage and very likely avoid early withdrawal penalties.)

FINDING THE STRONGEST BANKS AND SAVINGS & LOANS

Use the following pointers to check out banks and S&Ls yourself:

1. Figure out whether you are dealing with a bank or a savings and loan institution. Banks report to the Federal Reserve Board. S&Ls report to the Office of Thrift Supervision.

2. Know what questions to ask. For example, get your bank's latest financial statements and use them to apply the special three tests given at the end of this chapter.

Figure 8.2. Problems Grow

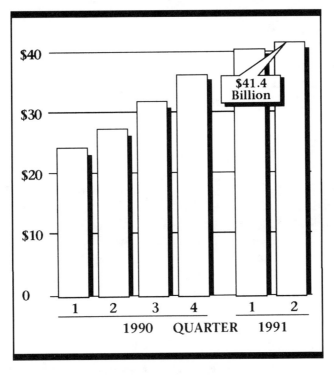

*Includes loans 90 days past-due

Source: FDIC and USA Today

ADDITIONAL WAYS TO CHECK OUT YOUR BANK'S SAFETY

Government regulatory bodies can provide you with general information, but are not obligated to tell you if your bank is in trouble. You can contact either of the following:

For Banks—FDIC, Office of Consumer Affairs, 550 17th Street NW, Washington, DC 20429; 1-800-424-5488 or (202) 898-3356.

For S&Ls—Office of Thrift Supervision, Office of Community Investment, Division of Consumer Rights, 1700 G Street NW, Washington, DC 20552; (202) 906-6237.

For Credit Unions—Office of Public and Congressional Affairs, National Credit Union Administration, 1776 G Street NW, Washington, DC 20456.

Ninety percent of all credit unions are insured up to $100,000 per account by the National Credit Union Administration. As with the FDIC, if you have a joint account or similar accounts (such as two IRAs) worth more than $100,000, you may be out of luck should your credit union fail.

You can obtain evaluations of banks within your state or across the United States from:

Weiss Research, Inc., P.O. Box 2923, West Palm Beach, FL 33402; 1-800-289-9222. Weiss Research evaluates and rates more than 12,500 banks and 2,500 savings and loans. The ratings range from A+ (excellent) to F (failed or in the process of failing). In addition to providing immediate ratings over the phone and follow-up reports (see "Preserving the Safety of Your Deposit Accounts"), Weiss also offers a *Watchdog Service.* For a fee of $19 per quarter ($10 per quarter for each additional institution), you will get a *Personal Safety Brief* every time they receive new information on your institution that causes the safety rating to change.

VeriBanc, Inc., P.O. Box 461, Wakefield, MA 01880; 1-800-442-2657 (1-800-44BANKS), (617) 245-8370. VeriBanc rates every federally insured bank, S&L and credit union in the country, some 27,000 institutions in all. Using a color and star system, they provide a quick view of an institution's strength and a plain-English description of what the ratings mean. You may receive VeriBanc's ratings immediately over the telephone for a charge of $10 for the first institution and $3 for each additional. A credit card may be used to charge telephone orders.

SAFETY TIP

A First: A Brokerage Rating Service

On November 15, 1991, Weiss Research, Inc., announced that they would begin rating the safety of brokerage firms.

According to Martin D. Weiss, President of Weiss Research, *"The investor faces numerous dangers—including commingling of securities, bad record keeping and a possible freeze of customer accounts—when dealing with some unsafe brokers. Furthermore, although many institutions rarely commit fraud, they may be vulnerable to a major market decline."*

Known for their *conservative* ratings of banks and insurance companies, Weiss Research will rate the safety (using capital, liquidity, risk and leverage considerations) of over 200 brokerage firms as follows:

A or Excellent means the company has followed a conservative policy and has excellent scores on all or nearly all of our indicators. It is liquid, has little debt, does not take extra business risks, and has more than enough capital to withstand even the most adverse market conditions.

B or Good means the company offers good security and has the resources to deal with a cyclical market decline. However, in the event of a major bear market or other severe disruption, this would need to be re-evaluated on the basis of the most current data.

C or Fair reflects a company that is currently stable and should remain viable as long as financial markets do not deteriorate significantly from current levels. However, this company has failed to demonstrate that it will be able to withstand any adverse market conditions.

D or Weak suggests that the company has failed to demonstrate that it can adequately protect customers from its financial weaknesses. The weaknesses may include insufficient capital, low liquidity, or high levels of risk.

E or Very Weak is a brokerage that has significant weaknesses in one or more areas. It has failed some of the basic tests that Weiss uses to identify financial strength. Therefore, even in favorable market conditions, customers could incur significant risk.

F or Failed (or near failure) suggests the company has failed to meet the SEC's minimum capital requirements. Unless an infusion of capital could be arranged, it will most likely have to be liquidated or sold to another firm.

Here are the results of their first survey: Out of 221 companies, 12 were rated "A" (excellent), 115 as "B" (good), 80 as "C" (fair), 13 as "D" (weak) and one as "E" (very weak).

The Five Highest Rated

Atlanta/Soshoff Management Corporation	A	Needham and Company, Incorporated	A –
Lipper Analytical Securities Corporation	A	Allen and Company, Incorporated	A –
NYLIFE Securities, Incorporated	A		

To receive a letter grade for your brokerage firm, contact Weiss Research, Inc., 2200 N. Florida Mango Road, West Palm Beach, FL 33409; 1-800-289-9222. You will be charged $15 per rating over the phone, or you can receive a one-page *Personal Safety Brief* for $25. A 150-page Brokerage Safety Directory is available for $189, and includes ratings for over 200 brokerage firms.

In addition, you can order a variety of other plain-English reports that go into detail about the data behind the ratings. You can also obtain lists of the strongest banks in your area with their *Blue Ribbon Bank Report* ($35) or their customized *City/County Report* ($50). VeriBanc publishes a quarterly newsletter, *The Banking Safety Digest.* If you wish, you can also receive the same news releases on the industry that over 2,500 major print and electronic media receive.

Federal Financial Institutions Examination Council, U.B.P.R., 1776 6th Street NW, Washington, DC 20006; (202) 357-0177. (Each request costs $40.)

NEWSLETTERS THAT DISCUSS BANK SAFETY

Because the status of banks can change very rapidly as different sectors of the economy change, it is best if you can learn to monitor your bank yourself. The following newsletters can be of great help in this regard.

Safe Money Report, (formerly *Money & Markets*), Martin D. Weiss, Editor, Weiss Research, P.O. Box 2923, West Palm Beach, FL 33402; 1-800-289-9222. Since this newsletter is published by (possibly) the toughest financial rating service, this is a unique publication that goes one step beyond. Besides monitoring the safety of financial institutions, it provides you with ways of profiting from the instability as well.

The Retirement Letter, Peter Dickinson, Editor, Phillips Publishing, 7811 Montrose Road, Potomac, MD 20854; 1-800-722-9000. This newsletter regularly monitors banks in the United States and offers alternative conservative investment ideas.

Bank Stock Analyst, P.O. Box 15381, Chevy Chase, MD 20825; (301) 654-5205. As a subscriber to *Growth Stock Outlook* (designed for brokers, institutions and investors who recognize the risks and rewards of investing in vigorously growing companies), you receive complimentary copies of *Bank Stock Analyst;* or if you would like a copy, they sell for $50.

BROKERAGE HOUSES: HOW SAFE ARE THEY?

About 12,000 U.S. brokerage firms contribute to an insurance program referred to as the Securities Investor Protection Corporation (SIPC). It has about $500 million in its fund, with a $1 billion credit line with the government.

The SIPC is supported by the member brokerage firms—it is not a government-funded agency, nor does it regulate the industry. If a member firm fails, a trustee is appointed to liquidate the firm and, in some cases, transfer the customer accounts to another brokerage house.

When a brokerage house fails, the accounts are often simply transferred to another firm. If not, then all securities shown on your monthly statement, plus any cash, will be sent to you over a period of several months. If your broker "fast-talks" you into a security and you can prove a case of fraud against him, the SIPC will sometimes cover that as well.

SIPC insurance covers up to $500,000 per customer, and includes up to $100,000 held in cash in the brokerage account. However, this insurance covers only cash and securities such as stocks, bonds, notes, CDs, money market funds, and warrants. It does not cover commodities or commodity options.

Many brokerages carry insurance besides the SIPC insurance. Check with your brokerage house on what is covered. If you want to know more about the SIPC, contact:

SIPC, 900 17th Street NW, Washington, DC 20006; (202) 371-8300.

MUNICIPAL BOND COVERAGE

Municipal bonds are insured by a number of insurance companies, in the event of a default. The three main companies are:

Municipal Bond Investors Assurance (MBIA), 113 King St., Almond, NY 10504; (914) 765-3893. It is the largest, and a unit of MBIA, Inc.

American Municipal Bond Assurance Indemnity Corporation (AMBAIC), a unit of Citicorp.

Financial Guaranty Insurance Company (FGIC), 175 Water St., New York, NY 10038; (212) 607-3009. Owned by General Electric Capital Corporation.

Many experts express doubts that, in the event of a major recession, any of these companies could truly cover the widespread defaults that could occur.

MUTUAL FUNDS

About the only way you can purchase a mutual fund that is insured is by buying one that owns a portfolio of municipal bonds backed by private insurers. Anything else is a marketing gimmick or worse. Recently the SEC has warned funds to stop using the word "insured" or "guaranteed" in their advertising efforts.

MORTGAGE-BACKED SECURITIES

Brokers like to promote Government National Mortgage Association securities (Ginnie Maes) because the government insures the timely payment of principal and interest. But as with bond funds, the government does not guarantee a Ginnie Mae's yield or its life span. As interest rates decline, homeowners with high-rate mortgages tend to refinance them at lower levels. Instead of a steady income paid over the years, Ginnie Mae investors may get all their principal back well before the security matures—causing possible tax complications.

INSURANCE COMPANIES: THE LATEST FINANCIAL DEBACLE

"There is a crisis of confidence in the insurance industry today," says Senator Howard Metzenbaum. And rightfully so.

State regulators had taken control of 34 insurers by the third quarter of 1991, compared to 32 in 1990. In 1988, only 13 were seized. (See Figure 8.3.).

While the vast majority of insurers are healthy, of 1,269 life insurers with assets of $5 million or more, 91 are potentially at risk due to real estate and junk bond investments.

According to *Myers Finance and Energy,* "The dominoes began to fall last April when California regulators seized the assets of First Executive, which had 400,000 customers and more than $10 billion in assets. May marked the collapse of another Los Angeles insurance giant, First Capital Life, which was seized

Figure 8.3.   Insurance Company Failures

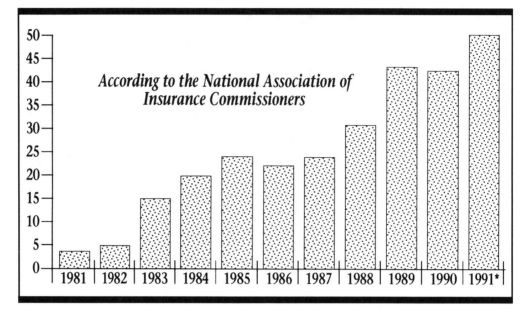

According to the National Association of
Insurance Commissioners

*MFE projection

Source: Myers Finance & Energy

after its number one lender, Citicorp, tried to force it into bankruptcy. It had $4.5 billion in assets and 190,000 life insurance policyholders."

John Dingel, Chairman of the House Energy and Commerce Committee, stated "The parallels between the present situation in the insurance industry and the early stages of the savings and loan debacle are both obvious and deeply disturbing."

He merely echoes the opinions of experts across the country. It has been estimated that a serious recession could wipe out 20% of America's insurance companies. Unlike the S&L industry, there is no federal insurance to insure the insurers!

Even more disturbing is the fact that insurance companies are required to furnish far less financial information than are banks. This means that government regulators have only a hazy idea of the actual health of the $2 trillion insurance industry.

CATEGORIES OF INSURANCE

Insurance in this country operates under four different categories: Life, property and casualty, health insurance, and reinsuring the risks on the other three. As an industry, insurance is regulated on a state, rather than a federal, level. (See Figure 8.4.)

Because of the housing slump, property and casualty insurance is already in deep trouble. But the worst sector at the moment is life insurance, mainly because of the insurance revolution that began in the 1970s.

It started when interest rates rose in the late 1970s and raced to new heights in the early 1980s. Responding to policyholders who demanded better returns than the 4% they were earning on whole life policies, the industry changed its emphasis. For example, universal life policies were introduced that could allow you to vary your death benefit and premium and take advantage of rising interest rates.

By 1985, universal life made up 38% of the total insurance sales. In 1980,

Figure 8.4. Insurance Revolution

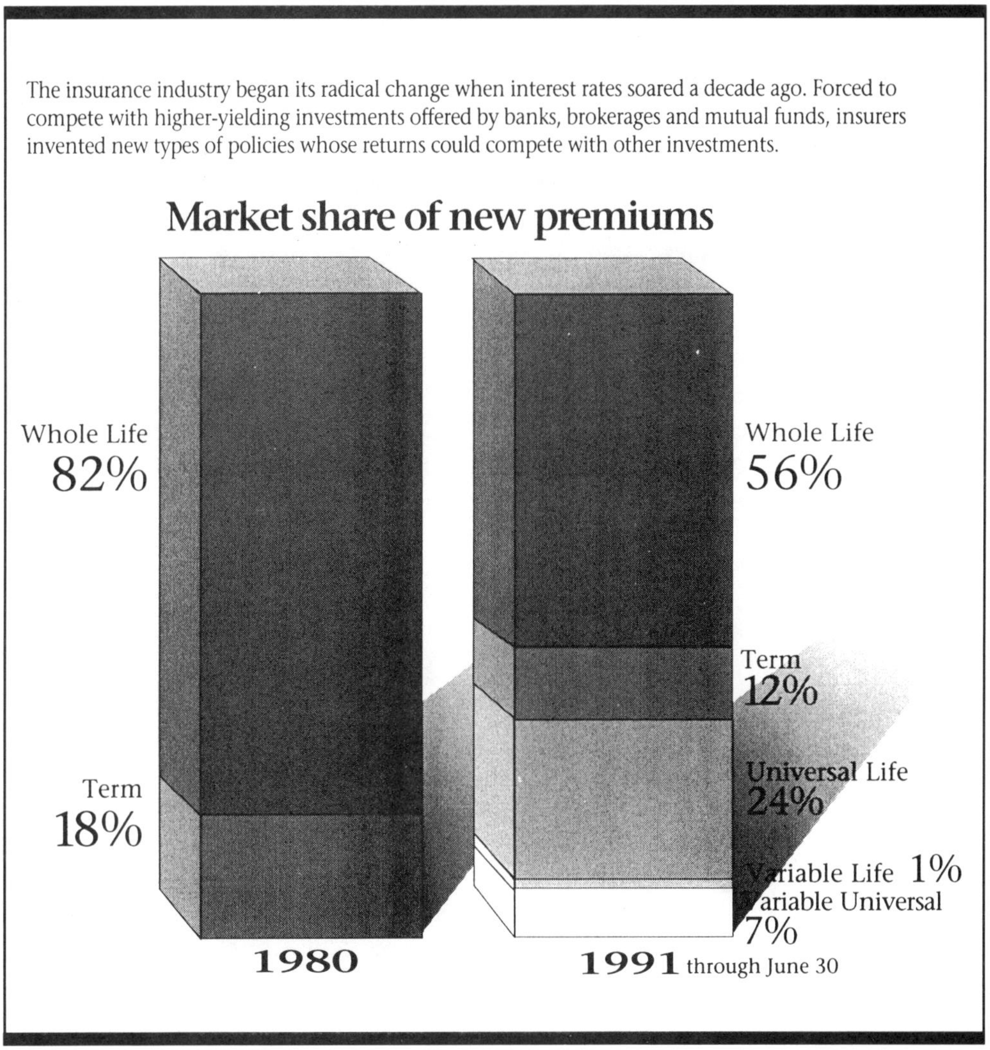

The insurance industry began its radical change when interest rates soared a decade ago. Forced to compete with higher-yielding investments offered by banks, brokerages and mutual funds, insurers invented new types of policies whose returns could compete with other investments.

Market share of new premiums

Whole Life
82%

Whole Life
56%

Term
12%

Universal Life
24%

Term
18%

Variable Life **1%**
ariable Universal
7%

1980   **1991** through June 30

Source: Life Insurance Marketing and Research Association

insurance companies sold nearly twice as much in life insurance premiums as in annuity premiums. By 1990, sales of annuity contracts exceeded life insurance premiums by a margin of 5 to 3. Additionally, Guaranteed Investment Contracts (GICs) became the mainstay investment for 401(k) plans.

Unfortunately, to keep pace with the higher yields offered by other investments, insurance companies sought out riskier, higher-yielding investments. Insurers could not profit simply with reliable, low-yield investments such as government bonds. Instead, they turned to riskier investments, such as high-yield corporate bonds, junk bonds, and real estate, in hopes of higher returns.

Then the trouble began. In the late 1980s, real estate values declined, with many mortgage holders defaulting on their loans. Meanwhile, the junk bond market plummeted as investors worried about the recession and the downfall of Drexel Burnham Lambert, the biggest brokerage firm in the junk bond business.

On the average, insurers had 11.4% of their bond holdings in junk bonds after 1990 and 24% tied into real estate—of which 5% were in repossessed property and mortgages whose payments were 90 days late or in default. The weakest companies had junk bond and nonperforming real estate holdings far exceeding the average. Executive Life, for example, had 82% of its $10.1 billion bond portfolio in junk bonds. Nearly 10% of the $5 billion real estate holdings of Mutual Benefit of New Jersey was in mortgages more than 90 days past due.

The 10 largest life insurers (see Table 8.1) hold $162 billion in mortgages and real estate. That's more than 50% of the total industry holdings. The chart shows the percentage of risky real estate and mortgages held by these insurers. Aetna, Connecticut General, Equitable, John Hancock, and Travelers appear to be in the worst condition.

FINDING THE SAFEST INSURANCE COMPANIES

If there can be a good side to this news, it is: The insurance industry is really not in as desperate straits as it sounds. Of the 1,269 insurers, fewer than 100 had high-risk assets in 1990 larger than the firm's net worth. Of those, 34 had risky assets that amount to 200% of their net worth—15 are now under state controls. (For a partial list see Table 8.2).

"For the most part, the insurance industry didn't get into the junk bonds to the degree that this company [Executive Life] did. Thank God that's the case," says John Garamendi, the California State Insurance Commissioner.

Finding the worst insurance company is more difficult than finding the best, because there is no single reliable source for rating them. A.M. Best is the oldest and most often referred to insurance rating company in the United States. But its standards are not nearly as high as Standard & Poor's and Moody's ratings of banks. Weiss Research is possibly the strictest rating service.

For example, of the largest life insurers listed, Table 8.3 shows how the various services rated them.

As you can see, big is not necessarily the safest. Equitable Life appears to be

Table 8.1. 10 Largest Life Insurers

The ten biggest life insurance companies, ranked by assets, and the percentage of their investments in mortgages and real estate.

Company	Mortgage/ real estate as pct. of invested assets	Pct. of mortgages/ real estate that is risky	Total mortgage/ real estate in billions
Prudential Ins. Co.	27.9%	1.5%	$28.8
Metropolitan Life Ins.	30.3%	2.6%	$27.2
Teachers Ins.	44.0%	4.1%	$21.5
Aetna Life Ins. Co.	54.2%	6.8%	$20.9
New York Life Ins.	18.7%	3.6%	$6.9
Equitable Life Assur.	37.4%	6.7%	$13.0
John Hancock Mutual	44.6%	5.5%	$12.8
Northwestern Mutual	23.5%	2.6%	$6.7
Travelers Ins. Co.	49.4%	18.3%	$13.7
Conn. General Life	42.1%	4.0%	$10.4

Source: USA TODAY analysis of National Association of Insurance Commissioners data.

in the worst shape, while Metropolitan Life, New York Life and Northwestern Mutual have the highest ratings.

Here is a list of the safest insurance companies with assets over $4 billion according to Weiss Research (as of the 3rd quarter of 1991). Each has ratings of A or better:

State Farm A+

Northwestern Mutual A

Continental Assurance A−

Guardian Life A−

New York Life A

Hartford Life A

Metropolitan Life A−

In addition, see Table 8.4.

The weakest, receiving D+ or less with assets over $4 billion are:

Kemper Investors D+

Fidelity & Guaranty D+

Table 8.2. Low on Liquid Assets

Asterisks indicate companies under state control.

Insurer, state	Total assets (billions)	Liquidity rate
Executive Life Ins Co., Calif.*	$10.2	38%
UNUM Life Ins Co., Maine	$4.4	38%
Kemper Investors Life Ins Co., Ill.	$5.5	38%
Mutual Benefit Life Ins Co., N.J.	$13.0	41%
Northwestern Natl Life Ins Co., Minn.	$4.7	41%
Sun Life Co. of America, Md.	$5.2	41%
John Alden Life Ins Co., Minn.	$2.5	42%
John Hancock Mutual Life Ins Co., Mass.	$29.6	42%
Aetna Life Ins Co., Conn.	$39.8	44%
United of Omaha Life Ins Co., Neb.	$4.4	50%
State Mutual Life Asr Co. of Amer., Mass.	$5.8	51%
Principal Mutual Life Ins Co., Ind.	$23.7	52%
Mutual Life Ins Co. of New York, N.Y.	$14.6	63%
Nationwide Life Ins Co., Ohio	$9.2	65%
Minnesota Mutual Life Ins Co., Minn.	$5.1	66%
Allstate Life Ins Co., Ill.	$14.8	67%
Connecticut General Life Ins Co., Conn.	$26.7	68%
Provident National Asr Co., Tenn.	$7.8	68%
Variable Annuity Life Ins Co., Texas	$11.7	70%
Anchor National Life Ins Co., Calif.	$2.1	73%
First Capital Life Ins Co., Calif.*	$4.0	74%
Executive Life Ins Co. of New York, N.Y.*	$3.2	75%
Horace Mann Life Ins Co., Ill.	$1.6	75%

Source: Michael Conn Associates, USA TODAY research

Equitable Life Assurance D
Mutual of New York D–
United Pacific D
Anchor National D

Table 8.3.   Rating the Top 10 Insurers

	A.M. Best	Standard & Poors	Moody's	Weiss Research
Aetna Life Insurance	A+	AA+	Aaa	C+
Conn. General Life	A+	AAA	Aaa	C+
Equitable Life Assurance	A+	A	A	D
John Hancock Mutual	A+	AAA	Aaa	C
Metropolitan Life Insurance	A+	AAA	Aaa	A–
New York Life	A+	AAA	Aaa	A
Northwestern Mutual	A+	AAA	Aaa	A
Prudential Insurance Co.	A+	AAA	Aaa	B
Teachers Insurance (TIAA)	A+	AAA	Aaa	B–
Travelers Insurance Co.	A	A+	nr	C

nr (no rating)

Source: July/August 1991 Annuity & Life Insurance Shopper

In Table 8.5, you will find a list of the top 50 (safest) insurance companies. These companies have been compiled from the ratings provided by all of the rating services as of mid-1991. Be aware that these ratings change (upward or downward) frequently, so don't rely entirely on these ratings. (See page 174.)

WHO RATES INSURANCE COMPANIES

Weiss Research, P.O. Box 2923, West Palm Beach, FL 33402; 1-800-289-9222. Weiss Research rates over 1,700 life, health, and annuity insurers, using a scale of A+ (excellent) to F (failed or in the process of failing). Weiss is the only service that updates its information every quarter. You can receive an immediate rating over the phone for $15 per insurer or you can obtain a one-page *Personal Safety Brief* ($25 per insurer), or the *Personal Safety Report,* an in-depth report, for $45.

A.M. Best & Co., Ambest Road, Oldwick, NJ 08858. Call (908) 439-2200 and ask for your insurer's code. Then call 1-900-420-0400 ($2.50 per minute). Ratings range from A+ (superior) to C– (fair).

Standard & Poor's Corp., 25 Broadway, New York, NY 10004. Ratings range from AAA (superior); AA+, AA, AA– (excellent); to B+, B, B–, CCC, CC and C (speculative); and D (in default).

Moody's Investors Service, Inc., 99 Church Street, New York, NY 10007. Ratings range from Aaa (exceptional) to C (lowest).

Table 8.4. Top Insurance Companies

(Highest Overall Rated Insurance Companies)

Company Name	Assets In Billions	A.M. Best Rating	S & P Rating	Moody's Rating	Weiss Rating
Allstate LIC	$ 14.82	A+	AAA	Aa1	B
Comm. Union LIC	.55	A+	nr	nr	B+
Commonwealth LIC	4.59	A+	AAA	Aa3	B+
Continental Assurance	9.89	A+	AA+	Aa1	A–
First Colony LIC	4.45	A+	AA+	nr	B+
Franklin LIC	4.59	A+	nr	Aa2	B+
Great Southern LIC	.69	A	A	nr	B–
Guardian LIC of Am	6.16	A+	AAA	Aaa	A–
Hartford LIC	11.62	A+	AAA	Aa2	A
IDS LIC	15.58	A+	nr	Aa1	B–
Jefferson Pilot LIC	3.93	A+	AAA	nr	A+
Kansas City LIC	1.59	A+	nr	nr	B+
Liberty Nat'l LIC	2.20	A+	AAA	nr	B–
Life Insurance Co/S'west	.98	A+	nr	nr	B–
Life Insurance Co/VA	4.82	A+	AA	Aa3	B
Lincoln Benefit	.09	A+	AAA	nr	B
Lincoln Nat'l LIC	18.79	A+	AA+	Aa3	B+
Mass Mutual LIC	27.23	A+	AAA	Aaa	B
Metropolitan	103.23	A+	AAA	Aaa	A–
Mutual of America LIC	4.96	A+	AA	Aa2	B+
Nat'l Home Life Assur	5.33	A+	AA	nr	B+
National LIC	4.04	A–	A+	nr	B–
Nationwide LIC	12.34	A+	AAA	Aaa	B–
New York LIC	39.88	A+	AAA	Aaa	A
N'western Mutual LIC	31.38	A+	AAA	Aaa	A
Ohio Nat'l LIC	2.64	A+	nr	Aa2	B–
Pacific Mutual LIC	9.78	A+	AAA	Aa2	B
Peoples Security LIC	3.05	A+	AAA	Aa3	B–
Protective LIC	1.89	A+	AA	nr	B+
Prudential Ins Co./Am	133.46	A+	AAA	Aaa	B
Secur. Conn LIC	.89	A+	nr	nr	B

Table 8.4. (continued)

(Highest Overall Rated Insurance Companies)

Company Name	Assets In Billions	A.M. Best Rating	S & P Rating	Moody's Rating	Weiss Rating
State Farm LIC	12.13	A+	AAA	Aaa	A+
Surety LIC	.07	A+	AAA	nr	B
United of Omaha	4.37	A+	nr	Aa2	B
Variable Ann. LIC	12.46	A+	AA+	Aa2	B–
Volunteer State LIC	.54	A+	AA+	nr	A+
Wash. Nat'l Ins Co.	1.71	A+	nr	nr	B–
Western Nat'l LIC	4.37	A+	A–	A3	B

nr: no rating

Note: Some of these ratings are as much as 12 or more months old. We suggest that you contact the specific rating services or obtain the latest copy of Annuity & Life Insurance Shopper for up-to-date information.

Compiled by CMAI from data furnished by: Annuity & Life Insurance Shopper (July/August 1991).

WHO INSURES THE INSURERS?

Many states have established insurance guaranty associations to help pay claims to policyholders of failed insurance companies. However, like FDIC insurance on banks, should there be a string of failures, there will not be enough money to cover it all.

Business Week reported, *"The state guaranty funds could easily be overwhelmed by multistate, multibillion-dollar insolvencies. A wave of insurance collapses could have a domino effect. It could overwhelm often weak and understaffed state regulators [and] drag down healthy companies. Many analysts think a hair-curling shakeout is inevitable."*

Furthermore, these are state insurance programs—not federal—and each state has different levels and types of coverage that may conflict with another state. If your insurance company is headquartered in a state other than your state, the legal complications and paperwork could be horrendous in the event of a failure.

Table 8.6 is a list of liability limits per state. You should confirm the coverage by calling your particular State Insurance Commissioner (the phone numbers are also provided). (See page 178.)

Table 8.5. The Two Largest Blue Ribbon Banks in Each State

Commercial Bank Name	City	State	Profitability Ratio (%)	Equity/ Assts Ratio (%)	Liquidity Ratio (%)	Average Assets ($)	Average Equity ($)	Annualized Net Income ($)
National Bk of Alaska	Anchorage	AK	1.39	10.68	71.06	1,979,498,000	212,313,000	27,542,000
*First NB of Anchorage	Anchorage	AK	2.42	17.21	97.63	1,175,131,500	202,246,000	28,396,000
Amsouth Bk Birmingham NA	Birmingham	AL	1.25	7.73	59.43	7,616,212,000	588,647,500	95,394,000
First Alabama Bk	Montgomery	AL	1.25	8.09	43.55	6,167,022,000	498,868,000	77,170,000
Union NB of AR	Little Rock	AR	0.55	9.24	77.64	536,331,000	49,542,500	2,974,000
Simmons First NB	Pine Bluff	AR	0.83	7.62	79.86	507,938,500	38,721,000	4,226,000
*Farmers & Merchants Bk of L	Long Beach	CA	2.00	16.23	97.61	1,415,442,500	229,741,500	28,248,000
Santa Barbara B&TC	Santa Barbara	CA	1.36	7.73	45.76	850,240,000	65,721,000	11,532,000
First NB In Boulder	Boulder	CO	1.26	8.27	49.74	343,074,500	28,370,000	4,322,000
United Bk Greeley NA	Greeley	CO	0.77	11.82	64.90	194,825,000	23,038,000	1,496,000
Thomaston Svg Bk	Thomaston	CT	0.75	11.05	47.08	216,259,500	23,895,500	1,624,000
*Savings Bk Of Danbury	Danbury	CT	0.97	12.35	67.31	190,295,000	23,503,000	1,854,000
Citizens Bk Washington NA	Washington	DC	0.70	8.48	46.25	207,179,000	17,561,000	1,452,000
*National Capital Bk of WA	Washington	DC	1.49	18.14	71.38	99,707,500	18,082,500	1,488,000
Baltimore TC	Selbyville	DE	1.61	11.86	48.22	209,109,500	24,801,500	3,358,000
Sun Bk South FL NA	Fort Lauderdale	FL	1.18	8.63	54.71	2,232,822,000	192,626,500	26,436,000
Peoples Bk of Lakeland	Lakeland	FL	0.95	10.89	91.94	556,288,000	60,569,000	5,282,000
*Trust Co Bk	Atlanta	GA	1.68	8.51	76.61	7,444,810,500	633,905,500	125,330,000
Trust Co Bk of Middle GA NA	Macon	GA	1.62	8.97	48.42	513,314,000	46,031,000	8,300,000
GECC Financial Corp	Honolulu	HI	2.12	10.76	70.04	761,209,500	81,909,500	16,162,000
*Davenport B&TC	Davenport	IA	1.56	12.51	135.84	1,849,804,000	231,370,500	28,946,000
National Bk of Waterloo	Waterloo	IA	1.08	7.94	67.18	510,059,000	40,483,500	5,522,000

Bank	City	State						
Affiliated Bk	Franklin Park	IL	0.64	8.03	51.57	1,389,543,000	111,543,000	8,848,000
Amcore Bank NA	Rockford	IL	1.07	8.13	49.84	831,722,500	67,586,500	8,878,000
Old NB in Evansville	Evansville	IN	1.06	10.25	53.24	977,436,000	100,225,000	10,386,000
Citizens NB of Evansville	Evansville	IN	1.21	8.44	48.73	793,253,000	66,956,000	9,618,000
First NB in Wichita	Wichita	KS	1.01	8.31	53.98	917,019,500	76,185,500	9,262,000
First NB of Hutchinson	Hutchinson	KS	0.79	8.36	96.65	219,515,500	18,342,000	1,730,000
Mid America B&TC	Louisville	KY	1.09	10.13	65.67	913,784,000	92,559,500	9,954,000
Citizens B&TC	Paducah	KY	1.01	9.37	49.94	461,259,500	43,219,000	4,666,000
*Calcasieu Marine NB	Lake Charles	LA	0.55	10.73	79.67	837,864,000	89,916,000	4,634,000
*First Interstate Bk Sthrn L	Thibodaux	LA	0.79	8.24	76.43	504,717,500	41,598,500	4,008,000
Peoples Svg Bk	Worcester	MA	0.67	7.87	48.84	919,347,500	72,386,000	6,114,000
Cambridge Svg Bk	Cambridge	MA	0.50	11.02	56.46	522,415,500	57,560,000	2,612,000
Mercantile Safe Dep & TC	Baltimore	MD	1.41	8.75	50.17	2,046,530,500	179,118,000	28,826,000
*Farmers NB of Maryland	Annapolis	MD	1.09	8.21	73.90	518,764,500	42,591,500	5,664,000
Camden NB	Camden	ME	1.49	8.20	51.64	288,962,000	23,709,000	4,318,000
Androscoggin Svg Bk	Lewiston	ME	0.74	10.68	62.20	183,522,500	19,593,500	1,364,000
*Citizens Commercial & Svg B	Flint	MI	0.75	8.34	61.64	1,295,711,000	108,093,500	9,672,000
Huntington Bks of MI	Troy	MI	1.34	9.01	52.98	1,246,852,000	112,336,000	16,754,000
National City Bk	Minneapolis	MN	0.62	9.14	53.17	464,548,500	42,464,000	2,902,000
Commercial St Bk	St Paul	MN	0.77	7.81	59.18	276,340,500	21,583,500	2,126,000
Boatmens First NB of K	Kansas City	MO	0.89	8.34	60.21	2,864,575,000	238,895,500	25,582,000
United Missouri Bk Kc Cy NA	Kansas City	MO	1.29	9.03	95.88	2,388,664,000	215,653,500	30,844,000
Bank of Mississippi	Tupelo	MS	1.08	8.78	57.43	1,556,831,500	136,672,500	16,748,000
Peoples B&TC	Tupelo	MS	0.87	9.11	68.92	638,098,000	58,114,000	5,532,000
First Security Bk of Bozeman	Bozeman	MT	1.29	9.03	65.59	159,978,000	14,447,500	2,068,000
*Farmers St Bk	Conrad	MT	1.18	24.10	116.10	74,016,000	17,835,500	872,000
*Security BTC	Salisbury	NC	1.57	12.56	76.59	358,763,500	45,058,500	5,626,000
Bank of Granite	Granite Falls	NC	2.08	11.98	44.32	324,993,500	38,925,000	6,754,000
*First NB ND	Grand Forks	ND	1.22	7.91	60.25	292,966,000	23,172,000	3,564,000

Table 8.5. (continued)

Commercial Bank Name	City	State	Profitability Ratio (%)	Equity/ Assts Ratio (%)	Liquidity Ratio (%)	Average Assets ($)	Average Equity ($)	Annualized Net Income ($)
First American Bk West	Minot	ND	1.13	8.01	66.01	285,916,500	22,909,000	3,242,000
Firstier Bk NA	Lincoln	NE	1.35	8.17	61.89	1,029,582,500	84,081,500	13,870,000
Abbott Bk	Alliance	NE	0.94	7.75	49.48	292,129,500	22,635,000	2,746,000
*Portsmouth Svg Bk	Portsmouth	NH	0.60	14.17	72.58	278,576,500	39,464,500	1,670,000
First NB of Portsmouth	Portsmouth	NH	0.92	12.54	61.26	220,431,000	27,649,000	2,028,000
*United Counties TC	Cranford	NJ	1.14	8.52	80.83	1,321,221,000	112,598,000	15,016,000
Union County Svg Bk	Elizabeth	NJ	1.46	13.04	85.17	350,034,000	45,629,000	5,110,000
First NB of Farmington	Farmington	NM	1.01	7.87	94.00	359,795,500	28,333,000	3,620,000
First NB of Dona Ana City	Las Cruces	NM	0.80	8.14	52.01	321,786,000	26,179,500	2,572,000
Nevada St Bk	Las Vegas	NV	1.41	8.83	48.88	310,826,500	27,433,500	4,380,000
*American B of Commerce	Las Vegas	NV	0.93	8.61	70.37	132,482,000	11,404,000	1,238,000
Manhattan Svg Bk	New York	NY	1.84	8.64	54.05	5,994,393,000	517,640,000	110,398,000
Norstar Bk of Upstate NY	Albany	NY	1.26	8.25	64.34	4,568,530,500	376,814,000	57,574,000
Star Bk NA	Cincinnati	OH	1.44	8.53	42.29	3,079,877,500	262,653,500	44,350,000
*First NB of Ohio	Akron	OH	1.06	8.93	55.76	2,087,935,500	186,386,000	22,214,000
First Interstate Bk of NA	Oklahoma City	OK	2.05	8.50	49.43	821,720,000	69,805,500	16,868,000
Bancfirst	Oklahoma City	OK	0.80	8.14	61.99	682,253,500	55,566,000	5,478,000
Pioneer Tr Bk NA	Salem	OR	2.63	13.44	95.43	104,796,500	14,089,500	2,760,000
*National Security Bank	Newport	OR	1.40	10.62	52.48	101,612,500	10,787,000	1,422,000
*Dauphin Deposit B&TC	Harrisburg	PA	1.51	8.62	62.76	3,022,092,000	260,492,000	45,492,000
Fulton Bk	Lancaster	PA	1.60	8.60	46.99	1,121,567,000	96,473,500	17,988,000
ROIG Commercial Bk	Humacao	PR	0.81	8.53	70.36	451,492,500	38,503,000	3,644,000
*Centreville Svg Bk	West Warwick	RI	1.52	16.81	76.44	275,311,000	46,278,000	4,182,000

First NB	Orangeburg	SC	0.90	8.52	64.08	263,345,500	22,435,000	2,368,000
*Conway NB	Conway	SC	0.92	8.83	84.63	21,481,500	20,429,000	2,140,000
First NB in Sioux Fls	Sioux Falls	SD	0.93	8.02	49.04	296,064,000	23,737,500	2,764,000
Dial Bk	Sioux Falls	SD	3.85	14.83	13.02	212,329,000	31,496,000	8,176,000
National Bk of Commerce	Memphis	TN	1.34	7.59	75.54	1,732,215,500	131,506,000	23,144,000
American NB&TC	Chattanooga	TN	1.02	8.12	54.15	1,242,217,000	100,907,500	12,722,000
*American St Bk	Lubbock	TX	1.16	9.48	102.37	532,837,000	50,496,000	6,182,000
First NB of Abilene	Abilene	TX	1.13	8.92	73.80	471,758,000	42,065,000	5,354,000
American Investment Bk NA	Salt Lake City	UT	1.71	8.71	55.18	154,598,000	13,472,000	2,644,000
Central B&TC	Springville	UT	1.64	11.29	54.83	119,881,500	13,530,000	1,970,000
Jefferson NB	Charlottesville	VA	1.00	8.78	49.26	1,569,064,500	137,781,000	15,682,000
Farmers & Merchants NB	Winchester	VA	1.08	8.51	47.88	468,680,500	39,908,000	5,042,000
Citizens Svg B&TC	St Johnsbury	VT	0.89	9.10	46.09	66,480,500	6,047,500	592,000
*First Independent Bk	Vancouver	WA	1.63	13.36	91.58	412,155,000	55,062,000	6,708,000
*Skagit St Bk	Burlington	WA	1.08	8.98	61.18	216,472,000	19,437,500	2,330,000
Bank One Appleton NA	Appleton	WI	1.18	8.08	67.35	398,758,500	32,232,000	4,716,000
First NB of Kenosha	Kenosha	WI	1.49	10.01	82.98	381,322,500	38,157,500	5,668,000
First Huntington NB	Huntington	WV	1.13	7.88	62.04	514,495,500	40,520,000	5,832,000
Commerce Bk Charleston NA	Charleston	WV	1.03	7.89	54.98	459,736,500	36,291,500	4,746,000
Key Bk Wyoming	Cheyenne	WY	1.53	8.33	49.72	625,745,000	52,124,500	9,576,000
*Rock Springs NB	Rock Springs	WY	1.52	13.53	104.32	199,283,500	26,961,000	3,022,000

This table is based on the Federal Reserve Board Reports of Condition and Reports of Income for the bank reporting period ending 6/30/91 and earlier periods. The most recent of this data was released by the Federal Reserve Board on 10/2/91.

*Has been a BLUE RIBBON BANK for the last eight consecutive quarters or more.

Table 8.6. Life and Health Insurance Guaranty Associations

		LIABILITY LIMITS				
State	Coverage	Aggregate Benefits	Death Benefits	Cash Values	PV of Annuities	Insurance Commissioner's Phone Number
Alabama	I	$300K	–	$100K	–	(205) 269-3554
Alaska	R	$300K	$300K	$100K	$100K	(907) 465-2515
Arizona	I	$300K	–	$100K	$100K	(602) 255-5400
Arkansas	R	$300K	$100K	$100K	$100K	(501) 371-1325
California	R	$250K	$250K	$100K	$100K	(213) 736-2551
Colorado	R	$300K	$300K	$100K	$100K	(303) 866-6400
Connecticut	R	$300K	$300K	$100K	$100K	(203) 566-5275
Delaware	R	$300K	–	$100K	–	(302) 739-4251
Dist. of Col.	N	–	–	–	–	(202) 727-8000
Florida	R	$300K	–	$100K	–	(904) 488-3440
Georgia	R	$300K	–	$100K	–	(404) 656-2056
Hawaii	R	$300K	$300K	$100K	$100K	(808) 586-2790
Idaho	R	$300K	–	$100K	–	(208) 334-2250
Illinois	R	$300K	$300K	$100K	$100K	(217) 782-4515
Indiana	R	$300K	–	$100K	–	(317) 232-2385
Iowa	R	$300K	–	$100K	–	(515) 281-5705
Kansas	R	$200K	$100K	$100K	$100K	(913) 296-3071
Kentucky	R	–	$300K	$100K	$100K	(502) 564-3630
Louisiana	N	–	–	–	–	(504) 342-5900
Maine	R	$300K	–	$100K	–	(207) 582-8707
Maryland	R	All contractual obligations				(301) 333-6300
Massachusetts	R	$300K	$300K	$100K	$100K	(617) 727-3333
Michigan	R	$300K	$300K	$100K	$100K	(517) 373-9273
Minnesota	R	$300K	–	$100K	–	(612) 296-6907
Mississippi	R	$300K	$300K	$100K	$100K	(601) 359-3569
Missouri	R	$300K	$300K	$100K	$100K	(314) 751-4126
Montana	R	–	$300K	–	–	(406) 444-2040
Nebraska	R	$300K	$300K	$100K	$100K	(402) 471-2201
Nevada	I	$300K	–	$100K	–	(702) 687-4270
New Hampshire	I	$300K	–	$100K	–	(603) 271-2261
New Jersey	N	–	–	–	–	(609) 292-5363
New Mexico	I	$300K	–	$100K	–	(505) 827-4535
New York	R	$500K	–	–	–	(212) 602-0492
North Carolina	I	$300K	–	–	–	(919) 733-7343
North Dakota	R	$300K	$300K	$100K	$100K	(701) 224-2440

Table 8.6. (contintued)

LIABILITY LIMITS

State	Coverage	Aggregate Benefits	Death Benefits	Cash Values	PV of Annuities	Insurance Commissioner's Phone Number
Ohio	R	$300K	$300K	$100K	$100K	(614) 644-2658
Oklahoma	R	$300K	$300K	$100K	$300K	(405) 521-2828
Oregon	I	$300K	–	$100K	–	(503) 378-4271
Pennsylvania	I	$300K	–	$100K	–	(717) 787-5173
Puerto Rico	I	–	$300K	–	–	(809) 722-8686
Rhode Island	R	$300K	$300K	$100K	$100K	(401) 277-2246
South Carolina	I	$300K	–	–	–	(803) 737-6117
South Dakota	R	$300K	$300K	$100K	$100K	(605) 773-3563
Tennessee	R	$300K	$300K	$100K	$100K	(615) 741-2241
Texas	R	$300K	$300K	$100K	$100K	(512) 463-6464
Utah	R	$300K	$300K	$100K	$100K	(801) 530-6400
Vermont	I	–	$300K	–	–	(802) 828-3301
Virginia	R	$300K	–	$100K	–	(804) 786-3741
Washington	R	$500K	$500K	–	$500K	(206) 753-7301
West Virginia	R	–	$300K	–	–	(304) 348-3386
Wisconsin	I	$300K	–	–	–	(608) 266-0102
Wyoming	R	$300K	$300K	$100K	$100K	(307) 777-7401

Coverage: R (Residents Only) means that the state's guaranty fund covers only its own residents, regardless of where the failed insurer is domiciled. Some of these states (the ones that adopted relevant language in the 1987 version of the NAIC Model Act) also provide coverage to nonresidents under special conditions. Many states have not adopted this language.

I (Domiciled Insurers Only), means that the state's guaranty association covers a failed company only if it is domiciled in that state. If the insurer is domiciled there, then the guaranty fund will meet the claims of policyholders in all 50 states.

N (No Coverage) means that the state currently does not have any life or health insurance guaranty association.

Liability Limits: Aggregate Benefits – This coverage applies to the aggregate benefits for all lines of insurance.

Death Benefits – Maximum liability with respect to any one life.

Cash Values – Maximum liability for cash or withdrawal value of life insurance.

PV of Annuities – Maximum liability for the present value of an annuity contract.

Source: Annuity and Life Insurance Shopper

GUARANTEED INVESTMENT CONTRACTS

Insurance companies guarantee a set return on funds sold to pension and profit-sharing plans such as 401(k) plans, but unlike Treasury bonds or insured depositors, guaranteed insurance contracts (GICs) are guaranteed because the insurer says so – not the federal government. If the insurance company goes belly up, so may its GIC.

To date, no GIC insurer has failed, but you should be concerned about the health of the company backing your GICs in your 401(k) plan. Check its credit rating with your corporate benefits office. If the rating is less than BBB, you might switch to other options.

RESOURCES

Annuity & Life Insurance Shopper, United States Annuities, Editor: Hersh Stern, 98 Hoffman Road, Suite 100, Englishtown, NJ 07726; 1-800-872-6684. Published monthly, this publication lists the rates, premium calculations and contract specifications of various annuity programs. In addition, it lists the major insurance companies and their individual ratings from A.M. Best, S&P, Moody's, and Weiss rating services.

The Donoghue Group, P.O. Box 19535, Seattle, WA 98119; (206) 281-1615, regularly issues reports on insurance companies, as well as on banks.

Insurance Safety Directory, the only source of ratings updated quarterly, is destined to replace the A.M. Best directory as the most quoted source of insurance ratings.

VeriBanc, Inc., P.O. Box 461, Wakefield, MA 01880; 1-800-442-2657 (1-800-44BANKS), (617) 245-8370. VeriBanc rates every federally insured bank, S&L, and credit union in the country, some 27,000 institutions in all. You may receive VeriBanc's ratings immediately over the telephone for a charge of $10 for the first institution and $3 for each additional. A credit card may be used to charge telephone orders.

VeriBanc rates about 13,200 banks, 2,900 savings and loan associations and 14,000 credit unions. Using a key code of colors and stars, investors can get a quick idea of each institution's strength. The charge is $10 per bank, or you can get a list of the strongest banks in your area with VeriBanc's *Blue Ribbon Bank Report,* priced at $35. They also publish a quarterly newsletter and will even give information over the phone if you urgently require a rating on your local bank.

Weiss Research, Inc., P.O. Box 2923, West Palm Beach, FL 33402; 1-800-289-9222. Weiss Research has one of the most objective and elaborate rating systems for banks, insurance companies and, just recently, brokerage houses. You can learn the safety rating of your financial institution by phone for $15 per institution – and Weiss Research will accept credit cards for payment. You can also obtain a one-page *Personal Safety Brief* for $25 per institution (three reports for $55); the *Personal Safety Report,* an in-depth report, for $45 (three for $95); or the *Watchdog Service,* a continuous monitor service, for $19 per quarter.

In addition, Weiss Research publishes an *Insurance Bank, S&L, and Brokerage Safety Directory* (a listing and rating of all companies in each financial industry, $189); a quarterly *Safety Directory* update for $84 per quarter; and various other financial publications and newsletters. For a complete list of their services, call 1-800-289-9222 and ask for a copy of their *Safety Products and Services* brochure.

(We would like to thank Dr. Warren G. Heller, VeriBanc, and Martin Weiss, Weiss Research, for their assistance in compiling this chapter.)

Tables 8.7 and 8.8 show the 50 largest banks and S&Ls in the country, as well as how they are rated by VeriBanc, Inc., the nation's premiere bank-rating firm. VeriBanc's ratings range from green (most preferred) to red (least preferred). In addition to the color code, stars are used to indicate the institution's future prospects: "***" or three stars is best and no stars or "U" (unrated) is worst. A green color code with three stars would indicate a bank with no foreseen problems. (See pages 182 and 184.)

Table 8.7. Rating the 50 Largest Federally Insured U.S. Commercial & Savings Banks

Bank Name	City	State	Total Assets ($)	Equity ($)	Equity to Assets (%)	Net Income for Quarter ($)	Loss As A Percentage of Equity (%)	Color Code and Star Rating	Excess Problem Loans (i) to Equity (%)
Citibank NA	New York	NY	159,858,000,000	8,436,000,000	5.28	36,000,000	+	Green/**	81.07
Bank of America Nt & Sa	San Francisco	CA	97,074,000,000	4,928,000,000	5.08	243,000,000	+	Green/**	60.82
Chase Manhattan Bk NA	New York	NY	76,215,556,000	3,330,552,000	4.37	6,467,000	+	Yellow/U	105.76
Morgan Guaranty TC of NY	New York	NY	74,098,844,000	3,581,074,000	4.83	168,694,000	+	Yellow/**	0.00
Manufacturers Hanover	New York	NY	55,926,000,000	2,912,000,000	5.21	83,000,000	+	Green/**	29.81
Security Pacific NB	Los Angeles	CA	54,961,196,000	3,140,902,000	5.71	48,702,000	+	Green/**	38.69
Bankers TC	New York	NY	53,186,000,000	2,247,000,000	4.22	159,000,000	+	Yellow/*	24.08
Wells Fargo Bk NA	San Francisco	CA	52,571,676,000	3,434,368,000	6.53	33,898,000	+	Green/***	15.77
Chemical Bk	New York	NY	49,405,000,000	2,298,000,000	4.65	74,000,000	+	Yellow/U	109.62
Bank of New York	New York	NY	38,264,079,000	2,115,385,000	5.53	45,603,000	+	Green/***	26.87
NCNB Texas NB	Dallas	TX	34,181,458,000	1,808,161,000	5.29	109,384,000	+	Green/***	0.00
First NB of Chicago	Chicago	IL	32,221,205,000	1,813,562,000	5.63	36,714,000	+	Green/***	10.80
First NB of Boston	Boston	MA	25,220,456,000	1,127,693,000	4.47	-16,763,000	1.49	Yellow/U	30.10
Mellon Bank NA	Greensburg	PA	25,196,889,000	1,545,886,000	6.14	49,611,000	+	Green/***	6.38
Continental Bk NA	Chicago	IL	24,929,000,000	1,757,000,000	7.05	11,000,000	+	Green/***	22.48
Republic NB of NY	New York	NY	23,336,019,000	1,658,059,000	7.10	40,136,000	+	Green/***	0.00
NCNB of NC	Charlotte	NC	22,486,485,000	1,044,468,000	4.64	23,625,000	+	Yellow/*	14.18
NBD Bk NA	Detroit	MI	22,305,684,000	1,382,619,000	6.20	59,531,000	+	Green/***	4.47
First Insterstate Bk CA	Los Angeles	CA	20,242,960,000	1,128,789,000	5.58	19,317,000	+	Green/***	3.18
First Union NB NC	Charlotte	NC	16,802,064,000	880,846,000	5.24	12,853,000	+	Green/**	31.92
First Union NB FL	Jacksonville	FL	16,800,848,000	1,401,414,000	8.34	23,052,000	+	Green/***	11.72
Wachovia Bk N Carolina NA	Winston-Salem	NC	16,724,401,000	1,229,655,000	7.35	55,555,000	+	Green/***	0.00
Pittsburgh NB	Pittsburgh	PA	16,624,156,000	889,022,000	5.35	63,223,000	+	Green/***	0.00
Union Bk	San Francisco	CA	16,610,807,000	1,078,914,000	6.50	36,540,000	+	Green/***	14.01

Bank	City	State						
Green Midland Bk NA	Buffalo	NY	16,516,549,000	5.79	−5,414,000	0.57	Yellow/*	78.14
National Westminster Bk USA	New York	NY	15,361,183,000	5.05	−43,107,000	5.55	Yellow/*	80.24
Corestates Bk NA	Ardmore	PA	15,306,256,000	6.46	43,101,000	+	Green/***	19.64
NCNB NB of Florida	Tampa	FL	14,401,382,000	4.77	17,184,000	+	Yellow/**	9.25
New Bank of New England NA	Boston	MA	14,036,401,000	3.21	0	0.00	Yellow/U	566.30
Sovran Bk NA	Richmond	VA	13,807,166,000	6.27	11,430,000	+	Green/***	21.30
First Fidelity Bk Na NJ	Newark	NJ	12,841,580,000	4.79	34,169,000	+	Yellow/*	24.86
Bank One Texas NA	Dallas	TX	12,762,545,000	6.71	32,226,000	+	Green/***	0.00
Maryland NB	Baltimore	MD	12,560,133,000	3.89	−53,230,000	10.88	Yellow/U	47.61
Citizens & Southern NB	Atlanta	GA	12,466,741,000	7.25	40,196,000	+	Green/***	0.00
Seattle-First NB	Seattle	WA	12,031,581,000	7.28	40,361,000	+	Green/***	2.66
Comercia Bk	Detroit	MI	11,815,485,000	5.98	36,891,000	+	Green/***	2.59
State Street B & TC	Boston	MA	11,786,323,000	6.07	25,990,000	+	Green/***	0.11
Norwest Bk Mn NA	Minneapolis	MN	11,750,971,000	4.62	19,222,000	+	Yellow/**	10.54
Southeast Bk NA	Miami	FL	11,026,691,000	3.39	−139,522,000	37.28	Red/U	57.23
Shawmut Bk NA	Boston	MA	10,970,830,000	5.73	−18,158,000	2.89	Yellow/**	16.97
United States NB	Portland	OR	10,848,430,000	8.05	33,579,000	+	Green/***	11.28
Connecticut NB	Hartford	CT	10,554,619,000	5.77	−32,903,000	5.40	Yellow/*	36.04
First Bk NA	Minneapolis	MN	10,451,197,000	7.11	49,875,000	+	Green/***	0.00
Harris T&SB	Chicago	IL	10,424,076,000	5.78	13,978,000	+	Green/***	17.39
Crestar Bk	Richmond	VA	10,359,459,000	5.99	13,742,000	+	Green/**	39.37
Manufacturers NB	Detroit	MI	10,200,786,000	5.76	27,055,000	+	Green/***	0.00
Fleet NB	Providence	RI	9,921,715,000	5.50	2,222,000	+	Green/**	40.42
Bank of Tokyo TC	New York	NY	9,921,020,000	4.45	3,687,000	+	Yellow/*	74.35
Northern TC	Chicago	Il	9,864,043,000	5.50	25,443,000	+	Green/***	0.00
Bank of Hawaii	Honolulu	HI	9,803,161,000	5.69	26,445,000	+	Green/**	0.00

(i) Excess problem loans (EPL)– The amount of all acknowledged problem loans less the loan reserve balance.
Bank reporting date is 6/30/91.
Federal Reserve Board release date is 10/2/91. Reporting period is quarterly.
("#" means bank's equity equals zero) ("+" means the bank is profitable) ("−" means the bank's equity is less than zero)

Source: VeriBanc Inc.

Table 8.8. Rating the 50 Largest Federally Insured Savings & Loan Associations

Savings and Loan Name	City	State	Total Assets ($)	GAAP Net Worth ($)	GAAP Net Worth to Assets (%)	Net Income for Quarter ($)	Loss As A Percentage of Equity (%)	Color Code and Star Rating	EPL (i) To GAAP Net Worth (%)
Home Savings of America, FA	Los Angeles	CA	40,673,870,000	2,522,564,000	6.20	65,035,000	+	Green/**	47.82
Great Western Bank, FSB	Beverly Hills	CA	37,250,409,000	2,206,302,000	5.92	81,620,000	+	Green/**	52.89
World S & LA, A FS & IA	Oakland	CA	22,918,147,000	1,440,389,000	6.28	65,570,000	+	Green/***	13.89
Glendale Federal Bank, FSB	Glendale	CA	20,475,791,000	921,969,000	4.50	-136,312,000	14.78	Yellow/U	54.23
California Federal Bank, A FSB	Los Angeles	CA	19,006,130,000	1,092,152,000	5.75	-5,663,000	0.52	Yellow/*	73.82
First Nationwide Bank, A FSB	San Francisco	CA	18,804,884,000	1,220,143,000	6.49	-31,757,000	2.60	Yellow/*	69.67
American Savings Bank, FA	Stockton	CA	16,903,807,000	705,940,000	4.18	47,789,000	+	Yellow/*	9.68
Homefed Bank, FSB	San Diego	CA	16,309,384,000	459,005,000	2.81	-113,589,000	24.75	Red/U	279.14
Citibank, Federal Savings Bank	San Francisco	CA	13,097,500,000	1,989,653,000	15.19	39,478,000	+	Green/***	5.42
The Dime Savings Bank of NY, FSB	Garden City	NY	10,269,637,000	453,837,000	4.42	-37,112,000	8.18	Yellow/U	196.55
First Federal of Michigan	Detroit	MI	9,568,843,000	402,309,000	4.20	5,544,000	+	Yellow/*	7.88
Great American Bank, A FSB	San Diego	CA	9,523,603,000	87,247,000	0.92	-70,273,000	80.54	Red/U	2,027.50
Standard Federal Bank	Troy	MI	9,149,942,000	492,239,000	5.38	15,442,000	+	Green/***	6.74
Coast Federal Bank, FSB	Los Angeles	CA	8,993,230,000	248,563,000	2.76	22,226,000	+	Red/U	76.39
Household Bank, FSB	Newport Beach	CA	8,865,075,000	456,244,000	5.15	16,788,000	+	Green/***	18.00
Anchor Savings Bank, FSB	Northport	NY	8,446,512,000	351,958,000	4.17	31,759,000	+	Yellow/U	13.10
Crossland Savings, FSB	Brooklyn	NY	8,405,598,000	62,448,000	0.74	-123,067,000	197.07	Red/U	1,288.71
First Gibraltar Bank, FSB	Dallas	TX	8,095,654,000	404,074,000	4.99	25,720,000	+	Yellow/**	14.29
Pacific First Bank, A FSB	Seattle	WA	7,473,717,000	615,429,000	8.23	9,248,000	+	Green/***	25.56
New West FS & LA	Stockton	CA	7,152,721,000	10,000	0.00	0	0.00	Red/U	0.00
The Talman Home FS & LA of Ill	Chicago	IL	5,849,706,000	361,074,000	6.17	9,587,000	+	Green/U	5.99
Franklin Sa	Ottawa	KS	5,825,787,000	-34,209,000	- 0.59	-850,000	-	Red/U	346.26
Sunbelt Federal Savings, FSB	Irving	TX	5,640,331,000	-109,280,000	- 1.94	-10,053,000	-	Red/U	0.00
Fidelity Federal Bank, A FSB	Glendale	CA	5,567,137,000	236,583,000	4.25	7,418,000	+	Yellow/*	18.33
First FS & LA of Rochester	Rochester	NY	5,442,904,000	194,967,000	3.58	4,972,000	+	Yellow/*	57.73

Institution	City	State	Assets	EPL	%	Profit	Rating	Ratio
Carteret Savings Bank, FA	Newark	NJ	5,354,370,000	39,898,000	0.75	373.42	Red/U	785.33
Commercial FB, A FSB	Omaha	NE	5,073,878,000	174,673,000	3.44	+	Yellow/*	75.31
Chevy Chase Savings Bank, FSB	Chevy Chase	MD	5,004,161,000	162,936,000	3.26	9.85	Yellow/U	329.88
Transohio Savings Bank	Cleveland	OH	4,847,922,000	129,152,000	2.66	+	Red/U	137.21
Sears Savings Bank	Glendale	CA	4,790,817,000	197,558,000	4.12	+	Yellow/*	34.64
Metropolitan Federal Bank, FSB	Fargo	ND	4,676,371,000	247,147,000	5.29	+	Green/***	24.29
Western Federal Savings & Loan	Marina Del Rey	CA	4,662,044,000	200,161,000	4.29	0.22	Yellow/U	61.87
Georgia Federal Bank, FSB	Atlanta	GA	4,592,651,000	298,544,000	6.50	+	Green/***	13.16
Columbia Savings, A FS & LA	Englewood	CO	4,515,984,000	245,017,000	5.43	+	Green/***	0.00
Citizens Federal Bank, A FSB	Miami	FL	4,201,106,000	215,738,000	5.14	+	Green/***	16.70
TCF Bank Savings, FSB	Minneapolis	MN	4,089,863,000	161,505,000	3.95	+	Yellow/*	34.33
Downey S & LA	Newport Beach	CA	4,064,438,000	278,002,000	6.84	+	Green/***	4.88
Northeast Savings, FA	Hartford	CT	4,033,785,000	186,005,000	4.61	+	Yellow/*	61.71
Columbia S & LA, FA	Beverly Hills	CA	3,932,537,000	−976,248,000	−24.82	−	Red/U	14.56
Southwest Federal Savings	Dallas	TX	3,907,998,000	−474,514,000	−12.14	−	Red/U	61.04
Perpetual Savings Bank, FSB	McLean	VA	3,749,012,000	57,932,000	1.55	136.12	Red/U	582.63
Capital FS & LA	Topeka	KS	3,629,075,000	325,686,000	8.97	+	Green/***	3.31
St Paul Federal Bank for Savings	Chicago	IL	3,618,180,000	220,461,000	6.09	+	Green/***	10.47
Guardians & LA	Houston	TX	3,601,283,000	86,190,000	2.39	+	Red/U	312.56
American Savings of Florida, FSB	Miami	FL	3,487,739,000	125,978,000	3.61	+	Yellow/*	93.66
Farm & Home Savings Association	Kansas City	MO	3,474,238,000	176,495,000	5.08	+	Green/***	31.53
Astoria FS & LA	Long Island City	NY	3,419,448,000	245,320,000	7.17	4.00	Yellow/*	76.62
San Francisco FS & LA	San Francisco	CA	3,356,893,000	172,602,000	5.14	+	Green/**	35.16
Guaranty Federal Savings Bank	Dallas	TX	3,286,287,000	143,557,000	4.37	+	Yellow/**	2.82
Third FS & LA	Cleveland	OH	3,279,523,000	304,430,000	9.28	+	Green/***	4.41

(i) Excess problem loans (EPL). The amount of all acknowlegded problem loans less the loan reserve balance.

S&L reporting date is 6/30/91.

Office of Thrift Supervision release date is 10/1/91.

Reporting period is quarterly.

("#" means S&L's equity equals zero)

("+" means the S&L is profitable)

("−" means the S&L's equity is less than zero)

Source: VeriBanc Inc.

APPENDIX: HOW TO EVALUATE YOUR BANK

While you can order reports on your bank from firms such as Weiss Research and VeriBanc, there is a certain satisfaction (not to mention cost savings!) in performing a "bank examination" for yourself. With the permission of Dr. Warren G. Heller, author of *Is Your Money Safe?* and Research Director for VeriBanc, Inc., we present you with three specific tests taken from his book. Each of these tests checks on a critical part of your bank's, S&L's, or credit union's operations. Over the last several years, virtually no institution that has been closed by regulators has "passed" all three tests. (The few failures that did leak through with good scores gave fraudulent or falsified data on their reports, or were subject to exceedingly unusual circumstances.) The tests form the core of the rating system used by the bank research firm, VeriBanc, Inc.

To give you an idea of how effective these tests are, the chance of failure for an institution that passes them is less than one in 3,000 per year. This minuscule probability is *less* than the chance of bank failure during the 1950s, 1960s, and 1970s—the "good old days" when worry about bank problems was nonexistent. Now, even if you could get your hands on the FDIC's secret problem bank list, and avoided the institutions on it, your odds would be slightly worse (about one in 2,500 per year) than if you use the results of these three tests. (The FDIC would do better if they could react to the bank data faster, since they use variants of these same criteria. The FDIC's problem is that some banks fail within a few months of a field audit of their latest financial filing, while it can take months to assign an institution to the problem bank list.)

(Note: Figure 8.5 is a worksheet to assist you with this evaluation.)

TEST ONE: DOES YOUR INSTITUTION HAVE ADEQUATE CAPITAL?

A financial institution such as a bank, S&L, or credit union does business by lending out money that it has borrowed from its depositors. Thus, its business is controlling investments of other people's funds. In addition, it uses (and, of course, controls) money and other items of value that belong to the institution's owners. This portion is called "equity," also often referred to as "capital." The total of the institution's equity plus the investments that really belong to others is called "assets."

It is both good business practice and a federal requirement for financial institutions to have a stake in the monies they control; that is, a certain percentage of their assets must consist of equity. In fact, if the equity of an institution drops to zero or less, the institution is "insolvent." For this reason, equity is often referred to as a financial cushion. It allows an institution to withstand temporary periods of unprofitability without having to go out of business.

To start our first test, obtain from your bank, savings and loan association, or credit union a copy of its latest "statement of condition." This may also be called a counter statement, a balance sheet, or a financial summary. Sometimes larger banks simply distribute copies of their annual report. If you are using the latter, find the page that is called "consolidated balance sheet" or a similar name. You can also use an institution's quarterly "call report."

The key word to look for is "assets." Under this heading, you will find a list of the bank's different assets and amounts in each assets category. The information you need is often at the bottom, next to the heading "Total Assets." This is usually the largest amount of money given on the page.

Now, if your institution is an ordinary bank, you will need to find an item called "equity," "shareholders' equity," or "total equity." If you are examining a savings and loan association, this item is called "net worth." If your bank has the word "mutual" in its name, there will not be an entry on the balance sheet for equity or net worth. In that case, find, near the bottom of the page, the amount given for "surplus." Whatever this item is called—equity, net worth, or surplus—divide it by the "total assets" and express the result as a percentage.

If the result exceeds 5%, the institution's equity is above usual norms for financial institutions and, unless it has severe difficulties with problem loans (see Test Three, which follows), it is not likely to be receiving strong regulatory scrutiny. A ratio between 6.0% and 7.5% is considered quite good. Above 7.5% is superb.

If equity is between 3% and 5% of assets, the institution may be considered weak. However, some regulatory authorities allow the institutions under their jurisdiction to operate with equity as low as 3% of assets (S&Ls, for example). If the equity-to-assets ratio is below 3%, the institution is almost surely receiving considerable attention from its regulatory authorities. The reason why its equity is so low certainly deserves your close attention too.

Needless to say, if the institution's equity is negative (often indicated by a number printed within parentheses), you know immediately that it is insolvent. Only recently, with the federal banking regulatory system overloaded by the crisis, have insolvent banking institutions continued to operate for very long.

Of course, measures of capital other than equity are used. Among them is "tangible net worth," which involves the subtraction of goodwill and other intangible assets before forming the ratio with assets. Currently, S&Ls are required to possess tangible net worth that is at least 1.5% (rising to 3% of assets by 1994).

Another measure is "risk-based capital." Risk-based capital requirements account for the varying degrees of safety among different kinds of assets owned by the bank.

TEST TWO: IS YOUR INSTITUTION LOSING MONEY?

Even though earning money is the purpose of any business, profitability can sometimes be elusive. Banking, like any other endeavor, encounters difficulties that cause institutions to suffer losses. One way of measuring the seriousness of the losses is to pose the question, "How long could the present rate of loss continue before the institution's equity would be used up?"

For this test, you will need to look at the "income" portion of your financial institution's statement. The income statement is usually presented separately from the balance sheet information used in Test One, above. For many institutions, it is present on another page. The name for this table of figures is usually "Statement of Income," "Report of Income," "Income and Expenses," "Statement of Operations" or some similarly worded item.

First look toward the bottom of the income statement and find the entry for "net income." Note whether or not this item is negative or set within parentheses. (Recall that parentheses designate a loss.) If the institution is profitable, it can be considered to have "passed" the income test. Otherwise, copy the amount of the net loss the institution suffered.

The other important item you will need from the income statement is the period of time to which the statement applies. This is usually one year, but sometimes the most recent six months or four months of income is presented. Be sure to record the appropriate number of months with the loss figure you copied above.

You will now want to examine how serious the institution's losses are. Divide the net loss figure (you can drop the parentheses or negative sign) by the number of months over which the loss accumulated (the second figure you copied). This will establish the average loss rate per month over the period.

Now, divide the average rate of loss per month into the same equity you used in Test One. The result is the number of months over which the institution can continue to sustain such losses before it runs out of equity. If the institution should continue to lose money at the same rate (it may or may not, of course), it could become insolvent in the number of months you have just calculated.

If the number of months is 12 or less, the losses are clearly quite serious. However, if the institution could tolerate losses this large for more than a year, the losses are somewhat less threatening.

TEST THREE: CAN PROBLEM LOANS SINK YOUR INSTITUTION?

Tests One and Two indicate your institution's condition as of the date of its financial statement. In addition, the amount of money that an institution has lent, but for which repayment is late or in doubt, needs to be considered. Many institutions keep loan loss reserves to provide a first line of defense against borrowers who default. Thus, the total dollar amount of problem loans in excess of an institution's loan loss reserve, measures the potential degree to which its equity could suffer from future losses. Problem loans can be a better indication of what may lie ahead than current amounts of equity and earnings. This test has more of a "What does the future hold?" flavor than Tests One and Two.

All of the data needed for this test are usually not available in the small financial statements or newspaper tables that the bank issues. You will need either an annual report, a specially issued "disclosure report" or the call report. To begin, you will need to add up the institution's problem loans. These will typically include loans that are seriously past due (usually 90 days or more), loans in nonaccrual condition (unlikely to be repaid) and loans that have been restructured (because of borrower's difficulty in repaying). Add these items up to obtain the bank's total problem loans.

Then, find the item called "loan loss reserves" or "balance of reserve for loan losses." Compare the loan loss reserve balance with the total problem loans above. If the loan loss reserves exceed the total problem loans, the institution passes this test so easily that no further calculations are needed.

However, if total problem loans exceed loss reserves, it is important to know how much the excess is. Subtract the loan loss reserves from the total problems to obtain the excess problem loans. Compare excess problem loans to equity (the same amount used in Test One). If excess problem loans exceed equity, the institution could be headed toward insolvency. In other words, if all of the problem loans turned out to be completely worthless, it would take more equity than is available at the bank to make up for the losses involved.

To see how large a bite the problem loans could take out of equity, subtract excess problem loans from equity to obtain discounted equity. Divide discounted equity by total assets and express the result as a percentage. If the result is less than 4%, the situation is sufficiently serious that the regulators could be paying close attention to the institution.

TEST SUMMARY AND A CAUTION

Three tests for a banking institution's health are:

1. Is its equity more than 5% of assets?
2. Did it have positive net income (i.e., was it operating profitably) recently?
3. Are its problem loans in excess of its loan loss reserve; and if so, is this excess serious enough to reduce equity below 4% of assets?

If an institution passes all three tests, recall that, other things being equal, its odds for continued survival are better than 3,000-to-1. If the tests provide mixed results (i.e., a combination of passes and fails), varying conclusions can be drawn about the institution's safety.

However, in applying the three tests, you should keep two things in mind. One is that conditions may change. Thus, up-to-date financial information is important. The second is that other "things" are not always equal and, therefore, the tests are not infallible. They measure only three (admittedly very important) aspects of a financial institution's operations. Other, normally less important, factors can take center stage when circumstances are right. If you observe signs that an institution is having serious financial problems, do not ignore them just because the numbers from the three tests look good. The following sections provide examples.

OTHER SIGNALS THAT PROBLEM BANKS SOMETIMES DISPLAY

Detecting financial weakness in a bank, S&L, or credit union can be an art as much as a science. In addition to the analytical tools described in the foregoing sections, you can use your intuition when evaluating a bank's safety. For example, the following events should arouse your suspicions:

- Frequent news stories of irregularities, firings, changes of auditors, criticized commercial transactions, and so forth.
- Ongoing media discussion of the presence of, or repeated visits by, regulatory officials, bank examiners, or similar activities.
- Persistent rumors repeating a theme of financial problems.
- Reorganizations of top management, particularly if there have been other reorganizations in the recent past.
- Disclosure of large amounts of lending to bank "insiders."
- Announcements of new stock offerings, especially if the reasons for the new issue are vague: for example, "recapitalization."
- The institution is new. New banks, S&Ls and credit unions have many of the same problems encountered by other kinds of new business. Their greater risk of "not making it" is well known to regulatory authorities, who tend to watch young institutions more closely.

HOW OFTEN DOES A BANK'S HEALTH NEED TO BE CHECKED?

The simple answer is: continuously. Insofar as possible, you should always "have your antenna up" to receive signals about the safety of the institutions with which you bank. These signals can come from friends, newscasts or even from the bank. Relying too heavily on financial data alone could cause you to miss important problem signals. Nonetheless, numbers tell a very strong story even within the normal limits on the availability and freshness of financial data. Banks and S&Ls file new financial reports with their regulators every three months. It takes the regulatory authorities another three to four months to release the data to the public. Thus, for example, data from the quarter ending December 31 typically becomes available around April 15.

This delay is not as serious as it might first appear. For example, the three tests discussed earlier in the chapter are based on data that is available to the public before institutions actually fail. Studies have shown that decline at an institution often occurs slowly enough that there is time to find out and act before the regulators do. If you keep up to date with your bank's financial health on a quarterly basis, you are working with the latest "hard" information available.

The foregoing observations are based upon how long it often takes downturns to set in at healthy banks. When dealing with an institution that you know is already shaky, you need to follow the press and any other information sources continuously. You should review your options and alternatives according to a predefined schedule, at least monthly.

Again, we would like to thank Dr. Warren G. Heller for his assistance in compiling this chapter. The information above was taken from Dr. Heller's book, *Is Your Money Safe?* (Berkeley Publishing, New York, NY). We highly recommend that you obtain a copy of this book. It is available in bookstores or from VeriBanc, Inc., P.O. Box 461, Wakefield, MA 01880.

Figure 8.5.   How to Evaluate Your Bank Work Sheet

Test One
Does Your Institution Have Adequate Capital?

1-1. Obtain a copy of the "statement of condition" from your institution and enter the "total assets" figure.   _____

1-2. Enter either the "total equity," "net worth" or "surplus" figure.   _____

1-3. Divide the equity (1-2) by total assets (1-1) to obtain the institution's *equity percentage.*   _____

An equity percentage of 5% or above is considered above-average equity, 6% to 7.5% is considered good, and 7.5% or above is superb. An equity percentage of 3% to 5% is a sign of a weak condition; and below 3%, the institution is sure to recieve considerable attention from its regulatory agency. Any negative figure means the bank is insolvent.

Test Two
Is Your Institution Losing Money?

2-1. From the income portion of your financial institution's statement, enter the "net income" figure, which is usually located at the bottom of the income statement.   _____

Note: If this figure is negative or in parentheses, the institution is losing money.

2-2. Enter the period of time (in months) to which the statement applies (usually 12 months).   _____

2-3. To determine the seriousness of the institution's losses, divide the net loss figure (2-1) by the number of months (2-2) to compute the *average loss per month.*   _____

2-4. Divide the average loss per month (2-3) into the equity from Test One (1-2).   _____

This figure provides the number of months in which the institution can continue to sustain such losses before it runs out of equity. If the institution should continue to lose money at the same rate, it could become insolvent in the number of months you have just calculated. If the number of months is 12 or less, the losses are quite serious.

Test Three
Can Problem Loans Sink Your Institution?

Obtain an annual report, disclosure, or call report from your institution. (You will not find this information in the "statement of condition" that you used in Tests One or Two.) Add up the following items:

3-1. Total loans that are past due (usually 90 days or more).　　　_____

3-2. Total loans in non accrual condition (not likely to be paid).　　+ _____

3-3. Total restructured loans (because of borrower's difficulty in repaying).　　+ _____

3-4. *Total Problem Loans*　　= _____

3-5. Enter an item called *"loan loss reserves"* or "balance of reserves for loan losses."　　_____

If loss reserves (3-5) exceed problem loans (3-4), your institution passes this test and no further calculations are needed. However, it total problem loans exceed loss reserves:

3-6. Subtract loan loss reserves (3-5) from total problem loans (3-4) to determine the *excess problem loans.*　　_____

3-7. Enter the institution's equity (1-2) from Test One above.　　_____

If excess loans (3-6) exceed equity (3-7), the institution could be headed toward insolvency. In other words, if all of the problem loans turned out to be completely worthless, it would take more equity than is available at the bank to make up for the losses involved.

3-8. To determine how large a bite the problem loans could take out of equity, subtract excess problem loans (3-6) from equity (3-7) to obtain *discounted equity.*　　_____

3-9. Divide discounted equity (3-8) by total assets (1-1) from Test One.　　_____ %

If the percentage is less than 4%, the situation is sufficiently serious that the regulators could be paying close attention to your institution.

See the test summary on page 189 to review your test results and the overall condition of your institution.

9

Foreign Bank Accounts for Safety and Privacy

"When you travel, remember that a foreign country is not designed to make you comfortable. It is designed to make its own people comfortable."

Clifton Fadiman

There are as many foreign bank account options as there are reasons to diversify your assets overseas. The key is to pick a bank and a nation that best fit your individual needs. To help you, this chapter takes you on a world tour of banking and provides additional helpful hints such as:

- Reasons to open an overseas account,
- Eight specific suggestions on how to transfer funds overseas,
- How to open an overseas account (that allows you to hold up to nine currencies) for as little as $10,
- Two excellent international banking consultants, and
- A way to earn 20% yields on a foreign currency investment.

The major reason most people give for opening an account overseas is diversification. But there are other very valid reasons, many of which are more important in light of the current investment environment.

For instance, while it is possible to invest in hard-currency-denominated vehicles without ever leaving America (as we have described in Chapter 4), *any investment in the United States* is subject to scrutiny by whomever has access to the data bank containing information on that transaction.

This means that ex-spouses, creditors, anyone who thinks they have grounds for a lawsuit against you, and of course the IRS, can instantly find out exactly where all your assets are invested.

We certainly don't encourage reneging on any debt. It is much better to *choose* to live up to your commitments, rather than have compliance forced upon you. And we don't advocate cheating on your taxes but, as Supreme Court Justice Learned Hand related, "Anyone may arrange his affairs so that his taxes shall be as low as possible; he is not to choose the pattern that best pays the treasury. And nobody owes any public duty to pay more than the law demands."

As we stated earlier in this book, you not only have to think in terms of being in the *right investment* in these turbulent times, but also must have that investment in a *safe financial institution.*

With the banking and S&L crisis getting worse by the day and insurance companies showing continued signs of strain, the likelihood of banking "holidays" and collapses, not unlike those of the Great Depression, is very real.

Look what happened in Rhode Island on January 1, 1991. Hours after being sworn in, Governor Bruce Sundlun ordered a bank holiday. In this situation, he closed all banks and credit unions covered by a private insurance fund that nearly ran out of money when the fund covered an insolvent member. This affected around 300,000 accounts totalling $1.7 billion in assets.

Until very recently, we could sit back and say "it can't happen here." After all, the U.S. dollar is a reserve currency. The rest of the world could not afford to allow our banking system to collapse because it would take the world economy with it.

That, however, may be changing.

A NEW ROLE FOR THE U.S. DOLLAR

Over the past few years, the U.S. dollar has lost some of its dominance as the world reserve currency.

European nations whose currencies belong to the ECU (European Currency Unit) "basket" have been keeping inflation rates down and following sound monetary principles. As part of the European Community agreement, they are required to keep their currency value fluctuations within a narrow range.

Because of this stability, the ECU has been growing in importance. In fact, it was thought that both the ECU basket of currencies and the German mark would continue to gain on the U.S. dollar as the next reserve currency.

However, with the breakdown of the Soviet and Eastern Bloc economies, it appears this rise to dominance has subsided temporarily. The strain on United Germany's economy, for example, has renewed concerns of inflation and thereby weakened the German mark. Other European countries are feeling similar strains. If the ECU continues to develop, there may still be a changing of the guard; but meantime, the U.S. dollar should maintain its dominance as the world's currency through 1992.

THE EUROPEAN COMMUNITY

Beginning January 1, 1993, any bank in any member nation of the European Economic Community can get a license to open banks in any other member nation without further approval. There will be a common bank capital requirement, under which all banks must maintain the same amount of capital to protect against insolvency.

This will give banks in the European Community more freedom to become megabanks than American banks have currently.

Interestingly, we tend to look back on history and believe that changes happen suddenly. They do not. This is why history is replete with disasters. Economic life is a lot like the story of the frog in the frying pan. If you put a frog into hot water, he will immediately jump out. But if you put him into lukewarm water and then SLOWLY turn up the heat, he never realizes his danger until it's too late.

Today, although you may not feel in financial danger, you should take an objective reading of the economic "temperature" around you.

Although experts disagree on the severity of the recession and the other mounting U.S. financial problems, the fact remains that our economy is in danger. You owe it to yourself to diversify your investments so that your assets are not all vulnerable to the policies of just one country.

When times get tough, governments resort to tough measures. That could mean exchange controls, confiscation of certain assets, or even forced repatriation of hard-currency-denominated investments—all in preparation for a devaluation of the U.S. dollar.

So if you have hard-currency investments in the United States, they are vulnerable to this kind of decree. And if you have a small nest egg abroad, that may be the only part of your wealth that is worth anything when it is all over.

ADVANTAGES OF FOREIGN BANKS

The two primary advantages of having a foreign bank account are:

1. *Privacy.* The portion of your assets that you have deposited overseas is shielded from creditors and others.

2. *Security.* While foreign banks do not have a foreign equivalent of FDIC insurance, this actually works in their favor. It makes them more respon-

sible in their lending practices, and the reserve requirements for foreign banks are usually higher than in the United States. By not having insurance, the banks police themselves so that they don't need insurance.

A WORLD TOUR OF BANKING: SWITZERLAND

Swiss banks are considered the *safest* and *most conservative in the world.* They are also known throughout the world for their strict secrecy. It is a crime in Switzerland to reveal information, even to the authorities, about a client's account *unless a crime has been committed under Swiss law.*

The Swiss deposit account is a cross between a checking and savings account. It will pay interest, yet you can withdraw small amounts of cash with little or no advance notice. The account can be denominated in any major currency you wish.

The amount of interest you receive depends on the amount of funds in the account and the type of currency. Yields offered by Swiss banks are generally slightly lower than those offered by banks of other countries. You may sacrifice some yield, but you will have greater privacy and safety.

To the negative, Switzerland imposes a 35% withholding tax on any Swiss franc interest you earn. This tax payment is 90% tax-deductible against your U.S. taxes.

If you hold CDs or other currency-equivalent interest-bearing securities in currencies other than the Swiss franc, the bank will usually suggest that you enter into a Trust Agreement with them. This releases you from the 35% withholding tax obligation. But, if the bank with which they have entered a currency agreement (on your behalf) goes under, it also releases the Swiss bank from any liability.

If you challenge a Swiss banker on this, he will tell you that they enter currency agreements with only top-quality foreign banks. This is true. Yet the fact remains that Swiss banks only stand behind their Swiss franc accounts—nothing else.

ARE THE DAYS NUMBERED FOR SECRET ACCOUNTS?

A May 20, 1991 article in *Business Week* reported: "The days are numbered for secret accounts. Switzerland succumbs to global pressure to drive out dirty money . . . 30,000 [secret] account holders will have until September 30, 1992 to reveal their identities or close their accounts."

According to Jean-Pierre Louvet, editor of *The Capital Preservation Strategist* (Globacor Consultants Ltd), this article was very misleading:

"Here are the important facts. To whichever *Swiss* governmental body this reporting will be made, it will not mean systematically that all *foreign* governmental departments will have access to such information. The Swiss will continue to reveal the contents held within banks accounts *only if and when they judge that a Swiss law or a bilateral agreement to which they are party has been broken or calls for disclosure* [emphasis added]. To state in a media-emphasized way that 'the days of secret accounts are over,' so as to imply that Switzerland is altering the very core of its banking system, is *totally inaccurate.*"

To support their argument that Switzerland was "less confidential," *Business Week* alluded to the President Ferdinand Marcos affair. Louvet continues: it is essential to differentiate between the concept of *freezing* of assets, as opposed to *confiscation* or automatic *repatriation.* Under Swiss law, the freezing of assets does not imply that the Swiss government has concluded formally that a legal impropriety has been committed. It reflects simply the fact that a dispute has arisen, and in order to avoid the premature disbursement of assets, these are frozen until resolution of the case is achieved."

". . . The fundamental reality about secret Swiss bank accounts is this: Contrary to popular belief, it has *never* been possible to own a 'secret' bank account in Switzerland. Whenever a numbered account is opened by a foreign or Swiss depositor, it has always been mandatory that two senior officials of the bank offering that service be aware of the *true* identity of the account holder . . . therefore, there was always *someone in Switzerland* to whom the Swiss government could go if it suspected the existence of an illicit transaction and say, based on Swiss law: We are concerned about the propriety of this depositor transaction. Swiss court action could then be taken. If proved in a Swiss court that an illicit transaction was being conducted, then the identity of the depositor would be revealed."

Therefore, you can still open a numbered or password "secret" Swiss account, provided the deposits are not related to a criminal activity. In their effort to keep drug money and other illicit operators out of Swiss banks, bank officials will require substantially more proof of ownership of an account. But contrary to the doom-and-gloom press, this will work in your favor, rather than against. If Switzerland can remove all the excuses for big government agencies to come calling—by cooperating with investigations of fraud, money laundering and organized crime—then the little guy is less likely to get caught in the crossfire.

Remember: Any foreign bank account must be reported to the IRS and the U.S. Treasury (if it individually, or accumulatively with other accounts, exceeds $10,000).

The three largest Swiss banks that provide services to American investors are:

Union Bank of Switzerland, Bahnohofstrasse 45, CH-8021 Zurich, Switzerland; Phone: 011-41 (01) 234-1111, Fax: 011-41 (01) 236-5111. Union Bank, the largest of the "Big Three" Swiss banks, is our favorite in terms of service.

U.S. Branch: 299 Park Ave., New York, NY 10171; (212) 715-3000.

Swiss Bank Corporation, Aeschen Vorstadt 1, CH-4002 Basel, Switzerland; Phone: 011-41 (061) 288-2020. This institution runs a close second to Union Bank in service.

U.S. Branch: 4 World Trade Center, New York, NY 10048; (212) 938-3500.

Credit Suisse (Swiss Credit Bank), Paradeplatz 8, CH-8022 Zurich, Switzerland; Phone: 011-41 (1) 333-1111, Fax: 011-41 (1) 332-5555. Credit Suisse (CS), the smallest of the "Big Three," has never been as customer-service-oriented as the other two banks. In addition, Credit Suisse is now part of a large financial service's company that includes CS First Boston and Bank Leu, as well as life insurance, energy, industry and service companies.

If any of the sister companies in this conglomerate fall into trouble, Credit Suisse will be expected to rescue them. The whole point of a Swiss bank is its "Swissness," and this business relationship puts a very "unSwiss" strain on a major Swiss bank.

U.S. Branch: 100 Wall St., New York, NY 10005; (212) 612-8225.

Harry Browne, *(Harry Browne Special Reports,* P.O. Box 5586, Austin, TX 78763) recommends the following Swiss banks:

Anker Bank SA (Formerly Banque Indiana and Banque Ankerfina), 50 Avenue de la Gare, P.O. Box 159, CH-1001 Lausanne, Switzerland; Phone 011-41 (21) 20-4741, Fax 011-41 (21) 23-9767. Contact: Mrs. Francine Misrahi or Mr. Jean Gander. The minimum to open an account is $5,000.

Cambio + Valoren Bank, Utoquai 55, P.O. Box 535, CH-8021 Zurich, Switzerland; Phone 011-41 (1) 252-2000, Fax 001-41 (1) 252-2658. Contact: Werner W. Schwarz or Jesus Arias. The minimum account is $100,000.

Overland Bank (Formerly Foreign Commerce Bank [Focobank]), Bellariastrasse 82, CH-8038 Zurich, Switzerland; Phone 011-41 (1) 482-6688, Fax 011-41 (1) 482-2884. Contact: Bruno Brodveck or Jean-Maurice Clerc. The minimum to open an account is $20,000.

Overland Bank has a representative office in Vancouver, B.C. as well. The address is: *Overland Financial Services, Ltd.,* 1450-1176 W. Georgia St., P.O. Box 48326, Vancouver, B.C. V7X 1A1, Canada; 1-800-663-8942 or (604) 682-3626, Fax (604) 682-6643. Contact: Mr. Adrian Hartmann. Overland Financial provides you ready access to Overland Bank, Switzerland during business hours and acts as your North American advisor on matters concerning overseas banking.

The Canadian office can provide you: 1) investment counseling, 2) personal contact to help you in operating a Swiss bank account, 3) counseling in the transfer of funds and international banking, 4) transmittal of investment instructions to the bank, and 5) mail forwarding between you and the Swiss bank (to preserve your privacy by preventing mail coming directly from Switzerland to your U.S. address).

They can also help you in obtaining loans in all major currencies against any marketable security you might have. You can obtain a Eurocard/MasterCard or a VISA card against your account and Overland can form a Swiss, Liechtenstein or Cayman Islands company for you.

Be aware, however, that Overland Financial Services is *not a bank.* They are a financial company that offers Swiss banking services with Overland Bank of Switzerland. For this service, they will charge you a fee. If you have no experience in foreign banking, they can teach you how to operate internationally. If you already know your way around foreign banking, then we suggest you deal directly with Overland Bank, Switzerland.

Overland offers certificates of deposit in the following currencies: Australian dollar, British pound sterling, Canadian dollar, Dutch guilder, German mark, Italian lira, Japanese yen, New Zealand dollar, Swiss franc, U.S. dollar and the ECU (see Table 9.1).

AUSTRIA

Austria competes with Switzerland for private banking customers. The advantage over Switzerland is that there is no withholding tax.

Also, most Austrian banks have much lower minimums to open accounts and since so few Americans currently bank there, Austria is not a country that the IRS chooses as their first target when it goes on a witch-hunt.

Austrian banks are less private than Swiss banks and, if our experience, Austrian bankers are far more difficult to do business with than either the Swiss or the Dutch. Therefore, we do not recommend any Austrian banks at this time.

THE NETHERLANDS

The major advantage that Dutch banks have over Swiss banks is that Dutch institutions personally guarantee your deposit if you hold CDs in currencies other than Dutch guilders.

In contrast, Swiss banks generally guarantee only Swiss franc currency deposits, with other currencies held in fiduciary (trust) accounts guaranteed by the

Table 9.1. Certificate of Deposit Rates From Overland Bank

(As of 10/17/91)

Currency	3 months	6 months	12 months
Swiss Franc	7.125%	7.000%	7.000%
Canadian Dollar	7.125	7.000	7.000
German Mark	8.125	8.370	8.375
Dutch Guilder	8.125	8.250	8.375
British Pound	9.250	9.125	9.125
Italian Lira	10.000	10.125	10.250
Japanese Yen	5.625	5.500	5.125
New Zealand Dollar	6.375	6.375	6.375
Australian Dollar	7.750	7.750	7.750
European Currency Unit	8.750	8.750	8.750

issuing bank (a German bank for German marks, etc.). Also, unlike Swiss banks, there is no tax (at source) on profits you make with a Dutch bank.

Other advantages include:

1. Dutch banks are considerably more flexible than Swiss banks. Therefore, for ease of trading and simply getting things done, we strongly recommend Dutch banks.
2. If you want the best yields in Europe and excellent service, we highly recommend a Dutch bank.

But don't expect total privacy. Bank secrecy is not built into Dutch laws, nor is it part of their way of thinking.

A Dutch bank that has an excellent reputation is:

ABN-AMRO Bank, P.O. Box 90, 1000AB Amsterdam, Netherlands; Phone: 011-31-20-282-764; FAX: 011-31-20-628-9898. Contact Edward Van Tongeren, senior vice president.

There is no minimum to open an account; but to hold a CD, you must have a minimum of 25,000 Dutch guilders (about U.S. $15,000) in your account.

AMRO Bank merged in 1991 with Algemene Bank, Nederland (ABN), making it the largest bank in the Netherlands, the seventh largest in Europe and the 16th worldwide.

CANADA

Americans can also open accounts in Canada to take advantage of the high yield on the Canadian dollar. However, the tax laws in Canada are a little strange. If you hold a savings account or certain types of money market accounts, the Canadian government withholds 25% of your interest.

If you put your money in a time deposit or a Guaranteed Investment Certificate (GIC) for five years or more, you are not subject to this tax.

A Canadian bank that we recommend is:

Bank of Nova Scotia, 44 King Street W, Toronto, Ontario M5H 1H1 Canada; (416) 866-6161; U.S. Headquarters, Bank of Nova Scotia, One Liberty Plaza, New York, NY 10006; (212) 225-5000.

HONG KONG

The *Hong Kong & Shanghai Bank* (also known as Hong Kong Bank) is not only Hong Kong's largest bank, but also one of the largest and most profitable banks in the world.

This bank's earnings have grown at a rate of over 19% over the past 15 years, and are expected to grow at an annual rate of 45% through 1993. It has more than 1,300 offices in 50 countries around the world and owns Marine Midland Bank in New York (the 17th largest bank in the United States).

YIELD TIP

Hold Up to Nine Currencies with Only $10

Hong Kong Bank's *CombiNation Savings Account* allows you to hold up to nine currencies in one passbook account with a minimum balance of *only U.S. $10!* Interest rates are high. In fact, you can possibly earn higher interest on currencies (the Swiss franc, for example) than you could earn in the country where the currency is native.

The currencies offered are: Australian dollar, British pound, Canadian dollar, German mark, Japanese yen, New Zealand dollar, Swiss franc, U.S. dollar and the ECU.

But what about the Chinese takeover in 1997? Given its diversification throughout the world, many analysts believe Hong Kong Bank will survive even the nationalization of its Hong Kong assets by the Chinese. But to be safe, Hong Kong Bank is planning to reorganize its operations under a British holding company. The bank already has joint operations with some branches of the British Midland Bank.

Until 1997, Hong Kong is still under British rule, so you have at least a few years to take advantage of these very high rates.

Hong Kong Bank offers two unusual high-yielding accounts for the investor interested in currency diversification:

The CombiNation Savings Account: This offers nine currencies in a single passbook account with an extraordinarily low minimum and high yields (see the "Yield Tip" for more information on this unique vehicle).

The Foreign Currency Time Deposit Account: This account provides even higher interest rates. You can choose among the same nine currencies for time periods ranging from two weeks to one year.

There is no withholding tax for foreigners in Hong Kong, and an overdraft (the ability to borrow cash without withdrawing from your account) can be arranged.

Hong Kong & Shanghai Bank, One Queens Road, Central, Hong Kong; Phone: 011-852-822-1111.

UNITED KINGDOM

National Westminster Bank is an excellent example of the best that Britain has to offer. It offers personal checking accounts in over 50 currencies, with no fees, provided you keep a minimum balance of 250 British pounds (about U.S. $500) or its equivalent in foreign currency.

Fixed-term deposits range from seven days to one year, and require a minimum of about U.S. $2,000. You can also purchase foreign currency securities and foreign currency certificates of deposit with National Westminster.

National Westminster Bank, 41 Lothbury, London EC2P, 2BP, England; Phone: 011-44-71 (01) 726-1000, Fax 011-44-71 (01) 588-5728.

U.S. BRANCHES OF FOREIGN BANKS

While U.S. branches of overseas banks afford you no privacy at all, this is a good way to get started in the overseas banking. Many U.S. branches of foreign banks will act as an agent for you if you wish to open an account with their head office. This enables you to talk face-to-face with people within the bank in which you wish to open an account. Two banks that we suggest are:

Bank International Luxembourg, 540 Madison Ave., New York, NY 10022; (212) 972-6060. This bank will help you open a German mark, Japanese yen, Swiss franc or U.S. dollar account for U.S. investors with its Luxembourg branch. The minimum is $100,000. However, they will want a letter of reference from your bank, and they will want to know where the money is coming from and what it will be used for.

Royal Bank of Scotland, 63 Wall Street, New York, NY 10005; (212) 269-1700. They offer interest-bearing British pound accounts to be held through their United Kingdom bank. In addition, they offer deposits to be held in the Channel Islands (the British tax haven) in all major currencies, for a minimum of 10,000 pounds (slightly under U.S. $20,000).

Royal Bank also offers a Currency Premium Account, that is a combination of a money market account and a current account. For this they require a minimum of U.S. $2,500. They also have a Gold Deposit Account, that increases the interest paid on a progressive scale—the more you invest, the higher the interest. The minimum investment is approximately U.S. $1,000.

If you wish to contact their overseas banks directly, you can contact:

Royal Bank of Scotland, Offshore Islands Manager, 44 Esplanade, St. Helier, Jersey, Channel Islands; Phone: 011-0534-26322. You can write to their head office at 36 St. Andrew Square, Edinburgh, EH2 2YB, Scotland, United Kingdom.

TWO EXCELLENT INTERNATIONAL BANKING CONSULTANTS

If you want to discuss your international banking requirements with someone in America, then we suggest you contact Otto E. Roethenmund.

Roethenmund is Swiss by birth, but American by nationalization. He understands the European mentality and is in an excellent position to judge European banks. Furthermore, he has lived and worked in the United States for many years, so he understands the special needs of Americans.

Roethenmund has been involved in international banking his entire life and is presently a consultant to both high-net-worth individuals and Swiss banks. He will be able to help you choose the right Swiss or international bank for you, and to give his advice on foreign currency investments and global investment opportunities in general. He can also introduce you to conservative overseas private banks that you could not gain access to on your own. The initial consultation is free.

Contact: *Otto E. Roethenmund,* Inter-Nation Capital Corp., 230 Park Avenue, Suite 650, New York, NY 10169; (212) 687-9415.

Another excellent source for international banking is *Rene Scholl,* vice president of ABN-AMRO Bank Switzerland of Zurich, Switzerland.

YIELD TIP

20% Yields in the Mexican Peso

A somewhat riskier, but *very* high-yielding foreign currency investment is in Mexican peso deposits. Mexican banks are now paying *close to 20%* on so-called Cuenta Maestra peso deposits, that are money market accounts in Mexican banks.

In 1985, the real returns in U.S. dollars were a negative 19.23%. In 1986 the returns began to turn around with .32%, then 86.34% in 1988, 28.13% in 1989. They continue to be high.

REMEMBER: There is a far *greater danger* in the Mexican peso than in any currency such as the British pound or German mark. But it appears Mexico's economy may be strengthening. So far under President Carlos Salinas, Mexico is breaking from its Third World shackles, and is moving toward free enterprise and a healthy economy. Inflation and interest rates, once firmly entrenched at 150% levels, have been reduced to under 20%. Foreign debt, the budget deficit and tariffs have all been reduced, and foreign currency reserves and peso demand are up.

In short, the Mexican peso is still a somewhat unsound currency. As long as the rate of devaluation continues to decline and there is no panic selling of the peso, U.S. investors should do well. Mexican banks are government owned, and in a banking collapse, they could just print enough money to bail out the banks (sounds familiar).

At the moment there seems little chance of a repeat of 1982, when foreigners were suddenly told that their U.S. dollar deposits were being devalued with the peso. However, this investment is speculative. Don't put money into the peso that you cannot afford to lose.

For interested investors, Eugene Latham serves as an American intermediary between Mexican banks and U.S. depositors. According to our sources, he is paid 0.5% commission *by the banks,* so the interest you earn is the same as if you went directly to the bank. We suggest, however, that you make your checks payable directly to the bank where you plan to open your account. The minimum is 10,000,000 pesos, which is about U.S. $4,000.

For more information, write or call Eugene Latham, Apdo Postal 10-7111, Mexico, DF, 11000, Mexico; Phone: 011-52-5-540-07-95.

Scholl is a very knowledgeable banker who speaks excellent English and, unlike most Swiss bankers, understands how Americans think. ABN Bank Switzerland is the Swiss branch of ABN Bank, the largest bank in the Netherlands.

As a result, you can get the "best of both worlds." Under Swiss law, any Swiss branch of a foreign bank has to become a full-fledged Swiss bank so that the Swiss government can enforce its very strict secrecy laws on it. It also means that you can have a "numbered" account if you wish. (Only a few top executives of the bank know to whom such an account belongs.)

Here you have *Dutch flexibility* with *Swiss secrecy*—a terrific combination. However, ABN-AMRO Switzerland requires a minimum of U.S. $50,000 to open an account.

Contact *Rene Scholl,* Pestalozzistrasse 18, Zurich, Switzerland; Phone: 011-411-252-0088-8032.

HOW TO OPEN A FOREIGN BANK ACCOUNT

The mechanics of opening a foreign bank account are similar in most countries. Unless you speak the local language and understand the local customs, the only foreign banks that you will be able to do business with are foreign branches of American banks and banks of Switzerland and the Netherlands.

American banks have the disadvantage of automatically reporting to the IRS any interest you accrue in your account. Even if you plan to pay all your taxes, that direct link from an overseas account to an American data bank leaves very little room for privacy.

Despite which country or currency you decide to have your assets in, most of your financial transactions can be accomplished through the banks or consultants mentioned earlier. In particular, the larger Swiss and Dutch banks are typically one-stop investment houses.

EIGHT SUGGESTIONS FOR TRANSFERRING FUNDS OVERSEAS

Once you have chosen a bank, there are several ways you can transfer funds to the account. Some suggestions are:

1. DO NOT SEND CASH. If the money gets lost, you will have no way of tracing it.
2. Write a check on your personal account and mail it to the bank. Ask them to open an account for you, and state what currency you would like in the account.

   With the passage of the Bank Secrecy Act, U.S. banks are required to photocopy any check over U.S. $100. So if you are concerned about privacy, don't use personal checks. Instead, use your money market fund, if you have one. Presently, there are no requirements to photocopy money market transactions.

3. Purchase a bank cashier's check made out to you, and then endorse it over to your chosen foreign bank. Your local bank will provide such a check for you. More privacy is achieved if you take the check to a second bank and exchange it for their check.

4. Purchase a cashier's check made out directly to the new bank (this, of course, provides less privacy).

5. Purchase money orders for less than U.S. $1,000. For privacy, pay in cash and don't put your name (or the bank's name) on the money order until after you have purchased it.

6. Fly to your chosen bank and open an account in person with cash, government bonds, T-bills, or checks.

7. Make a direct bank transfer. This is done by merely telling your local bank how much you want to send and to where, and they do the rest.

8. Some Swiss banks have travelling agents who come to the U.S. periodically. They will meet with you and open an account for you. Once your account is opened, you can use it as you would use an American account (i.e., have a checking or deposit account). Or you can use it like a brokerage account in which you can buy stocks, shares, currency contracts, bonds and all kinds of commercial and government paper.

Again, do not open an account with the American branch of a foreign bank if you want privacy. Also, most American branches of foreign institutions are not geared to individual investments, and will normally accept only large accounts ($500,000 or more).

While the minimum for most foreign banks is higher than that of your friendly neighborhood American bank, some will open an account for you with only a few thousands dollars.

To get your money out of a foreign bank account, you simply write, call or fax the bank and give them instructions to mail or wire you your money. You can send out or bring back up to $10,000 a day into the United States without any reporting requirements.

A WORD OF CAUTION

While cracking down on money laundering, drug lords, and the BCCI's of the world, the U.S. government has passed several new laws that affect banking dramatically. So be careful. If you are accused of violating these laws, they can seriously affect your personal and financial well-being. *Do not, under any circumstances, willfully break any U.S. law.* Remember, your goal is to diversify and protect your investments along with exerting your right to privacy.

RESOURCES

Harry Browne Special Report, P.O. Box 5586, Austin, TX 78763. Harry Browne offers all-round investment advice with emphasis on the international aspects of investing.

Capital Preservation Strategist, Globacor Consultants Ltd, Jean-Pierre Louvet, editor, P.O. Box 1618, Gainesville, Georgia 30503; (404) 536-0309. Jean-Pierre Louvet writes an international investment newsletter that shares the European viewpoint of world economics and investments. Globacor also offers private international consulting services. They can introduce you to competent and, up to now, impeccably honest, legal or fiduciary institutions in Switzerland and elsewhere. For information call 011-44-628-990.

Dessauer's Journal, Editor: John Dessauer, Limmat Publications, Inc., P.O. Box 1718, Orleans, MA 02653; (617) 255-1651. An excellent newsletter that reports on foreign currencies and all five major world stock markets.

Forecasts & Strategies, Mark Skousen, editor, Phillips Publishing, Inc., 7811 Montrose Road, Potomac, MD 20854; 1-800-722-9000.

Fullermoney, Editor: David Fuller, Chart Analysis Ltd., 7 Swallow Street, London, WIR 7HD, United Kingdom; 011-4471-439-4961. Another excellent newsletter that reports on international markets.

International Financial Statistics gives interest rates and monetary figures for all the countries of the world. Available in most libraries.

Myers Finance & Energy, P.O. Box 3082, Spokane, WA 99208; (509) 534-7132. John Myers writes a very good, internationally oriented market newsletter.

Rand McNally Bankers Directory provides a listing of international banks, addresses, phone numbers, and officers. The directory is available in most libraries.

Resident Abroad, Marketing Department, Greystoke Place, Fetter Lane, London EC4A 1 ND, England. This is a monthly magazine covering all aspects of living abroad—offshore unit trusts (mutual funds), insurance programs (annuities), individually managed accounts, and items of privacy and lifestyle trends.

— 10 —

Rating the Safety of *Foreign* Banks, Brokerage Houses, and Insurance Companies

---

"What affects men sharply about a foreign
nation is not so much finding or not finding
familiar things; it is rather not finding them in
the familiar place."

G. K. Chesterton

International investment scams are one of the most prominent forms of investment fraud. But with proper care, you may have less to fear from dealing directly with foreign institutions than from those at home in the United States.

This chapter gives you common-sense rules to gauge the reliability of overseas banks, brokerages and insurance companies, including . . .

- Seven steps to protect yourself against international fraud,
- Which foreign banks are the safest and why "big is not better,"

- How to find a safe overseas bank,
- The world's 100 best banks,
- The world's 100 largest banks.

As noted earlier, fraud in the investment industry is on the rise—particularly in the overseas investment area.

"International scams are now the fastest-growing fraud problem state regulators are dealing with," says M. Douglas Mays, the Kansas state securities commissioner and president of the North American Securities Administrators Association (NASAA).

The reason seems obvious: It is much easier to escape U.S. law from overseas.

The fact is, most international scams are conducted from within the United States. They apparently work better because Americans feel safer when fellow Americans offer them an easy way to invest abroad. Ironically, you will have less to fear from dealing directly with an overseas agent than you do from dealing with local agents for overseas operations.

SEVEN STEPS TO PROTECT YOURSELF AGAINST FRAUD

1. Never give your credit card number to anyone who has telephoned you.

2. If it sounds too good to be true, IT PROBABLY IS. In other words, avoid any investment that promises unrealistically high, above-market rates of return, or unrealistic turnaround of your investment. Compare these rates to typical rates of return of other similar investments.

3. Beware of any opportunity that offers "privacy" or suggests that you operate in the "gray area of the law." These scams are successful because the victims seldom come forward when they lose money, for fear they are already criminals.

4. Be cautious of anyone who offers you an investment that is "guaranteed" or cannot, in any way, result in a loss of your funds.

5. Don't accept any offer that is operated through a corporation in Liechtenstein, the Cayman Islands, the Bahamas, Bermuda, Andorra, and similar tax havens. Any operation that needs a "letter-box" corporation through which to conduct their business is likely to be a scam.

    That does not mean there is anything wrong with having a tax haven company. It merely means that if somebody is conducting a mail order or telephone order business through one, you have absolutely no protection should it later prove to be a fraud. If you need a tax haven company, form your own!

6. If the person you are dealing with is a foreigner, and you are not used to dealing with people from that particular country, then enlist the help of a friend who is. Each nationality has its own way of thinking, and it is not easy to judge a person's honesty if you don't understand the customs of his or her country.

7. Check, recheck, and then check again any overseas investment offer that seeks you out, rather than you seeking it out. Or better yet, "just say no" to any unsolicited offshore offer that is presented to you.

THE SECURITY ADVANTAGES OF FOREIGN BANKS

Among the world's banks, U.S. institutions have been lagging behind for years. Currently no U.S. institution stands among the world's top 20.

World bankers will look back on 1991 as a year of reckoning—a time when the lending excesses of the 1980s came back to haunt lenders from New York to Tokyo to London. "In most countries the earnings of major banks were disappointing, but there was no cause for concern as regards to their underlying financial strengths," noted the Bank for International Settlements (BIS) in a recent report.

Largely, the big European banks are in better shape than most U.S. banks. According to their June 1991 report, the BIS stated that European banks accounted for more than 75% of last year's $787 billion expansion in international bank assets.

In contrast, in the United States, more than half the 25 biggest banks reported weaker first-quarter earnings.

European banks are in somewhat better shape than U.S. banks for two reasons:

1. Because they have no FDIC cushion under them, European banks have been more responsible than U.S. banks and have not made as many unsound loans.

2. Unlike U.S. banks, European banks have the freedom to operate like most other businesses. They can diversify their activities and thereby hedge their bets against any one portion of their portfolio going sour. American banks have been forced into such a narrow business focus that they often have few options that allow them to be both safe and profitable.

WHICH BANKS ARE THE SAFEST?

Although, for more than a decade many organizations have ranked the largest banks in the world, *Euromoney Magazine* says, "It is increasingly clear that, in banking, size has little relevance any longer." In their latest survey, *Euromoney* ranked the "World's Best 100 Banks" (see Table 10.1) in this manner:

"The bank must be profitable: it must have high return-on-equity and, to a lesser extent, return-on-asset figures. It must be managed tightly and cost-effectively with a low cost-to-income ratio. It must fund itself at the keenest possible rates and lend (or generate fee income) in ways that produce the highest possible return and therefore a high net interest margin."

If you examine Table 10.2, you will find that only 11 of these banks have made *Euromoney's* top 25 list. In other words, "big is not better," so forget the assets and watch the profit.

Table 10.1. Euromoney 100 Best Banks (1990 Rankings)

Rank	Bank	Score	Rank	Bank	Score
1	Banco Popular Espanol - Spain	85.74	51	NCNB Corp. - U.S.	65.75
2	Toronto-Dominion - Canada	84.74	52	Bayerische Landesbank - Germany	65.19
3	Bank One Corp - U.S.	83.44	53	Commerzbank - Germany	64.90
4	First Wachovia - U.S.	82.69	54	Credit Agricole - France	64.89
5	Banco Santander - Spain	80.65	55	Banque Nationale de Paris - France	64.73
6	Wells Fargo - U.S.	79.91	56	Royal Banke of Scotland - U.K.	64.45
7	National City - U.S.	79.28	57	Westpac - Australia	64.31
8	Deutsche - Germany	77.61	58	Industrial Bank - Japan	64.18
9	BankAmerica Corp - U.S.	77.28	59	Bayerische Bereinsbank - Germany	64.06
10	Banco Bibao Vizcaya - Spain	76.02	60	Republic New York Group - U.S.	63.99
11	Skandinaviska Enskilda - Sweden	75.50	61	Monte dei Paschi di Siena - Italy	63.86
12	Abbey National - U.K.	75.27	62	Creditanstalt-Bankverein - Austria	63.70
13	Suntrust Banks - U.S.	74.58	63	Caja de Madrid - Spain	63.69
14	Nordbanken - Sweden	74.49	64	Banque Indosuez - France	63.51
15	NBD Bancorp - U.S.	74.40	65	Union Bank of Findland - Finland	63.37
16	Robobank - Netherlands	74.36	66	Kansallis-Osake-Pankki - Finland	63.35
17	National Australia - Australia	73.52	67	Fuji - Japan	63.24
18	Compagne Bancaire - France	72.86	68	Banca Popolare di Novara - Italy	62.92
19	Security Pacific - U.S.	72.47	69	Groupe des Banques Populaires France	62.11
20	Credit Suisse - Switzerland	71.95	70	First Chicago - U.S.	61.99
21	Union Bank - Switzerland	71.53	71	Hong Kong & Shanghai Banking Corp	61.72
22	Banco Hispano Americano - Spain	71.33	72	Mitsubishi Trust & Banking - Japan	61.50
23	Crediop - Italy	70.93	73	Kredietbank - Belgium	61.20
24	Bank of Scotland - U.K.	70.74	74	Sumitomo Trust & Banking - Japan	61.15
25	Credit Local de France - France	70.36	75	Hypo-Bank - Germany	61.01
26	Royal Bank of Canada - Canada	70.26	76	DG Bank - Germany	60.96
27	Fleet/Norstar - U.S.	70.11	77	Banca Commerciale Italiana - Italy	60.44
28	First Union - U.S.	70.07	78	Dai-Ichi Kangyo - Japan	60.39

29	Barnett Banks - U.S.	69.97	79	Bank of Tokyo - Japan	60.14
30	Paribas Group - France	69.64	80	Unibank - Denmark	60.07
31	Dresdner - Germany	69.47	81	Banco Espanol de Credito - Spain	59.93
32	Barclays - U.K.	69.16	82	National Westminster - U.K.	59.88
33	Swiss Bank Corp - Switzerland	69.13	83	Long-Term Credit Bank - Japan	59.76
34	Commonwealth Bank - Australia	69.02	84	Yasuda Trust & Bank - Japan	59.62
35	NMB Postbank - Netherlands	68.55	85	Mellon - U.S.	59.64
36	Citizens & Southern/Sovran - U.S.	68.46	86	Kyowa - Japan	59.36
37	Societe Generale - France	68.19	87	Credito Italiano - Italy	59.29
38	Sanwa - Japan	68.11	88	Tokyo Trust & Banking - Japan	58.95
39	Mitsubishi - Japan	68.00	89	Swiss Volksbank - Switzerland	58.90
40	ABN/AMRO - Netherlands	67.90	90	Credit Industriel et Comm - France	58.62
41	Credit Lyonnais - France	67.85	91	Den Danske - Denmark	58.47
42	PNC Financial - U.S.	67.78	92	Mitsui Trust & Banking - Japan	58.38
43	Banco Central - Spain	67.38	93	Joyo - Japan	57.18
44	Westdeutsche Landesbank – Germany	67.13	94	Bank of Nova Scotia - Canada	56.95
45	Sumitomo - Japan	67.12	95	Ashikaga - Japan	56.86
46	Australia & New Zealand Bank	66.80	96	Hokuriku - Japan	56.45
47	Istituto Mobilair Italiano - Italy	66.62	97	Bank of Montreal - Canada	56.31
48	Istituto Bancario San Paolo di Torino - Italy	66.57	98	Daiwa - Japan	56.30
49	Carpiplo - Italy	66.51	99	Shizuoka - Japan	56.15
50	Canadian Imperial Bk of Commerce	66.42	100	TSB - U.K.	56.01

The Euromoney Rating Method

To qualify for inclusion in the top 100, only banks with equity above $1.3 billion were analyzed. Weights were assigned to the following categories: return on equity - 15%; return on assets - 10%; real profitability - 10%; cost-to-income - 5%; net interest margin - 5%; total net income - 5%; credit ratings - 25%; analysts' opinion - 25%. Objective data are those reported at the fiscal year-end 1989 - supplied by IBCA Limited, London. Credit ratings are those as of October 30, 1990. The analysts' survey was conducted in October, 1990.

Source: Euromoney Magazine

Table 10.2. The World's 100 Largest Banks

Asset Rank 1990	Bank	Assets in U.S. Dollars (in billions)	Deposits in U.S. Dollars (in billions)	Asset Rank 1990	Bank	Assets in U.S. Dollars (in billions)	Deposits in U.S. Dollars (in billions)
1	Dai-Ichi Kangyo Bank Ltd - Japan	428.167	339.683	51	Royal Bank of Canada - Canada	98.927	84.887
2	Sumitomo Bank Ltd - Japan	409.160	318.281	52	Bank of Yokohama - Japan	98.403	73.897
3	Mitsui Taiyo Kobe Bank - Japan	408.754	330.799	53	Monte dei Paschi di Siena - Italy	97.934	80.116
4	Sanwa Bank Ltd - Japan	402.698	300.739	54	Bank of America - United States	94.763	77.027
5	Fuji Bank - Japan	399.545	299.685	55	Banca Commerciale Italiana - Italy	92.846	76.699
6	Mitsubishi Bank - Japan	391.528	310.331	56	Canadian Imperial Bank - Canada	89.893	77.134
7	Credit Agricole Mutuel - France	305.205	224.198	57	Zenshinren Bank - Japan	84.502	76.840
8	Banque Nationale de Paris - France	291.872	246.019	58	Credito Italiano - Italy	82.564	68.475
9	Industrial Bank of Japan - Japan	290.067	240.288	59	Norddeutsche Landes Bank - Germany	82.144	77.427
10	Credit Lyonnais - France	287.330	241.002	60	Chuo Trust & Banking - Japan	81.135	73.472
11	Deutsche Bank AG - Germany	266.286	241.609	61	Skandinaviska Enskilda - Sweden	80.240	47.934
12	Barclays Bank - U.K.	258.983	212.712	62	Groupe Des Banques - France	78.507	56.040
13	Tokai Bank - Japan	249.751	192.352	63	Bank Melli Iran - Iran	78.262	69.708
14	Norinchukin Bank - Japan	249.666	196.682	64	Westpac Banking Corp - Australia	77.680	54.418
15	Mitsubishi Trust & Banking - Japan	237.695	214.036	65	Hokkaido Takushoku Bank - Japan	77.385	59.909
16	National Westminster - U.K.	232.512	204.157	66	Banco de Brasil - Brazil	75.767	21.710
17	Bank of Tokyo	223.184	168.427	67	Generale Bank - Belgium	75.416	69.684
18	Societe Generale - France	219.983	147.626	68	Banco di Napoli - Italy	73.505	58.798
19	Sumitomo Trust & Banking - Japan	218.916	199.007	69	Chase Manhattan - U.S.	73.360	59.862
20	Mitsui Trust & Banking - Japan	210.934	185.052	70	Nordbanken - Sweden	72.734	55.025
21	Long-Term Credit Bank - Japan	200.678	171.610	71	Bank of Montreal - Canada	71.786	62.763
22	Dresdner Bank - Germany	186.935	174.440	72	National Australia Bank - Australia	68.595	55.028
23	Union Bank of Switzerland	183.442	149.696	73	Bank of Nova Scotia - Canada	68.079	55.639
24	Yasuda Trust & Banking - Japan	175.552	156.337	74	Banque Indosuez - France	68.002	47.269

Rank	Bank			Rank	Bank		
25	Daiwa Bank - Japan	171.238	146.483	75	Australia & New Zealand Group - Aust.	67.916	56.554
26	Citibank - U.S.	155.394	112.586	76	Morgan Guaranty Trust - U.S.	67.627	37.847
27	Swiss Bank Corp - Switzerland	151.260	129.660	77	Svenska Handelsbanken - Sweden	64.720	44.797
28	Hong Kong & Shanghai - Hong Kong	148.488	133.579	78	Banco Bilbao Vizcaya - Spain	63.921	55.495
29	Commerzbank - Germany	144.165	134.662	79	Deutsche Girozentrale - Germany	63.509	43.939
30	Toyo Trust & Banking – Japan	141.744	125.406	80	Banque Bruxelles Lambert - Belgium	63.309	56.524
31	Bayerische Vereinsbank - Germany	137.747	129.183	81	Chiba Bank - Japan	62.646	50.965
32	Banca Nazionale del Lavoro - Italy	137.713	112.986	82	Sparbankemas Bank - Sweden	62.169	26.013
33	Deutsche Genossenschaftsbank - Germ.	136.453	96.935	83	Danske Bank - Denmark	61.879	52.900
34	Westdeutsche Landesbank - Germany	135.824	125.810	84	Banco di Roma - Italy	61.819	49.576
35	Istituto Bancario San Paolo - Italy	133.486	102.490	85	Sudwestdeutsche Landesbank - Germany	58.974	55.697
36	Nippon Credit Bank - Japan	128.321	102.898	86	Caja de Ahorros y de Pensiones - Spain	58.862	49.683
37	Aigemene Bank Nederland - Netherlands	122.042	101.180	87	Hessische Landesbank - Germany	58.102	48.299
38	RoboBank - Netherlands	119.728	81.650	88	Manufacturers Hanover Trust - U.S.	56.560	41.384
39	Credit Suisse - Switzerland	117.345	103.232	89	Hokuriku Bank - Japan	56.305	44.330
40	Bayerische Hypotheken - Germany	116.410	107.679	90	Royal Bank of Scotland - U.K.	56.279	48.114
41	Midland Bank Pic - U.K.	114.501	101.531	91	Credit Commercial de France - France	55.674	40.915
42	Amsterdam-Rotterdam Bank - Netherlds	112.460	96.557	92	Bank Saderat Iran - Iran	55.144	47.440
43	Banque Paribas - France	111.555	98.616	93	Security Pacific National - U.S.	55.032	45.376
44	Kyowa Bank - Japan	111.546	90.519	94	Kredietbank N.V. - Belgium	54.761	49.172
45	Lloyds Bank - U.K.	105.987	96.744	95	Bank of Seoul - Korea	54.225	46.820
46	Saitama Bank - Japan	105.634	87.385	96	Creditanstalt-Bankverein - Austria	54.007	35.443
47	Bayerische Landesbank - Germany	103.772	96.148	97	Shizuoka Bank - Japan	53.949	46.082
48	NMB Postbank Group NV - Netherlands	102.894	99.505	98	Wells Fargo - U.S.	53.659	42.716
49	Shoko Chukin Bank - Japan	102.672	93.804	99	Bankers Trust - U.S.	52.939	28.844
50	Cassa di Rispamio - Italy	99.946	78.238	100	Banco Espanol de Credito - Spain	52.356	33.876

Source: American Banker. Compiled from the world's 1,200 largest banks as of December 31, 1990.

To convince you further that the largest banks may not mean the safest, let's look at another illustration. Many U.S. rating services are determining the safety of a bank by examining its equity ratio—by dividing the capital worth of the institution by its assets. Of the ten largest banks, not one of the them has an equity ratio above the Bank for International Settlement's recommended 8% level. A safe level should be around 25% to 30%.

The International Bureau of Credit Audits, based in London, offers this list of the six best, AAA-rated banks:

Barclays (United Kingdom)

Deutsche Bank (Germany)

Robobank (Netherlands)

Swiss Bank Corporation (Switzerland)

Credit Suisse (Switzerland)

Yet, you must remember that, particularly with Swiss banks, far less information is known about their balance sheets than for U.S. banks. We have all seen how tough it is in this country to rate a bank—even when its balance sheet is public knowledge.

Moreover, the real art of finding a sound bank lies in projecting its strength, not just today, but far into the future as your investment rests in its care. Similar to the United States, several countries are experiencing recession-like economies and other economic calamities that have affected their banks. Bank earnings are suffering, real estate values are falling and bad loans are increasing.

To help you select the strongest foreign institution, the following discussion presents some general assessments of specific countries' financial institutions.

BRITISH FINANCIAL INSTITUTIONS

British banks have typically done better than banks of many other nations. Most British banks are well above the 8% Bank for International Settlements (BIS) minimum equity ratio, but again, is it enough? Due to a worsening economy, Britain's banks have seen their earnings drop. The three major banks (Lloyds, Barclays and National Westminster) have tripled their bad loans reserves from the year previous.

As far as British insurance companies are concerned, you can take comfort in the fact that the British have been in the insurance business longer than most. British insurance companies are generally much better run than those in the United States. Lloyd's of London, for example, is the granddaddy of all insurance companies.

British brokerage houses are such specialized operations that we would strongly advise against using them. You can do everything you might want through an American house, or through a Dutch or Swiss bank.

GERMAN FINANCIAL INSTITUTIONS

At the moment, German banks are very strong. It remains to be seen how well they fare with the incorporation of East Germany, and whether their high capital ratio can withstand the extra strain.

During 1991, it became increasingly apparent that the unification of East and West Germany was taking its toll on the economy. A nation that has prided itself on fighting inflation (since its 1920 hyperinflation experience) and having a strong economy, saw their annual budget deficit rise to 190 billion marks. Both taxes and unemployment have risen sharply as well.

"We will soon see the light at the end of the East German tunnel," says Himar Kopper, chairman at Deutsche Bank AG, Germany's largest bank. "The creation of a unified banking system will allow the country to develop into an engine of economic growth in Europe."

Though German banks remain strong, there was a case of a fairly large German bank failing in the mid-1970s, in which depositors lost a lot of money. When the government was asked why it didn't step in to support it, the answer was that if they helped one, where would it stop?

There is an aspect to the German mentality that is like no other. Germans will accept disasters that would cause a major outcry in other nations. The most surprising thing about the bank failure in the 1970s was not that a major German bank failed and nobody did anything about it. It was the fact that even the depositors resigned themselves to their losses.

While the German mark is a strong currency and an excellent investment choice, we would not recommend buying marks through a German bank. Instead, you should consider investing through either a Dutch bank (where the deposits are guaranteed), or through a U.S. bank.

We also advise very strongly against attempting to deal with a German insurance company directly. The Germans are the most over-regulated people in the Western World, and trying to negotiate your way through the maze of legalities is like walking through a mine field. If you want a German annuity or other insurance, then either obtain it through an insurance consultant, or through a non-German bank. That way, you also have someone to check the safety of the company with which you are doing business.

SWISS FINANCIAL INSTITUTIONS

The best-known banks in Europe are, of course, the Swiss banks. The four biggest banks all have a capital ratio of more than 15%, and the Swiss authorities impose more stringent loan regulations on their banks than are required by BIS standards or accepted by most other countries, including the United States.

But even the Swiss have economic problems they must face. According to *Investment Strategy* (Geneva, Switzerland), "Although Switzerland's economy has been in the grip of a recession for two quarters now, the rate of inflation has continued climbing (to a year-on-year rate of 6.6% in June [1991]). The steadily rising cost of living is tying the Swiss National Bank's hands and preventing any softening in the restrictive monetary policy line to which it has been adhering over the last two or three years."

The Swiss government debt load on a per-capita basis is only around $2,000, compared to $13,000 per person in the United States. Therefore, it appears that the Swiss financial system can withstand more strain at this time than ours.

As you can see from Figure 10.1, Switzerland's economy is rated by far the safest of the various economic systems in the world.

**Figure 10.1. International Economic Safety
Rating**

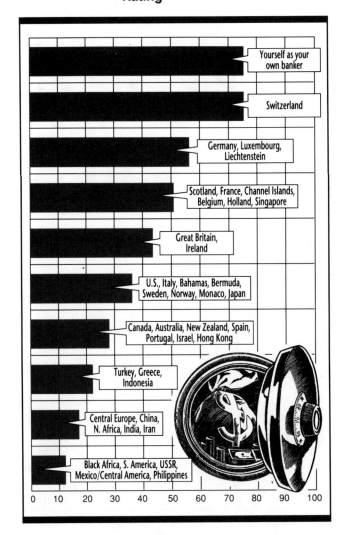

Ages refer to age of head of household

Source: CPS, J. P. Louvet

When a small Swiss bank has failed in the past, other banks have stepped in to help in order to preserve the image of Swiss bank stability. In fact, the Swiss banking industry is more like an exclusive guild than an open industry, so this type of cooperation is likely to continue in the future.

In general, the bigger Swiss banks have been more aggressive in expanding than the smaller banks. Credit Suisse, for example, is having problems because it is part of a holding company that also owns First Boston bank, which is having financial difficulties. As a result, earnings at Credit Suisse plummeted last year after a $587 million loss at First Boston.

A Swiss National Bank report stated that 95% of all Swiss mortgage lending is done either by Swiss Cantonal banks or the "big" banks. "The major Swiss banks are positioning themselves to become global universal banks on a whole-sale basis," says Pierre de Weck of Union Bank of Switzerland in the United States. Universal banks make loans, underwrite corporate debt, and take positions in corporate securities.

Except for Credit Suisse, last year's bank earnings were in line with expectations. The move toward more open and comprehensive reporting has further underlined the inherent strengths of the leading banks. Profits are expected to make a powerful recovery this year and a period of underperformance may now have ended.

DUTCH FINANCIAL INSTITUTIONS

How safe are Dutch banks? We challenged our contacts at ABN-AMRO bank in Amsterdam to come up with an answer to that question, and here is what they told us:

1. "In case of a failure of a Dutch bank, the sum of DGld [Dutch guilders] 30,000 per account (approximately U.S. $18,000) is guaranteed under regulations of the Central Bank (DE Nederlandsche Bank N.V.).

2. "The last time a Dutch bank failed was in the 1950s (a very small bank, due to fraud).

3. "If a Dutch bank should get into trouble, it is most likely that the Central Bank or other banks would step in."

In reply to our questions specifically about ABN-AMRO bank, we received the following answers:

1. "ABN-AMRO reserves are sufficient to avoid possible future problems.

2. "ABN-AMRO's exposure to Third World countries in relation to their balance sheet is far less than U.S. banks.

3. "ABN-AMRO's exposure is more evenly spread over countries than are U.S. banks.

4. "ABN-AMRO's provisions for bad loans are far larger than U.S. banks because we started raising reserves sooner."

But this is what the Dutch bankers say about themselves: So how accurate is it?

From all indications, it's very close to the mark: Dutch banks have *always* been international banks. Because the Netherlands is such a small nation, its survival has always depended on overseas trade. The more truly international the perspective, the safer the financial institutions because foreigners are more prone to running scared than locals.

We are seeing this in the United States right now. American financial institutions are in far worse condition than most of the rest of the Western World. Yet, most Americans still feel more secure with their money in their local bank than having it in an overseas bank.

It is this vast local market that has enabled American banks to be so irresponsible. In the early 1980s, when Mexico threatened to renege on its U.S. loans, the fear that this crisis would collapse the banking system was a lot greater than the fear today when the banking system is in much worse shape.

Why? Inherent in human nature is the belief that what happens to the other guy cannot happen to us. We fear what is foreign and have a false sense of security about what we know. In a similar fashion, America's huge domestic market and inward-looking banking system is in large part the reason our bankers have been so irresponsible.

JAPANESE FINANCIAL INSTITUTIONS

The same syndrome is seen in all Japanese financial institutions—and for similar reasons.

Japan is probably the most inward-looking nation in the civilized world. For this reason, its financial institutions are the most irresponsible.

Also, new capital requirements, a weak real estate market, and the plunge in Japan's stock market hampered earnings at local banks. As a result the domestic scene is looking increasingly like the West.

Therefore, we are not including any Japanese financial institutions in our list of recommended overseas banks. Our advice is simply: *Leave well enough alone*. If any country could trigger an international collapse, it is more likely to be Japan than the United States.

HOW TO FIND A SAFE OVERSEAS BANK

Once you learn to evaluate your local bank using the methods outlined in Chapter 8, you can use the same techniques to evaluate your foreign bank. Just remember to seek out only those institutions with a *high capital reserve*, with a *low debt/liquidity ratio*.

Because it is far more difficult to check the safety of overseas institutions, we suggest that you stick with those we recommend in this book.

Otto E. Roethenmund, Inter-Nation Capital Corp., 230 Park Avenue, Suite 650,

New York, NY 10169; (212) 687-9415. (See Chapter 9 for more information on Mr. Roethenmund.)

Jean-Pierre Louvet, Globacor Ltd., 18 Kimbers Drive, Burnham, Green Lane, Berkshire, Great Britain SL1 8JE; U.S. Toll-Free 1-800-678-6091, or 44-628-660-990.

They offer private consultations, publications, and seminars on maximum safety banking, insurance and financial planning companies, and services.

11

Real Estate:
The Largest Cash Reserve

"Our houses are such unwieldy property that we
are often imprisoned rather than housed
by them."

Thoreau, 1854

For most Americans, their greatest single investment asset is their home. But as a result of the recession, the value of this asset has plummeted as real estate values dropped nationwide.

Since this book is dedicated to helping you protect all your wealth despite the economic times—and that includes your real estate—the following pages will give you the information you'll need to make potentially tough decisions in the years ahead, such as:

- A simple worksheet to figure out the *true market value* of any property BEFORE you buy it,

- How to find out if the Resolution Trust Corporation is about to auction off a property you might be interested in,

- An eight-point check list that will tell you if a property—including your home—is worth buying in today's market,

- How to save $80,000 interest on a $100,000 mortgage,
- Whether you should refinance your mortgage now that interest rates are at near 18-year lows, and
- How you can earn up to a 30% annualized return using your home's equity.

The fact that our homes can drop in value will be the harshest reality of the decade for millions of American families—a reality that will permanently alter where and how you live, particularly in your retirement years.

The real estate downturn that began in the oil patch in the 1980s has spread to such seemingly impervious markets as California, the Northeast, and even Hawaii.

The severity of this decline depends on several factors, including: How long the economic recession will last, how low S&L and insurance company asset sales will drive property prices, and how the banking crisis progresses.

Not even rock-bottom interest rates could heat up the housing or commercial real estate market in 1991. And that could spell worse trouble in 1992. In past recessions, housing has led the country out of the recession.

Why haven't low interest rates sparked the housing industry? The missing link may be in consumer confidence. As of September 1991, consumers were still concerned about the recovery. Will we see a double-dip recession, or slow sluggish recovery?

Additionally there are too many houses for sale. Nationally in July 1991, there were 2.4 million homes for sale, which is equivalent to a nine-month supply. Experts say the supply is growing.

What makes this real estate "crisis" especially dangerous is its subtlety—the way it can lull us into complacency and inaction at the very moment that our net worth may be plummeting. As noted investment analyst Peter Cavelti observes,

"Real estate is the only investment that no one remembers going down for sustained periods of time. The collapse of the debt pyramid and the severe trouble in which the banks find themselves make it likely that real property prices will be the most widely felt casualty of the coming five years.

"This could be another 1929 situation because real estate is the one area of the economy where, because we have had no experience with plunging real estate prices, we simply don't know how to stop them from falling."

THE ROOT OF THE PROBLEM

The current predicament had its genesis in the 1980s, when speculators overbuilt on both commercial and residential levels for the *then* known market. The problem grows today, in part because the baby-boom generation is now beginning to look for smaller houses as their kids enter college. In addition, the next generation in search of the American dream is a much smaller group.

RESIDENTIAL REAL ESTATE

During the 1980s, when money was easy, people moved to areas with obvious advantages of geographic beauty, job opportunities, good schools, cultural activities, and so forth.

Soon, too many people were chasing too few properties and facilities. Prices soared for prime real estate and luxury services. The very lifestyle that prompted a move in the first place was quickly priced out of reach for all but the very wealthy.

As a result, the areas that experienced the greatest growth during the 1980s are now showing the worst declines. The Southwest and Northeast are prime examples of this.

In addition, the new generation is not only a lot smaller numerically than the baby-boom generation (meaning there are fewer of them looking for houses in which to raise a family), but this generation is far less interested in having children than prior generations. (See Figure 11.1.)

If you own a house that could potentially become a dinosaur, then scale down. Take your money and run. The real estate market in private houses will eventually turn around, but probably not in the megahouses.

COMMERCIAL REAL ESTATE

During the 1980s, commercial buildings were built with little regard for those who would occupy them. The biggest miscalculation was the assumption that the growing need for office space during the 1970s and early 1980s would continue in the same upward trend.

That was the period in which the baby-boomers were entering the work force. Much to the dismay of ambitious developers, the expansion in the work force quickly leveled off.

In most markets today, there are simply not enough people to fill the huge, expensive steel and glass monuments that now stand empty.

And there will be even fewer people in the future. During the 1990s and beyond, the work force will actually be *contracting* as more people retire than become employed. This will spark a push for more automation to make up the production shortfall—and robots don't need houses or offices.

The business of the 1990s will generally operate in less space and with greater efficiency. In this age of personal computers, modems, and fax machines, there is often little need for an employee to travel to the corporate office. With more frequency, professionals are "telecommuting" from offices in their homes. This trend has already had a measurable impact on big-city downtown areas.

Moreover, the decline in interest rates holds little hope for either residential or commercial real estate, because people are not going to build or buy what they do not need. Even if interest rates fall to zero, there will continue to be more sellers than buyers for all types of real estate.

Figure 11.1. Residential Real Estate Market to Shrink

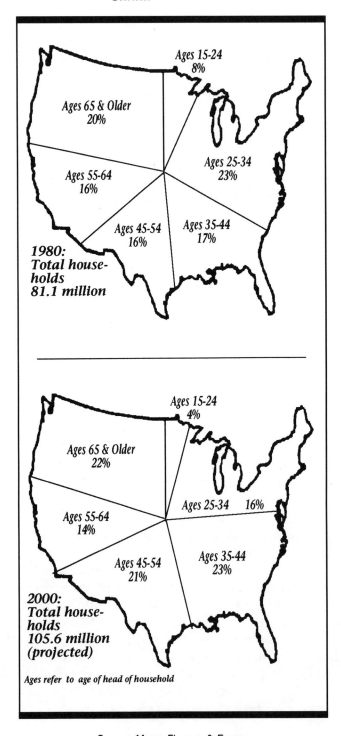

Source: Myers Finance & Energy

YIELD TIP

To Refinance or Not

When interest rates fall, homeowners are encouraged by finance companies to refinance their mortgages. Beware. *It is not always a good idea.*

If you are expecting to reduce your monthly payment, you may find out that lower rates may not translate into savings. Here are some points you should consider before refinancing:

1. *What will it cost to refinance?* Refinancing involves the same paperwork and closing costs you faced when you got your original loan. Finance charges, or points, plus the cost of title search and insurance, appraisal and attorneys may cost you 4% to 6% of the amount you wish to borrow. (And you can't deduct the points on your income tax return either.)

2. *Does your existing mortgage include prepayment penalties?*

3. *How long do you plan to say in your home?* Three years is considered the minimum time. If you have a $100,000 balance on your 30-year loan at 11.5% and want to refinance at 9.5%, your monthly payment would drop from $990 to approximately $840. That works out to an approximate annual savings of $1,800. But if closing costs average 5% (or $5,000), you would not break even until almost three years later.

Generally, it makes sense to refinance if the prevailing interest rate is at least 2% below that of your existing loan.

Thus, the problem with commercial real estate today isn't only that prices are falling, but that an awful lot of property may never find buyers or enough renters to survive.

REAL ESTATE INVESTMENT TRUSTS (REITS)

This is an industry that has had many problems since its inception in the early 1970s. Limit your exposure to a very few equity-oriented REITs that have a proven track record and high-quality, income-producing real estate. Generally, because of the S&L problems, the commercial real estate industry is not likely to be an attractive investment for the early 1990s—except in special situations.

THE CHANGING FACE OF REAL ESTATE IN THE 1990s

The real estate market in the 1990s will be dramatically different from that of the 1980s. Since the October 1989 Tax Reform Act was passed, all artificial returns created by prior tax legislation were removed, so that:

1. Real estate is no longer a delivery system for tax deductions.

2. For tax purposes, real estate investments (apart from your home) are now judged in cash flow terms—like any other business—rather than simply compared to other real estate projects as in the past.

3. Market value is determined purely by the operating bottom line.

4. And there is now an excess of real estate throughout the country.

John V. Kamin, Consulting Economist with *The Forecaster Moneyletter* (Forecaster Publishing Company, 19623 Ventura Blvd., Tarzana, CA 91356; (818) 345-4421) says:

"Change is a fact of life in all monetary markets, especially real estate. If you think things will not change, then that is unrealistic. Change is the only reality. You might as well embrace change, and make money out of it, that's my motto."

Here are 12 changes that John Kamin says will affect the markets during the 1990s:

Generally ...

1. Banks, under siege, have tightened their current lending, even as interest rates went lower. *The Moneyletter* observed that, these days, "banks will lend you money only if you can prove you don't need it!"

Residential ...

2. The number of listings of property for sale is up, in many markets in 1991. Listings in the San Fernando Valley region of homes for sale, for example, have tripled over recent years.

3. Despite a sluggish economy and weak housing markets, prices are still rising. The median price of a home in Southern California, for instance, is still creeping up. Nationwide median prices rose 4.7% in 1991 (see Table 11.1).

4. Construction costs are still rising. It simply costs more money to build a new house for the plumber, the electrician, and the tile installer. While new homes are being "dumped" on the market for auction prices, those who choose to build instead of buy find themselves paying higher—not lower—prices.

5. The RTC and buildings are *glutting* and saturating *certain markets*. The Santa Clarita Valley (California), as well as outlying areas such as Victorville, Lancaster, and Palmdale—retirement communities far from Los Angeles—are being glutted with auctions of unsold new homes. Texas is being glutted with properties for sale by the RTC.

Commercial ...

6. Increased vacancy rates. Depending on where you live, vacancy rates are climbing, especially in apartments, office buildings. Commercial property has also been affected, in some sectors.

Table 11.1. Deteriorating Southern California Real Estate Market

Downtown office vacancy rates

	March 1991	March 1990
Bakersfield	28.0%	30.8%
Fresno	34.1	26.4
Los Angeles	18.4	12.7
Orange County*	21.2	20.5
Ventura County*	26.1	20.3
National Average	17.4	13.1

Metropolitan rate, which had a national average of 19.4% at March 1991 vs. 16.0% at March 1990.

Source: *CB Commercial Real Estate Group Inc.*

Keep in mind, vacancy rates will differ widely from region to region. So, sloppy generalizations can cost you if you're a property buyer or owner. For example, at last measurement, Phoenix had a seven-year oversupply of office space available for rent. But Chicago, southern New Jersey, Washington, D.C. and a number of other places had tighter markets. Los Angeles was "average" on commercial, but oversupplied on high-priced upper-floor office space (see Table 11.2).

7. Tenants, many of whom are in trouble themselves, have become hard to keep. *"Treat your existing tenants well, but collect the rent,"* says Kamin.

8. As an owner or landlord, you may find yourself making deals to keep tenants in place. Some deals include, for example, the 13th month's rent free on a 12-month lease signing.
   Note: There is a lot of tenant-stealing going on. That's where agents and realtors approach your tenant directly and try to get him to move to their building and out of yours. Landlords can do the same thing. (See rollover risk below.)

9. The worst possible area is in office buildings. Office buildings, particularly upper floors, also have the worst vacancy rates, 20% to 50% in many cases. Be extremely careful in how you value upper-story offices. They will be harder to rent and won't bring nearly the dollars that street-level rentals will.

10. Buy modern energy-efficient buildings. You want to get the lowest air-conditioning costs, use solar heating, have more insulation and a modern

Table 11.2. Major Downtown Los Angeles Office Tower Vacancy Rates

The losers are developers and out-of-state lenders

Project *(Developer/Lender)*	Sq. Ft. (thousands)	Percent vacant
2 California Plaza *(Metropol. Struc./Citicorp)*	1,270	77%
Gas Company Tower *(Maguire Thomas/Sumitomo Bank)*	1,250	27%
777 Tower *(Prudential-Mitsubishi Est./ Citicorp-Mitsubishi Bank)*	1,023	67%
865 Figueroa *(Manufacturers Life Insurance Co., Canada)*	686	60%
550 S. Hope *(Koll/Ohbayashi America)*	565	55%
801 Figueroa *(R&T Dev./Misubishi Trust)*	435	82%
Figueroa Plaza II *(Raffi Cohen Ind./Barclays Bank, England)*	308	68%

Sources: Seeley Co., Cushman Realty Corp.

roof. What you don't want are energy-guzzling air conditioners or heaters, obsolete materials (such as fire-hazard wood shake roofs), inefficient watering systems, or asbestos insulation.

11. There is plenty of distressed property available—even in modern and newly built buildings! (For additional information on how to buy distressed property, we suggest that you get Kamin's *Negotiating* and *Distressed Property* books. They'll mean thousands to you.)
Remember, when buying property, offering prices are seldom attractive. If last year's property price was higher, you can bet that the asking price for the listing is higher too. So, if you're looking for an $800,000 property to be listed for $400,000, it's probably still listed at $800,000, not $400,000. Getting the asking price down to a bargain level is up to the buyer. The final price a seller will take is seldom offered in the inflated initial listing.

12. Finally, since the U.S. is embarked on a long-term deficit-financing inflationary policy, be extremely careful about long-term leases. They can be dangerous for landlords if inflation rises. You'll find most savvy land-

lords are now writing clauses calling for "Rent increases when Consumer Price Index increases" into their commercial and office rental contracts. (The clause is sometimes inserted into the residential rental leases as well.)

ROLLOVER RISK

There is a new risk facing the commercial real estate industry—rollover risk.

As commercial real estate vacancies continue to climb, tenants from well-planned and pricey buildings are being lured away to cheaper empty buildings. Some experts say that except for the credit squeeze, rollover risk is the single greatest obstacle to the recovery of the real estate market.

Although rollover risk is a normal part of real estate's boom-bust cycle, developers and bankers are more threatened this time because new financing schemes in the 1980s left properties leveraged more than ever before. Moreover, economists don't anticipate a return of the inflation of the 1970s that bailed the market out following that decade's slump. At the same time, many tenants are undergoing their restructuring to cut costs, thus they will cut their demands for office space and look for lower-cost facilities.

Particularly vulnerable are banks and insurers that have resisted writing down their bad real estate investments to current market value. Instead, they have argued, they should be allowed to stretch their write-offs until the market improves. Unfortunately, no one expects the commercial market to improve anytime soon.

SHOULD YOU BUILD IN TODAY'S ENVIRONMENT?

Before you embark on any real estate project, remember that any new construction you undertake *must be priced to yield a positive spread.*

Allen Cymrot, of Cymrot Realty Advisors, sums it up this way:

"[If] borrowing rates are more than the earning ability of real estate, that is called negative spread or 'the deterioration of profit margin.' This negative spread dramatically increases the occupancy levels necessary for breaking even. In today's real estate market, the difference between 80% leverage and no leverage (all cash) could mean the difference of 95% occupancy versus 30% occupancy required for breaking even."

As Table 11.3 shows, this geometric decline of cash flow can be disastrous to the bottom line. (This table assumes a capitalization rate of 8% and a cost of debt service of 12%.)

In today's market, no new construction should be undertaken unless there is a REAL NEED for the building—no building should be built on speculation.

Don't count on a market recovery until either mortgage rates are forced down to match current yields, or real estate prices are forced down to match current mortgage rates.

Table 11.3. The Effect of Leverage on Returns from Investment Real Estate

Basis: $100 Purchase Price

Income	$8.00	$8.00	$8.00	$8.00	$8.00	$8.00	$8.00
Down Payment (Investment)	100%	85%	70%	55%	40%	25%	10%
Debt	$0.00	$15.00	$30.00	$45.00	$60.00	$75.00	$90.00
Cost of Debt	$0.00	$1.80	$3.60	$5.40	$7.20	$9.00	$10.80
Net Cash	$8.00	$6.20	$4.40	$2.60	$0.80	$-1.00	$-2.80
% Return on Investment	8%	7.3%	6.9%	4.7%	2%	-4%	-28%

Source: Street Smart Real Estate Investing, Published by Dow Jones-Irwin 1988

SAFETY TIP

Seller Financing

Seller financing on property sale is becoming extremely dangerous—especially at these low rates.

Remember 1982, when the prime rate went above 16%? What if you had agreed to finance a new buyer's purchase of your property, for 10 years or more, at a low interest rate?

Here are two strategies you can follow in any market:

1. If you have property that is either hard to finance or to resell, consider giving buyers different prices. On a cash deal offer the lowest price. For terms of one to four years, for example, ask a higher price and don't agree to carry the buyer's note at less than 10% to 12% interest. And don't carry the loan for more than four years. Also, ask for a *substantial* down payment (of at least 25% to 40% up front).

2. When financing real estate sales, make sure you get your money monthly. Or at least quarterly. Nothing is more disappointing than to have a once-a-year payment and discover months later that the borrower is no-pay. It is better to find out early in the year by collecting your money monthly—especially if the borrower is getting into financial trouble.

This can also save you months in collection time and speed up foreclosure proceedings. Time is of the essence. Besides, you will collect your selling price faster with monthly payments.

HOW TO CALCULATE THE MARKET VALUE
OF AN INVESTMENT PROPERTY

In a market in which a property often has a greater chance of decreasing in value than increasing, the value of equity takes a back seat to the *earning power* of a property.

So before you buy an investment property, you must decide whether the income it generates is worth the trouble and potential risk. To illustrate what we mean, imagine that you are considering purchasing a $400,000 building. Here's how you can figure out the true market value of this or any commercial property:

First, assess how much you could rent it for in today's market. (This is easily done by pricing similar properties in the same area.) Let's suppose that you can earn $60,000 in rental income from that building per year, with $24,000 in non-mortgage expenses. This means you have $36,000 a year in income after expenses but before mortgage payments.

To see whether this represents a 9% return (for example) on your investment, you simply divide the $36,000 by .09 (9%) and you come up with the figure of $400,000. The building you are considering is priced correctly for what you want to achieve.

If you want a higher or lower return, the same formula works. Take the return after expenses and before mortgage payments and divide by .08 for an 8% return, by .10 for a 10% return, and so on.

It is important to note that this formula *does not take mortgage costs into account.* The reason is simple: The purpose of the exercise is purely to decide the VALUE of a property. How you purchase the property is a separate decision that can only be determined through a careful examination of your individual situation and the current cost of borrowing. (See Figure 11.2.)

FOUR WAYS TO INCREASE YOUR RENTAL INCOME

With so many vacancies available in the real estate markets, how do you increase your income (rent) without losing your tenants?

And, how do your combat those communities that impose rent controls (and there are many) that are making it increasingly difficult to make a profit?

A few suggestions are:

1. Add and charge for amenities. Some landlords are now providing extras such as VCRs, fax machine usage, movie rentals, safes, and satellite dish reception. The charges for these amenities are added to the rent.

2. Parking charges are often separated out, where they once were included. For example, what if you have a triplex where you have two retired widows in two of the units. Neither of these widows drives. You also rent to a young person with three junker cars who uses all three parking spaces. Shouldn't he pay more?

Figure 11.2.   How to Calculate the Market Value of an Investment Property

	Example	Your Figures
Determines the market value of a property and does not consider the mortgage costs.		
Potential Annual Rental Income	$60,000	_____
Estimated Annual Non-Mortgage Expenses	$24,000	_____
Net Annual Income (Before Mortgage Expenses/Payments)	$36,000	_____
Divided By		
Expected Percent Return	.09	_____
Correct Market Value (Based on income, expenses and expected return)	$400,000	_____
Enter Asking Price Of Property	$450,000	_____
Amount Overpriced or Underpriced	–$50,000	_____

(Subtract the asking price from the correct value. A positive figure means the property is under the market value to achieve your expected returns. A negative figure means the property is overpriced to accomplish your goals.

Landlords can do better by segregating parking charges and making each a separate charge, as local law allows.

3. Charge separately for storage areas that are used (and desired) by some tenants, while ignored by others. Let the rent charge reflect who uses the storage units, who needs extra units and who doesn't.

(Sometimes, parking charges and storage rents are *not covered* by rent-control ordinances, and can be marked up to full-ticket market! Be sure to check your local laws.)

4. Put utilities on separate meters. As a professional advisor to the Southern California Apartment Owners Association, John Kamin gave the following advice:

"In more than three decades of renting, where I frequently paid utilities for my tenants, I have never had a tenant come up to me and say, 'Thanks, Mr., for paying my water bill.' Never. Not once in nearly 30 years."

If a tenant doesn't appreciate it, why pay it?

Furthermore, when there are water shortages, power rationing, and other monopolistic proclamations affecting landlords and property owners, it is best if your tenants have separate meters installed, and pay their own utility bills. Let your tenants make up their minds about how much or how little energy, water, gas, and so on they wish to use. And let the tenants settle their own disputes with municipal monopolies when they arise.

EIGHT-POINT CHECKLIST TO BUYING REAL ESTATE TODAY

In the 1990s some real estate may not only fall to a fraction of its value, but may remain permanently empty and eventually be demolished.

So before you buy in the 1990s, ask yourself the following questions:

1. Is the area you are considering in a stable trend or in decline? If prices are declining, are they falling faster or slower than comparable areas? If faster, why? Would you want to own a business there, or would your elderly parents feel comfortable living there?

   In other words, whether you're buying commercial or residential property, *thoroughly research the area.*

2. Is the specific property priced in line with similar properties in the same area? Keep in mind that the 1990s will see a restructuring of American cities and suburbs as environmental concerns, and the aging of the baby-boom generation, create a trend toward a "less is more" mentality.

3. If you are looking at residential property, is there shopping, employment, and entertainment within 20 minutes travel time? John Kamin suggests sticking to major metro areas of one million people or more, where 85% of the U.S. population lives and works.

4. Is it an area where employed, law-abiding people live and work? For income properties, check the quality of present renters. Sometimes owners will fill a rental property with very short-term leases or use similar devices to create a false image when they put it on the market.

5. What will maintenance costs be for the building? Consider the going rates in the area for plumbers, electricians, roofers, and other workers.

6. Is the property you are considering conveniently located for the purpose for which you plan to use it?
   We can all take a lesson from one of the shrewdest real estate buyers in the world today: McDonald's. They research proposed locations very carefully before purchasing because they are not buying property, they are buying a *business*. They think in terms of the people who will use the building and the revenue these people will generate. So should you when you buy.

7. When you are comfortable with the answers to all the above questions, you should then look into the structural integrity of the building itself. Is the property in good shape? Check the entire building from roof to basement, from wiring to furnace.

   Consider a professional home or building inspection. Inspections are fast becoming a necessary part of most real estate sales today. Typically, a residential inspection will cost you $150 to $500. The American Society of Home Inspectors (ASHI) has set standards of practice for its members, which can be a starting point for choosing an inspector. For a copy, send $4 to ASHI, 3299 K St. NW, 7th Floor, Washington, DC 20007. Once you know what to look for, research the yellow pages for inspection companies in your area.

   Any defects must be dealt with before you buy. This is a buyer's market. You can demand, and get, perfection in any property you are planning to buy.

8. Is the property in danger of becoming an unrentable "dinosaur"? In particular, avoid multistory office buildings. Of all the illiquid real estate properties, office buildings are the hardest to resell or rent.

NOTE: This check list is also valuable in determining *whether you should stay in your current home*. If your home fails the test, you should get out while you can.

THE BOTTOM LINE: IS ANYTHING WORTH BUYING NOW?

The days of buying a piece of real estate and seeing it double or triple in value are over. In the 1990s you must look at the potential market value appreciation very carefully. In other words, calculate the potential return on your investment. You may be able to get a good price right now. But how long will it take to appreciate? And realistically, how much of a return can you expect? If you only expect a 3% return over a 10-year period, you had better look elsewhere.

There *will* be some terrific bargains in residential real estate, provided you follow our previous suggestions. As the S&L and bank debacle worsens and mortgage defaults grow at a record pace, real estate "fire sales" will continue to erupt. So if you are in the right place at the right time, you could find good property at vastly discounted prices.

As far as commercial real estate is concerned, consider it only if it is dras-

---

YIELD TIP

Profit from the S&L Crisis

One bank's disaster can become your dream home. As real estate woes continue, you may have the opportunity to find some great real estate at the federal Resolution Trust Corporation (RTC) sales.

But be careful and patient!

Uncle Sam's idea of a discount may not be your own, and prices could drop a lot further as the RTC gets more desperate to unload its huge backlog of property. Also inspect the home carefully, before you make an offer. Many of these homes are in need of serious repair. An excellent purchase price may be quickly offset by expensive repairs on the home.

For information on RTC sales, call the RTC at 1-800-348-1484. Ask for their Special Sales Event Calendar that lists current auction, sealed bid, and portfolio sales in your area—both residential and commercial. The calendar is updated approximately every two weeks. It will give you the auction contractor's name and phone number to obtain a specific list of properties to be auctioned.

Also, if you'd like help, there is a private partnership in New Mexico that works closely with the RTC. Tell them the type of property you would be interested in and they will let you know if such a property is to be auctioned. Contact: Ameral-Hays, 203 West Sixth Street, P.O. Box 2322, Roswell, NM 88202; (505) 623-2874.

---

tically discounted and if it can be used for any business serving an older community—health care, retirement leisure activities, and the like.

ALTERNATIVE REAL ESTATE INCOME-PRODUCING IDEAS

Since it is becoming much more difficult to make money in real estate (and chances are you already own costly debt-ridden property), three alternative ways that you can use your real estate to increase yields are:

Use creative financing,

Use a home equity loan to pay off consumer debt,

Consider the benefits of a reverse mortgage.

See Table 11.4.

Use Creative Financing

There are some very creative financing methods that will not only save you thousands of dollars of interest, but will allow you to build equity faster and pay your home off much quicker.

Table 11.4. Mortgage Rates

30-Year Fixed Rate

All-Time High:	18.63%	October 1981
1980's Low:	9.03%	March 1989
15-Year Low:	8.69%	Reached November 1991

Adjustable-Rate Mortgages (One-Year Rate)

All-Time High:	12.29%	July 1984
All-Time Low:	6.40%	November 1991

*Note: ARMs didn't become widespread until 1981, so
the September rates were the lowest to date.*

Home-Equity Credit Lines:

All-Time High:	23.50%	December 1980
All-Time Low:	9.50%	October 1986
Rate:	9.66%	November 1991

15-Year Mortgage: This type of mortgage is suddenly getting more attention. Interest rates have fallen so low that the higher payments of A 15-year mortgage are more affordable. The monthly payment on a 15-year is about 20% more than on a 30-year loan because more principal is paid. The prospect that home prices won't appreciate much in coming years is causing borrowers to look for other ways to build equity. a 15-year loan pays a mortgage faster. For example:

On a $100,000 loan, you would pay off $50,900 in principal after 10 years versus $9,800 on a 30-year at today's rates. Because the loan is paid faster, the total interest is much less than on a 30-year loan. Interest rates are ¼ to ⅜ points less than on a 30-year loan as well. With a 30-year at 9.5%, a 15-year would be 9.125% to 9.25%. For example,

30-Year Fixed-Rate Mortgage: $100,000 principal, interest rate 9.5%, monthly payment $841, total interest $202,760.
15-Year Fixed-Rate Mortgage: $100,000 principal, interest rate 9.125%, monthly payment $1,037, total interest $86,660: INTEREST SAVED $116,100.

Bi-Weekly Mortgages: Some banks are currently offering loans that permit you to pay off your loan faster and at lower interest rates. For example, a $75,000 bi-weekly loan at 10% could save you around $60,000 in interest over a 30-year fixed rate mortgage. Bi-weekly loans generally carry interest rates of about 0.25% below fixed-rate loans. Because you make 26 bi-weekly payments instead of 12 monthly payments a year, you will pay off the loan much faster.

Accelerated Mortgages: Even if you presently have a loan, you can take advantage of bi-weekly mortgages—without renegotiating, refinancing, or costly paperwork.

For example, with a $100,000, 30-year mortgage at 10.5% interest, you would save $82,104 in interest, build equity three times faster, and be debt-free nine years sooner.

There are many of these plans being advertised. But be careful, not all plans are legitimate. One plan that is well-recommended by many advisors is the Choice Mortgage Plan offered by Delaware Charter Guarantee & Trust Company. (Delaware Charter has been around for a long time.) Here's how Choice Plan works:

Instead of making monthly payments to your mortgage company, you will set up automatic bi-weekly drafts from your checking account to Choice Plan. For an initial start-up fee and per-payment fee of $3.50, Choice Plan will process your payments. Yes, you could do this yourself, but how many of us have the discipline to stick with a program like this.

For information on this program and a quote on how much you can save through this program, contact: Choice Plan, Delaware Charter Guarantee & Trust Company, 1013 Centre Road, Wilmington, DE 19899; 1-800-441-4303.

Use a Home Equity Loan to Pay Off Consumer Debt

By using a home equity loan to pay off your high-interest consumer debt, you could be earning the equivalent of 28% or more annual returns—risk-free. Here's what we mean.

Though interest rates have fallen during 1991, rates on credit card balances rose to their highest levels in more than 10 years. This is despite increased competition among credit card issuers and efforts by the Federal Reserve to cut the cost of funds for banks. According to the Bank Rate Monitor, the national average for credit card interest rates climbed to 18.94% as of September 1991 from 18.69% in 1990. Some rates have risen as high as 19.8% and more.

By converting your consumer debt to a home-equity debt, it can mean big savings. Suppose you have $5,000 in credit-card debt and your credit card charges the average rate of 18.94%. If you paid your debt in three years, you would shell out $6,593 in monthly payments of $183. With a home-equity loan at 10.5%, your total payments would shrink to $5,804 and your monthly payments would fall to $163. In three years, you would pay $804 interest on the home-equity line versus $1,593 on the credit cards—a 50% savings.

Furthermore, you can deduct the interest if you itemize your deductions. (consumer debt is no longer deductible.) If you're in the 28% federal tax bracket, the deduction lowers the average 10.5% interest rate to an after-tax rate of 7.6%—an additional $196.20 in savings.

According to Jane Bryant Quinn (author of *Making The Most Of Your Money),* the benefits of the debt conversion are "equivalent to a 28% to 30%

return on investment. I don't know where anybody's going to get a 28% to 30% return in a year, depending on their tax bracket. That's a fabulous return."

(With equity loan rates at near 8%, your return on investment will be several percentage points higher, making this an even more important program to follow.)

Consider the Benefits of a Reverse Mortgage

Reverse mortgages or home equity conversions are fairly new. For the most part (because of the FHA insurance programs that support this program), the minimum age is 62. Since this program really doesn't pay until you are older, most people who take these loans out are typically in their 70s.

The amount of money that you will receive on a reverse mortgage depends on how old you are, and how much equity you have in your home. These are all non-recourse loans, which means that you can never owe more than what the house is worth—even if you live to 105.

The loan amount can be paid to you in a number of ways (but carefully examine the results of each):

1. Lump sum.
2. Monthly, for as long as you live in the home.
3. You can get a line of credit and decide when you want to dip into it.
4. You can combine options 2 and 3.

Since the loans are tied to your life expectancy, the older you are, the more money you can get per month. In the monthly payment plan, you would receive the monthly payment as long as you survive or live in the home. If you (or your spouse) live longer than your life expectancy, you could actually receive more than the equity in your home.

(For couples, the bank will look at the joint life expectancy of the couple to determine the amount to be received.)

The interest on the loan is adjustable annually to 1.6% over the one-year T-bill rate. The rates and charges for these loans are almost the same as any fixed-rate mortgage. Just as you should in refinancing your home, consider the length of time you plan to live in the home before setting up a reverse mortgage. If it is only for three to four years or less, the cost of this program may be too expensive. However, it you live longer than expected, you will probably pay much less than the stated interest rate.

Benefits of a reverse mortgage: It requires no monthly payment, you need no income to qualify, the lender can look at your home's value only for repayment, and there are no prepayment penalties. Usually you will pay about $350 to close the mortgage because the other costs can be financed.

Caveats: Reverse mortgages are for those who wish to stay in their homes during their retirement years. They are owner occupant loans. So if you were to be placed in a nursing home (for 12 months or longer), this could cause the loan to come due. You would be left with only two options: pay off the loan or sell the home.

Most banks are not promoting these types of programs, so you need to ask. They are insured by the federal government and Fannie Mae is providing the money for them.

For more information, contact the American Association of Retired Persons who offers a free 47-page guide. Ask for the *Home-Made Money: Consumer's Guide to Home Equity Conversion.* Write to AARP Fulfillment D12469, 601 E St. NW, Washington, DC 20049.

The National Center of Home Equity Conversion offers a free fact sheet on reverse mortgages, also. Send a SASE to NCHEC Fact Sheet, Suite 300, 12120 E. College Dr., Marshall, MN 56258.

Or pick up a copy of *Retirement Income on the House,* Ken Scholen, author ($24.95, available at most bookstores.)

Check Your Flexible-Rate Calculations

If you have a flexible-rate mortgage on your property, double-check the new rate each time the bank updates it.

Usually a flexible-rate mortgage is calculated on the rate 45 days before the due date, and the rate is changed on each anniversary of the original mortgage date. Read the original agreement and double-check everything very carefully. Banks make mistakes—and seldom are they in your favor.

FINAL NOTE

If you keep your wealth out of harm's way (and even build it) using the strategies in this book, the time may come when you can use your wealth to buy prime property for pennies on the dollar.

Remember: *It ALWAYS pays to keep the big picture in focus.* In the 1930s, an investor named Arthur Wirtz used his cash to buy Chicago Stadium, an interest in a Detroit hockey arena and other properties for 10 cents on the dollar. After the depression ended, he became a millionaire many times over.

It could happen to you, too, provided you can keep your powder dry, sit out the hard times, and wait for the right time to buy.

RESOURCES

Peter Cavelti, Cavelti Capital Management Ltd., One Financial Place, 25 Adelaide Street East, Toronto, ONT M5C 1Y2, Canada. Peter Cavelti manages in excess of $500 million in precious metals and international assets.

The Complete Home Buyer and Seller Guide-1991 Edition, Communique Marketing, 1528 East 400 South, P.O. Box 178, Pleasant Grove, UT 84062; (801) 785-7043. This condensed real estate guide tells how to buy and sell homes in down markets, how to deal with contractors, and describes various mortgages (including some very creative methods) for buying real estate, and so on. For a copy, send $6.95 to the above address.

Allen Cymrot, Cymrot Realty Advisors, Inc., 12120 Edgecliff Place, Los Altos Hills, CA 94022; (415) 949-2236. Allen Cymrot is a nationally recognized advisor to real estate investors and businesses, and author of *Street Smart Real Estate Investing,* published by Dow Jones/Irwin.

The Forecaster Moneyletter, John Kamin, editor, 19623 Ventura Blvd., Tarzana, CA 91356; (818) 345-4421. John Kamin publishes a weekly investment newsletter and has written several books on real estate. He has no vested interest in recommending any particular property, as his sole interest in real estate has been investing for his own account.

We would like to thank both Mr. Cymrot and Mr. Kamin for their extensive help with this chapter.

Jane Bryant Quinn, author of *Making The Most of Your Money.* Available at most bookstores.

12

Investibles in the 1990s: Gold, Silver, Antiques, and Other Tangibles

"To be ignorant of what occurred before you
were born is to remain always a child. For what
is the worth of human life, unless it is woven
into the life of our ancestors by the records
of history?"

Cicero, 46 B.C.

I n the 1970s and early 1980s, gold, silver, and art were regarded as the ultimate cash equivalents as inflation soared out of control.

Many of you, during those inflation years, acquired one or more of these tangibles as cash equivalents to enable you to retain the value of your assets when currency values were falling.

In this chapter we will review the traditional inflation-oriented tangibles and attempt to explain where they are headed.

We also will uncover some of the less obvious tangibles that never became fashionable during the inflation years—tangibles that could offer you immense pleasure along with a tremendous opportunity for profit. Additionally, we will show you:

- Why the collectibles that made the headlines in the 1970s and 1980s will not be the winners in the 1990s,
- Three ways to build an "insurance" position in gold and silver bullion that will always be available and liquid,
- A gold investment that could generate significant profits for you even if the price of gold bullion doesn't budge a single dollar, and
- An undervalued and virtually undiscovered collectible that could outperform other collectibles in the 1990s.

To begin with, the rules for collectibles have changed. As David Gann, a governor of the American Numismatic Association, put it on CNN recently:

"... While coins appreciated 17% per year between 1981 and 1989, since then, with few exceptions, they have fallen badly. It is new era. Coins and other tangibles should now be bought primarily for their art and historic value, rather than as investments. However, having said that, many have fallen so far that, even as a hobby, there is little downside risk in buying at this point."

We are no longer living in an inflationary environment, which means that tangibles will no longer be acquired to escape devaluing currency. In most industrial countries, the bias is toward deflation, not inflation.

Also, the consumer is looking for value in anything he or she buys, and we will not see the outrageous prices paid for art and coins that we saw in the 1980s. Instead, collectibles will become, first and foremost, items people want to own and enjoy—and to show to their friends. However, by buying value, these items can become long-term conservative investments in their own right, which is why we refer to them as "investibles."

The aging baby-boomers are showing signs of being interested in a different set of collectibles than is the older generation.

For example, the "BMW generation" shows great interest in collecting antique cars and even airplanes—things that appeal to their more technological, scientific, and educational orientation.

You can expect old technology (antique cameras, scientific instruments, and mechanicals musical products—such as player pianos, music boxes, juke boxes, and so on) to become popular.

As as the most literate generation ever, the aging baby-boomer is entering a time in which Americans are searching for their identities in the midst of growing diversity and the increasingly unsettling ideals of "political correctness." Expect antique manuscripts, rare books, and antique documents that define the American character (i.e., documents of the Founding Fathers, newspapers and magazines of the Revolutionary and Civil Wars) to become increasingly popular. War, sports, and political memorabilia will increase in popularity as well.

In a moment, we will show you one collectible that has yet to take off, but appears ready to do so at any moment. But first let's discuss the direction of more widely known tangibles.

ART

According to Robin Duthy, in his survey of the world art market titled *Market Is Down But Not Out,* prices for 18th century British portraits and sporting paintings have dropped by 14% while most other categories have remained unchanged. American impressionists, whose value surged 200% in the three years prior to 1989, have dropped back 20%; but American art of the 1910–1940 period has seen a 34% rise.

French works, too, have had mixed results. Picasso has been particularly popular, with prices up 50% during 1989. A total of 248 of his works have been sold at an average of $460,000.

Sotheby's Art Index shows that the aggregate index, which includes ceramics, silver and furniture, as well as paintings, was down by 18% in the year ending July 1991. Between July and December 1991, the index declined a further 3%. This was entirely due to decreases in the paintings category. The drop was particularly marked for impressionist paintings, down 36%, and modern paintings, down 32%.

One of the main reasons why impressionist and modern paintings have dropped so badly is that the Japanese had been the main buyers of these works of art. Since the money-laundering scandals and dramatic drop in real estate values in Japan, the Japanese buying has virtually stopped.

This is very similar to what happened in the 1970s when Americans and others were buying rare stamps in order to secretly move money out of their native country and into tax havens.

Though you may be able to find some real bargains during 1992, you may be better off sitting on the sidelines instead. If you do venture into the market, please remember these tips:

1. Beware of telemarketing companies who offer art work at *unbelievable prices*—they may be fakes. Instead, buy only from reputable galleries or dealers unless you have the necessary expertise to determine an item's *true* value. You can obtain names through dealer associations or other collectors.

2. Talk to several art dealers, art consultants and advisors before making any purchase. As a rule, buy only when at least three experts are talking about the same artist or style. When experts talk about them, it's more likely that their value will increase shortly.

3. And remember: Art produces no income while it is hanging on the wall. You certainly may enjoy its beauty, but to make a profit (provided the art piece appreciates) you must attempt to sell it. Most famous masters, for example, do not have a ready market and, therefore, must be sold through an auction.

PRECIOUS METALS

In 1991 the price of gold dropped to a five-year low and silver dipped to a 15-year low. The obvious question is: Why would you want to own gold now? Gold doesn't pay interest or dividends and, based on so-called experts' projections, it won't be needed as an inflation hedge either.

In a moment, we will answer that question by showing you a very important reason to own gold and silver. But first, let's look at gold from the investment viewpoint.

THE TRUE VALUE OF GOLD

Only when a nation has a sound currency are its citizens truly free to use their money to buy whatever they please, either in their native land or overseas. In the absence of a sound currency, or in the case of a national crisis, gold remains the ultimate medium of exchange.

This is the reason every U.S. embassy is supplied with gold coins in case of an emergency.

In fact, the value of gold as survival money was recently demonstrated. Immediately after Saddam Hussein's tanks rolled into Kuwait, foreign exchange dealers all over the world ceased trading the Kuwaiti and Iraqi currencies. Those who managed to escape the conflict with only the local currency were penniless. Those with portable gold or U.S. dollars were able to preserve some of their wealth in a currency accepted in virtually any nation.

The value of gold as a reserve currency was further emphasized recently when the Group of Seven (G-7) agreed to loan eight Soviet Republics $1 billion and to defer more than $6 billion in debt payments for a year (including $3.6 billion owed to the G-7 nations themselves). As part of the original agreement, the G-7 (which includes the United States, Japan, Germany, Britain, Canada, France and Italy) requested that the Soviets put up half their gold reserves as collateral.

What is particularly significant with this action is that it is the first time in a decade that gold has been used in a major central bank transaction. Obviously gold is not dead and should be a part (about 5%) of every investment portfolio.

GOLD AND SILVER: AS AN INVESTMENT

There are two primary ways to view gold and silver: As an insurance policy (core holdings), or as a speculative investment.

In 1991, the price of gold fell to a five-year low and silver skidded to a 15-year low. With worries of deflation, rather than inflation, and slumping economies worldwide, the price and demand for both metals remained sluggish.

To be sure, bottoms of any financial market are always boring and saucer-shaped, so there is no way of knowing if gold and silver will move up much for several years, if at all.

SAFETY TIP

Buy Before a Crisis, Never During It

The lesson of the Gulf Crisis and Soviet Coup is that you should never buy gold in reaction to short-term developments. By the time you can get into the market after a crisis event, the price will be close to a peak. And once the situation is resolved, the price will quickly settle lower.

Even professional speculators (at least the ones still in business) prefer to concentrate on the long-term fundamentals driving the gold market.

In general, you should always remember that gold rises due to political crisis, inflation, and monetary crisis. You can't predict a political crisis. You can usually have a general idea of inflationary trends and expect a monetary crisis, but you can't predict precisely when they will occur.

One thing you can always do: Prepare for any of these three events before they occur.

Whether prices soar anytime soon, the fact remains that any commodity is a bargain at some price. At the 1991 price levels and as a component of a hard-asset "insurance policy," gold and silver are tremendous values at current prices. But as an investment, we prefer to stay by the sidelines.

THE IMPORTANCE OF A GOLDEN INSURANCE POLICY

If gold and silver have value in times of economic crisis, then it has never been more important for you to make sure that your "core holdings" are in place. There can be little doubt that the U.S. economy holds greater danger today than we have seen since the Great Depression. For example:

William Seidman, prior to his retirement as chairman of the FDIC, publicly stated that there was not enough money in the FDIC fund to cover the projected bank failures for 1991. He said, "[The banking industry] is bumping along the bottom of the recession. It doesn't look like it's getting much worse, but it doesn't look like it's getting much better either."

Though the number of projected bank failures was down in the first nine months of 1991 compared to the same period in 1990 (85 versus 160), the failures were larger than before. In 1990, failures averaged $65 million in assets. In 1991, they averaged $475 million. Just to cover projected failures through the end of 1991, it was projected that the fund would be at least $5 billion in the red. So don't bank on the FDIC.

Moreover, household debt (home mortgages and consumer debt) rose from $1.3 trillion at the end of 1980 to just under $3.4 trillion at year-end 1990.

Corporate debt exceeds $2.1 trillion, with about 28% of it in high-interest junk bonds and bank loans accumulated during the merger and acquisition mania of the 1980s. This is the reason why, for the first time since 1934, the net interest payments of U.S. corporations now exceed their *after-tax profits*.

And the 1990 budget accord quietly raised the federal debt ceiling to $4.145 trillion in hopes that it would be high enough to avoid an embarrassing vote until after the 1992 elections. The latest figures, however, suggest that the ceiling must be raised much sooner.

Add a sluggish economic recovery, continued inflation (despite what governmental figures report), and a host of other mounting troubles, and you can understand why experts strongly recommend that you allocate 5% or more of your total portfolio to a core position of hard assets such as gold and silver bullion.

THREE WAYS TO BUILD A CORE POSITION IN GOLD AND SILVER

If you're buying gold and silver to "squirrel" away in case of a dire emergency—one that requires having immediate access to a liquid asset—you need to purchase the *physical metal* and keep it readily available.

That rules out mining stocks, futures, options, and warehouse receipts. It leaves you with three basic options:

Gold and silver bullion,

Circulated coins,

Rare U.S. Coins.

Gold and Silver Bullion

Gold and silver bullion are sold as bars, rounds, and coins.

Bars are available in fractions of a troy ounce up to huge (and heavy!) 400-ounce gold and 1,000-ounce silver bars. Rounds are available in fewer sizes than bars, and they are seldom larger than an ounce. Except for that one point, the primary difference between a bar and a round is the shape. Gold and silver bars and rounds are manufactured by several companies, but you should buy only hallmark products such as Johnson-Matthey, Credit Suisse and Engelhard.

In contrast, gold and silver bullion *coins* are issues by a nation and are (supposedly) legal tender in that nation. Some examples are the U.S. American Eagle gold and silver coins (which can be placed in IRA accounts), Canadian Maple Leaf gold and silver coins, Chinese Panda gold and silver coins, and British Britannia gold coins.

When you purchase bullion, you pay a premium over the actual gold (spot) value to compensate for refining and manufacturing costs. For gold bullion, this premium can range as high as 12% for small fractional sizes and as low as a few percentage points for larger sizes and quantities. A one-ounce American Eagle gold coin, for example, should sell for about 4% to 5% above the actual gold value.

For silver bullion, the premiums will range a bit higher. A one-ounce American Eagle silver coin, for example, will trade for about $1.25 above the silver (spot) value, or a 30% premium at a silver price of $4.16 per ounce.

Circulated Coins

You can also build a core position by purchasing quantities of circulated U.S. gold and silver coins. These coins trade very close to their actual bullion value. Saint-Gaudens double eagles (that contain the equivalent of .9675 troy ounces of pure gold) trade in "very fine" condition for about 10% to 20% over their gold value.

YIELD TIP

An Historic Investment

One of today's best paper investments may well be paper itself—historic autographs, manuscripts, and documents.

According to Jeff Baker, a collector of historical and sports autographs for 20 years, *"autographs are among the few investments to have weathered the most perilous economic climates, rising in value without interruption throughout the last 10 years—by an average of about 20% per year for some of the most desirable items."*

The popularity of historic autograph collecting is spreading quickly. It is estimated that Americans will invest $100 million in autographs this year alone. Just a decade ago, there were only about 3,000 significant private collections of manuscripts in existence. Today, it is estimated that this number has increased to more than 12,000. Baker notes that *"on average, buyers will pay a full 15% to 20% more than the prices they paid last year."*

How high will prices go? It's hard to say, but the American manuscript still appears to be remarkably undervalued. An Emperor Hirohito-signed document, for instance, can trade for more than $100,000 in Japan. A George Washington-signed document, however, can still be acquired for only about $10,000.

Circulated silver coins can be purchased in bulk bags that are sold according to the total face value of the group. A $1,000 bag of .900 fine "junk silver" dimes, quarters or half dollars contains approximately 715 ounces of silver. Throughout 1990 and 1991, bags have traded for as low as 10 cents under spot to as much as 10% to 15% over the spot price of silver.

Rare U.S. Coins

Lesson No. 1 in the rare coin market is that "rare" is a relative term.

True ultra-rarities are immensely valuable U.S. coins of which only a few examples may exist in the highest grade known for the issue. In contrast, the most frequently encountered rare U.S. coins are common dates—called "generics" in the numismatic parlance. Thousands of generics may exist in any particular grade.

Rare U.S. coins are graded on a scale of 1 to 70, with the range of 60 to 70 being "mint state," or uncirculated. An MS-60 coin may have a few nicks and scrapes, but nonetheless it has never been circulated in commerce. An MS-70 specimen is perfect, and any grade MS-65 or above is generally considered a high-grade specimen.

The most liquid coins are those graded by either the Professional Coin Grading Service (PCGS) or the Numismatic Guaranty Corporation (NGC). You should never purchase a rare coin that has not been graded by one of these two organizations.

Rare U.S. coins have been through a devastating washout. To some, that spells opportunity. But investors have been waiting years now for a market turnaround, and we don't recommend buying unless you're a collector or prices begin a prolonged upturn.

Still, many investors consider profit potential a bonus in relation to another advantage these coins offer: *Privacy.*

Purchases of bullion (except for the American Eagle gold bullion coin) are reportable to the IRS. Your dealer reports the transaction when you sell the bullion. But purchases of any precious metal coin selling for more than 15% above its bullion value *are not reportable.*

IT PAYS TO BE PREPARED

Remember, your core precious metal position should be considered not as an investment, but as *insurance.* The danger of a currency and banking crisis is very real, and a position in readily accepted hard assets could someday be your fiscal salvation. As Thomas Jefferson observed:

"If the American people ever allow private banks to control the issue of their currency, the banks and the corporations that will grow up around them will deprive the people of all their property, first by inflation and then by deflation, until their children wake up homeless on the continent their father conquered."

Let's hope you never have to pay for food with gold and silver coins from your safe deposit box. But it pays to be prepared for anything.

INVESTIBLES: HISTORIC DOCUMENTS

Collectibles may encompass a variety of rarities—rarities that may include everything from antique photographic equipment to antique furniture to war or sports memorabilia. However, one of the most undervalued areas for the 1990s appears to be historic documents, including rare newspapers, historic autographs, and rare books.

There are many reasons why a growing number of people are collecting these historic items. One of the most prominent (but least important) is the profit motive.

Over the last few years, for example, autographic material of historic figures has begun to soar in value. Items signed by historic leaders such as George Washington, Thomas Jefferson, Patrick Henry and Ben Franklin, as well as more modern Americans such as Dwight Eisenhower, Harry Truman and even Marilyn Monroe, have been generating greater gains than many stocks, bonds and other more traditional "paper" investments.

But profits aren't the only reason why an increasing number of Americans are becoming amateur archivists. For example, new collectors are often shocked at the affordability of such rare documents and manuscripts. You can still acquire an authentic newspaper packed with vivid, first-hand accounts of dramatic Civil War battles for less than $100. And you can own a two-century-old document personally signed by George Washington for less than most stock, bond, or rare coin investments you may have ever made.

Amazingly, many of these rare documents and manuscripts (that have been around as long as written history) remain undervalued and virtually undiscovered.

Second, people are very impressed with historic documents and manuscripts. Show someone a $5,000 rare stamp, a $5,000 rare coin, $5,000 worth of IBM stock or a $5,000 signed presidential letter, and which do you think impresses him the most? Invariably, it's the presidential autograph.

The rarity of historic documents and manuscripts is another important factor to consider. How many newspapers have survived the passage of hundreds of years? In most cases, none at all. Of those few that remain, the vast majority are held in public institutions and will likely never be available to private collectors. Autographic material can be considered even more scarce, because each individual item is unique unto itself, with its own fascinating story to tell.

And finally, the potentially growing value of rare manuscripts and documents gives buyers a sense of security—a comforting feeling that their collection is rising in value even while they are enjoying their holdings and sharing them with friends and loved ones.

Consider markets like those of fine art, rare stamps, or rare coins and you'll find hundreds of these items selling for more than $20,000. At least fifteen 1804 silver dollars exist, yet each one is worth well over $1 million. In contrast, many rare documents, manuscripts, and autographs are absolutely unique, and still available at ground-floor prices.

A FINAL THOUGHT ABOUT HISTORIC DOCUMENTS

Though the investment potential of many historic manuscripts, books and autographs may be excellent as interest grows in this area of collectibles, the fact remains that you should never consider purchasing one of these historic items purely as an investment.

To earn a profit from an investment, you have to sell it. And that is one thing that few collectors of rare historic documents can bring themselves to do.

Instead, most collectors of paper Americana prefer to add to their collections.

Consequently, the supply of desirable items constantly shrinks as demand grows over time.

If you would like more information on historic documents, contact Jefferson Rarities, 2400 Jefferson Highway, 6th Floor, Jefferson, LA 70121; 1-800-877-8847. Jefferson Rarities offers many historic manuscripts, newspapers, and autographs for sale and also can provide you with additional information on how to purchase these items.

OTHER "INVESTIBLES" TO CONSIDER IN THE 1990s

The following is a list of a few examples of other "investibles" that may do well during the 1990s. For your convenience, we have included sources of additional information for each collectible:

Antique guns and Old West memorabilia: National Rifle Association, 1600 Rhode Island Ave. NW, Washington, DC 20036; 1-800-368-5714.

Butterfield & Butterfield, 220 San Bruno Ave., San Francisco, CA 94103; (415) 861-7500.

Antique furniture and fine art: Contact one of the following famous auction houses and ask for their most recent auction catalogs:

Christie's, 502 Park Ave., New York, NY 10022; (212) 546-1000.
Phillips, 406 E. 79th St., New York, NY 10021; (212) 570-4830.
Sotheby's, 1334 York Ave., New York, NY 10021; (212) 606-7000.

Antique cameras, photographs, and film: For more information, ask for auction catalogs from Christie's or Phillips listed above.

Collectible wines: Contact Christie's Wine Publications Department, 21–24 44th Ave., Long Island City, NY 11101.

Pocket watches and clocks: For more information, contact the National Association of Watch and Clock Collectors, 514 Poplar St., Columbia, PA 17512; (717) 684-8261.

RESOURCES

Blanchard Precious Metals Fund, 31 Madison Ave., 24th Floor, New York, NY 10010; 1-800-922-7771, in NY (212) 779-7979.

The Blanchard Precious Metals Fund is managed by Peter C. Cavelti, a very knowledgeable money manager, and invests in physical precious metals such as gold, silver, platinum and palladium, and in securities companies involved with precious metals. The fund may also invest in short-term instruments and government securities when the manager believes the precious metals markets may experience declines. The minimum to open an account is $3,000 ($2,000 for IRAs).

Dessauer's Journal, Limmat Publications, Inc., P.O. Box 1718, Orleans, MA 02653. Author John P. Dessauer.

Industry Council for Tangible Assets (ICTA), 666 Pennsylvania Ave. SE, Suite 301, Washington, DC 20003; (202) 544-3531. ICTA is a national lobbying group for tangible-asset dealers and investors.

Jefferson Rarities, 2400 Jefferson Highway, 6th Floor, Jefferson, LA 70121; 1-800-877-8847. Jefferson Rarities offers many historic manuscripts, newspapers and autographs for sale and also can provide you with additional information on how to purchase these items.

Numismatic Guaranty Corporation (NGC), P.O. Box 1776, Parsippany, NJ 07054; (201) 984-6222. Call for coin grading information and listing of authorized NGC dealers.

Professional Coin Grading Service (PCGS), P.O. Box 9458, Newport Beach, CA 92658; 1-800-447-8848. Call for information on how to get coins graded and for a listing of authorized PCGS dealers.

APPENDIX

Useful Names, Addresses & Phone Numbers

Note: All listings are in alphabetical order.

ULTRA-SAFE MONEY MARKET FUNDS

Benham Government Agency Fund, 1-800-472-3389.

Blanchard Government Money Market Fund, 1-800-922-7771.

Dreyfus U.S. Guaranteed Money Market Account LP, 1-800-782-6620.

Dreyfus Worldwide Dollar, 1-800-782-6620.

Evergreen Money Market Trust, 1-800-235-0064.

Fidelity Spartan, 1-800-544-8888.

INVESCO Treasurer's Money Market Reserve, 1-800-525-8085.

Neuberger and Berman Cash Reserves, 1-800-877-9700.

Templeton Money Fund, 1-800-237-0738.

Templeton Tax-Free Money Fund, 1-800-237-0738.

Vanguard MMR Prime, 1-800-662-7447.

TAX EXEMPT FUNDS

Benham National Tax-Free Trust, 1-800-472-3389.

Calvert Tax-Free Reserves Money Market Fund, 1-800-368-2748.

Capital Preservation Fund, 1-800-321-8321.

Dreyfus 100% U.S. Treasury, 1-800-782-6620.

Dreyfus Connecticut Municipal, 1-800-782-6620.

Dreyfus Michigan Municipal, 1-800-782-6620.

Dreyfus New Jersey Municipal, 1-800-782-6620.

Dreyfus Pennsylvania Municipal, 1-800-782-6620.

Dreyfus U.S. Treasury Money Market Account LP, 1-800-782-6620.

Evergreen Tax-Exempt Money Market Fund, 1-800-235-0064.

Fidelity Spartan Municipal Fund, 1-800-544-8888.

Fidelity Spartan U.S. Treasury Money Market Fund, 1-800-544-8888.

Fidelity Tax-Exempt, 1-800-544-8888.

Fidelity Tax-Free Bond Fund, 1-800-544-8888.

Fidelity U.S. Treasury Agency Fund, 1-800-544-8888.

Franklin Tax-Exempt Money Fund, 1-800-652-2301.

Lexington Tax-Free Money Fund, 1-800-526-0056.

Neuberger & Berman Government Money Fund, 1-800-877-9700.

Neuberger & Berman Municipal Money Fund, 1-800-877-9700.

Neuberger & Berman Municipal Securities Trust, 1-800-877-9700.

Scudder Tax-Free, 1-800-225-2470.

Strong Municipal Fund, 1-800-368-3863.

T. Rowe Price Tax Exempt, 1-800-638-5660.

Templeton Insured Tax-Free Fund, 1-800-237-0738.

USAA Tax Exempt, 1-800-531-8181.

UST Master Tax-Exempt Fund, 1-800-233-1136.

Vanguard California Tax-Free, 1-800-662-7447.

Vanguard Muni Bond, 1-800-662-7447.

Vanguard Muni Bond Short Term 1-800-662-7447.

Vanguard New Jersey Tax-Free, 1-800-662-7447.

Vanguard Ohio Tax-Free, 1-800-662-7447.

Vanguard Pennsylvania Tax-Free, 1-800-662-7447.

BOND FUNDS

Benham GNMA Income Fund, 1-800-472-3389.

Benham Treasury Note Fund, 1-800-472-3389.

Neuberger & Berman Limited Maturity Bond Fund, 1-800-877-9700.

Neuberger & Berman Ultra-Short Bond Fund, 1-800-877-9700.

Scudder Short-Term Bond Fund, 1-800-225-2470.

Templeton Income Fund, 1-800-237-0738.

Vanguard Intermediate-Term Portfolio, 1-800-662-7447.

Vanguard Short-Term Corporate Bond Portfolio, 1-800-662-7447.

TOP MUNICIPAL BOND FUNDS

Benham National Tax-Free Trust Fund, 1-800-472-3389.

Dreyfus Intermediate Tax-Exempt Bond Fund, 1-800-782-6620.

Fidelity Limited-Term Munis, 1-800-544-8888.

Fidelity Municipal Bond Portfolio, 1-800-544-8888.

IDS High-Yield Tax-Exempt Fund, 1-800-437-4332.

IDS Insured Tax-Exempt Fund, 1-800-437-4332.

IDS Tax-Exempt Bond Fund, 1-800-437-4332.

Scudder Tax-Free Target-1996, 1-800-225-2470.

Vanguard Muni Bond Intermediate, 1-800-662-7447.

Vanguard Municipal Bond Limited-Term Portfolio, 1-800-662-7447.

OTHER TAX-EXEMPT BOND FUNDS

Lexington Tax-Exempt Bond Trust, 1-800-526-0056.

Summit Tax-Exempt Bond Fund, contact Alex Green or Michael Spartz at (407) 629-1400, Fax: (407) 629-2470.

TOP DOUBLE AND TRIPLE TAX-EXEMPT FUNDS

Benham California Tax-Free Funds, 1-800-472-3389.

Dreyfus Tax-Exempt Bond Funds, 1-800-782-6620.

Fidelity Tax-Free Portfolios, 1-800-544-8888.

Vanguard Insured Long-Term Funds, 1-800-662-7447.

JUNK BOND FUNDS

Fidelity Capital and Income Fund, 1-800-544-8888.

Kemper High Yield Fund, 1-800-621-1048.

Merrill Lynch High Income A, 1-800-637-1022.

T. Rowe Price High Yield Fund, 1-800-638-5660.

Vanguard Fixed Income High Yield, 1-800-662-7447.

INTERNATIONAL MUTUAL FUNDS AND HARD CURRENCY PORTFOLIOS

Blanchard Short-Term Global Income Fund, 1-800-922-7771.

Blanchard Strategic Growth Fund, 1-800-922-7771.

Dean Witter Global Short-Term Income Fund, 1-800-869-FUND or (212) 392-2550.

Fidelity Global Bond Fund, 1-800-544-8888 or (617) 523-1919.

Fidelity Single Currency Portfolios, 1-800-544-8888 or (617) 523-1919.

G.T. Global Bond Fund, 1-800-824-1580.

G.T. Global Government Income Fund, 1-800-824-1580.

G.T. Global Growth Funds, 1-800-824-1580.

Huntington Advisors Global Cash Portfolio (GCP), 1-800-354-4111 or (213) 681-3700.

Huntington Advisors Hard Currency Portfolio, 1-800-354-4111 or (213) 681-3700.

Huntington Advisors High Income Currency Portfolio, 1-800-354-4111 or (213) 681-3700.

Huntington Advisors International Single Currency Portfolios, 1-800-354-4111 or (213) 681-3700.

Kemper Global Income Fund, 1-800-621-1048.

Kemper Short-Term Global Income Fund, 1-800-621-1048.

Kleinwort Benson International Equity Fund, 1-800-237-4218.

Lexington Worldwide Emerging Markets Fund, 1-800-526-0056.

PaineWebber Global Income Fund, 1-800-521-8840 or (212) 713-2000.

PaineWebber Short-Term Global Income, 1-800-521-8840 or (212) 713-2000.

Putnam Europe Growth Fund, 1-800-225-1581.

Putnam Global Growth Fund, 1-800-225-1581.

Putnam Governmental Income Trust, 1-800-225-1581.

Scudder International Bond Fund, 1-800-225-2470.

Scudder International Fund, 1-800-225-2470.

Shearson Short-Term World Income Fund, Global Currencies Portfolio, Single Currency Portfolio, Managed Currency Portfolio, Global Equity Account: Call either C. Taylor Walet, Jr. at 1-800-227-6121 or (504) 585-3900; or Martin Truax at 1-800-241-6900.

T. Rowe Price International Bond Fund, 1-800-638-5660.

T. Rowe Price International Stock Fund, 1-800-638-5660.

Templeton Developing Markets Trust, 1-800-237-0738.

Templeton Foreign Fund, 1-800-237-0738.

Templeton Global Utilities Fund, 1-800-237-0738.

Templeton World Fund, 1-800-237-0738.

OTHER RECOMMENDED FUNDS

Benham Capital Adjustable Rate Mortgage Fund, 1-800-472-3389.

Benham Target Maturity Funds, 1-800-472-3389.

Blackstone Income Trust: Contact Andy Clipper at (212) 272-7215.

Fidelity OTC Portfolio, 1-800-544-8888.

Fidelity Utilities Income, 1-800-544-8888.

Flag Telephone Investors, 1-800-767-3524.

Putnam High Income Convertible Bond Fund, 1-800-225-1581.

Rushmore American Gas Index, 1-800-621-7874.

SOURCES OF INFORMATION: MUTUAL FUNDS

Forbes Annual Fund Survey. Available at most libraries.

Investment Company Institute, 1600 M Street NW, Suite 600, Washington, DC 20036; (202) 293-7700.

Mutual Fund Education Alliance, 1900 Erie Street, Suite 120, Kansas City, MO 64116; (816) 471-1454.

National Institute of Business Management, Inc., 1328 Broadway, New York, NY 10001; 1-800-543-2054.

Standard & Poor's/Lipper Mutual Fund Profiles. This publication is available in most libraries.

BOOKS: MUTUAL FUNDS

IBC/Donoghue's Mutual Fund Almanac ($31.95 plus $3 shipping), 290 Eliot Street, Box 91004, Ashland, MA 01721, 1-800-343-5413.

IBC/Donoghue's Money Fund Directory ($24.95 plus $3 shipping), 290 Eliot Street, Box 91004, Ashland, MA 01721, 1-800-343-5413.

Individual Investor's Guide to No-Load Mutual Funds ($19.95), American Association of Individual Investors, 625 North Michigan Ave., Chicago, IL 60611.

Investor's Guide to Low-Cost Mutual Funds, Mutual Fund Education Alliance, 1900 Erie Street, Suite 120, Kansas City, MO 64116; (816) 471-1454. The guide's cost is $5, Investor Kit with 60-minute audio cassette and 48-page booklet is $10, or $12.50 for the combination of the guide and Investor Kit.

Investor's Guide and Mutual Fund Directory ($5), No-Load Mutual Fund Association, P.O. Box 2004, JAF Building, New York, NY 10116.

Mutual Fund Fact Book ($9.95) and *Guide to Mutual Funds* ($2.50), Investment Company Institute, 1600 M Street NW, Suite 600, Washington, DC 20036; (202) 293-7700.

Winning Mutual Fund Strategies for Uncertain Times, by Sheldon Jacobs, National Institute of Business Management, Inc., 1328 Broadway, New York, NY 10001.

PRIVATE ORGANIZATIONS THAT OFFER INFORMATION ON BANK, BROKERAGE, AND INSURANCE COMPANY SAFETY

A.M. Best & Co., Ambest Road, Oldwick, NJ 08858; (908) 439-2200 for condition of your insurance company.

Federal Financial Institutions Examination Council, U.B.P.R., 1776 6th Street NW, Washington, DC 20006; (202) 357-0177.

Moody's Investors Service, Inc., 99 Church Street, New York, NY 10007. Ratings on insurance companies.

National Organization of Life and Health Insurance Guaranty Associations (NOLHGA), 13873 Park Center Road, Suite 329, Herndon, VA 22071; (703) 481-5206.

Standard & Poor's Corp., 25 Broadway, New York, NY 10004. Ratings on insurance companies.

VeriBanc, Inc., P.O. Box 461, Wakefield, MA 01880; 1-800-442-2657 for the condition of your bank, S&L or credit union.

Weiss Research, Inc., P.O. Box 2923, West Palm Beach, FL 33402; 1-800-289-9222 for the condition of your bank, insurance company or brokerage house.

ADDITIONAL WAYS TO CHECK YOUR BANK'S OR BROKERAGE'S SAFETY

For Banks–FDIC, Office of Consumer Affairs, 550 17th Street NW, Washington, DC 20429; 1-800-424-5488 or (202) 898-3356.

For Brokerages–SIPC, 900 17th Street NW, Washington, DC 20006; (202) 371-8300.

For Credit Unions–Office of Public and Congressional Affairs, National Credit Union Administration, 1776 G Street NW, Washington, DC 20456.

For Municipal Bonds–Financial Guaranty Insurance Company (FGIC), 175 Water Street, New York, NY 10038; (212) 607-3009.

For Municipal Bonds–Municipal Bond Investors Assurance (MBIA), 113 King Street, Almond, NY 10504; (914) 765-3893.

For S&Ls–Office of Thrift Supervision, Office of Community Investment, Division of Consumer Rights, 1700 G Street NW, Washington, DC 20552; (202) 906-6237.

MISCELLANEOUS GOVERNMENT AGENCIES

Bureau of Public Debt, Division of Customer Service, 300 13th Street SW, Washington, DC 20239-0001.

Federal Reserve Bank of St. Louis, P.O. Box 422, St. Louis, MO 63166.

Social Security Administration Office. For a copy of your Personal Earnings and Benefit Estimate Statement, call 1-800-772-1213. To correct your records, call 1-800-537-7005.

U.S. Treasury's Continuous Recorded Line, (202) 874-4000.

Service Available	**Extension**
Treasury bill offerings	211
Treasury note and bond offerings	212
Treasury bill auction results	221

Treasury note and bond auction results   222

General information on Treasury bills   231

General information of Treasury notes and bonds   232

General information on the Treasury Direct system   233

Savings bond information   004

Requesting forms   241

Information on how to purchase Treasury securities   251

Information on how to redeem Treasury securities   254

To get specific questions answered   003

HOW TO BUY GOVERNMENT SECURITIES DIRECTLY FROM THE TREASURY

Walk-in addresses, phone numbers and mailing addresses of Federal Reserve banks.

(In alphabetical order by city)

Atlanta, GA, 104 Marietta Street NW, P.O. Box 1731, Atlanta, GA 30303; (404) 521-8657.

Baltimore, MD, 502 South Sharp Street, P.O. Box 1378, Baltimore, MD 21203; (301) 576-3300.

Birmingham, AL, 1801 Fifth Ave. N, P.O. Box 10447, Birmingham, AL 35202; (205) 252-3141, Ext. 215 or 264.

Boston, MA, 600 Atlanta Ave., P.O. Box 2076, Boston, MA 02106; (617) 973-3805 or 3810.

Buffalo, NY, 160 Delaware Ave., P.O. Box 961, Buffalo, NY 14240; (716) 849-5046.

Charlotte, NC, 401 South Tryon Street, P.O. Box 30248, Charlotte, NC 28230; (704) 336-7100.

Chicago, IL, 230 South LaSalle Street, P.O. Box 834, Chicago, IL 60690; (312) 322-5369.

Cincinnati, OH, 150 East Fourth Street, P.O. Box 999, Cincinnati, OH 45201; (513) 721-4787, Ext. 334.

Cleveland, OH, 1455 East 6th Street, P.O. Box 6387, Cleveland, OH 44101; (216) 579-2490.

Dallas, TX, 400 South Akard Street, Securities Dept., Station K, Dallas, TX, 75222; (214) 651-6362.

Denver, CO, 1020 16th Street, P.O. Box 5228, Terminal Annex, Denver, CO 80217; (303) 572-2473 or 572-2470.

Detroit, MI, 160 West Fort Street, P.O. Box 1059, Detroit, MI 48231; (313) 963-0080 or (313) 964-6157.

El Paso, TX, 301 East Main Street, P.O. Box 100, El Paso, TX 79999; (915) 544-4730.

Houston, TX, 1701 San Jacinto Street, P.O. Box 2578, Houston, TX 78295; (713) 659-4433.

Jacksonville, FL, 515 Julia Street, P.O. Box 2499, Jacksonville, FL 32231-2499; (904) 632-4245.

Kansas City, MO, 925 Grand Ave., P.O. Box 440, Kansas City, MO 64198; (816) 881-2783 or 881-2109.

Little Rock, AR, 325 West Capital Ave., P.O. Box 1261, Little Rock, AR 72203; (501) 372-5451, Ext. 288.

Los Angeles, CA, 409 West Olympic Blvd., P.O. Box 2077, Terminal Annex, Los Angeles, CA 90051; (213) 683-8546.

Louisville, KY, 410 South 5th Street, P.O. Box 32710, Louisville, KY 40232; (502) 568-9236 or 568-9238.

Memphis, TN, 200 North Main Street, P.O. Box 407, Memphis, TN 38101; (901) 523-7171, Ext. 225 or 641.

Miami, FL, 9100 NW 36th Street, P.O. Box 520847, Miami, FL 33152; (305) 593-9923.

Minneapolis, MN, 250 Marquette Ave., Minneapolis, MN 55480; (612) 340-2075.

Nashville, TN, 301 8th Ave. N, Nashville, TN, 37203; (615) 259-4006.

New Orleans, LA, 525 St. Charles Ave, P.O. Box 62630, New Orleans, LA 70161; (504) 593-3200, Ext. 3291.

New York, NY, 33 Liberty Street, Federal Reserve, P.O. Station, New York, NY 10045; (212) 791-6619, (212) 791-5823 (24-hour-recording).

Oklahoma City, OK, 226 Dean A. McGee Ave., P.O. Box 25129, Oklahoma City, OK 73125; (405) 235-1721, Ext. 182.

Omaha, NE, 2201 Farnam Street, Omaha, NE 68102; (402) 221-5633.

Philadelphia, PA, 10 Independence Mall, P.O. Box 90, Philadelphia, PA 19105; (215) 574-6680.

Pittsburgh, PA, 717 Grant St., P.O. Box 867, Pittsburgh, PA 15230-0867; (412) 261-7988.

Portland, OR, 915 SW Stark Street, P.O. Box 3436, Portland, OR 97208; (503) 221-5921 or 221-5931.

Richmond, VA, 701 East Byrd St., P.O. Box 27622, Richmond, VA 23261; (804) 643-1250.

Salt Lake City, UT, 120 South State Street, P.O. Box 30780, Salt Lake City, UT 84130; (801) 322-7911 or (801) 355-3131.

San Antonio, TX, 126 East Nueva Street, P.O. Box 1471, San Antonio, TX 78295; (512) 224-2141, Ext. 303 or 305.

San Francisco, CA, 101 Market Street, P.O. Box 7702, San Francisco, CA 94120; (415) 392-6640 or 392-6650.

Seattle, WA, 1015 Second Ave., P.O. Box 3567, Seattle, WA 98124; (206) 442-1650.

St. Louis, MO, 411 Locust Street, P.O. Box 442, St. Louis, MO 63166; (314) 444-8602.

RECOMMENDED BROKERS OR ADVISORS

Robert S. Berlin; Bear Stearns & Company, Inc., 245 Park Ave., Ninth Floor, New York, NY 10167; 1-800-926-0124. Knowledgeable on ECUs and other foreign investments.

John Bintz; Hutchinson, Shokey, Erley & Company, 135 South La Salle, Suite 1230, Chicago, IL 60603; (312) 443-1550, Fax (312) 443-7225. Specializes in personal portfolios of municipal bonds.

Andy Clipper; Bear Stearns & Company, Inc., 245 Park Avenue, New York, NY 10167; (212) 272-7215.

Alex Green; International Assets, 201 West Canton Avenue, Suite 100, Winter Park, FL 32789; (407) 629-1400, Fax (407) 629-2470. Specializes in bond funds.

Tom Hill; Merrill Lynch, Pierce, Fenner & Smith, Liberty Center, 14th Floor, Pittsburgh, PA 15222-3720; 1-800-937-0761. Specializes in fixed-income securities and ultra-conservative retirement assets.

Lyle Latvala (President); Market Timers, Hunt Tower, 200 Main Street, Suite 310, Gainesville, GA 30501; 1-800-451-2557 or (404) 531-9991. This is a small brokerage firm that will trade your account according to your favorite advisor or market letter writer.

Robert Meier, Fox Investments, 141 W. Jackson Blvd., Suite 1800A, Chicago, IL 60604; 1-800-621-0265. Specializes in options strategies for foreign currencies, precious metals, and stock indexes; plus special situation weather trades.

Paul or Jeff Merriman; Merriman Investment Management Company, 1200 Westlake Avenue North, Suite 700, Seattle, WA 98109-3530; 1-800-423-4893. Specialize in mutual fund market-timing and margin accounts.

Ron Miller; Shearson Lehman Brothers, 400 Perimeter Center, Terrace NE, Suite 290, Atlanta, GA 30346; 1-800-241-6900. Specializes in foreign bonds and foreign cash equivalents.

Michael Spartz; International Assets, 201 West Canton Avenue, Suite 100, Winter Park, FL 32789; (407) 629-1400, Fax (407) 629-2470. Specializes in bond funds.

John Train; Train Smith Investment Counsel, 667 Madison Ave., New York, NY 10021; (212) 888-7676.

Martin Truax; Shearson Lehman Brothers, 400 Perimeter Center, Terrace NE, Suite 290, Atlanta, GA 30346; 1-800-825-7171. Specializes in high-yield stocks with growth potential.

C. Taylor Walet, Jr.; Shearson Lehman Brothers, 909 Poydras Street, Suite 1600, New Orleans, LA 70112, 1-800-227-6121. A very knowledgeable and service-oriented broker.

Andrew Westhem; Western Capital Financial Group, Wealth Transfer Division, 1925 Century Park East, Suite 2350, Los Angeles, CA 90067; 1-800-423-4891. Specializes in estate planning.

U.S. FOREIGN EXCHANGE DEALERS FOR HARD-CURRENCY TRAVELER'S CHECKS

Guardian Safe Deposit, 2499 North Harrison, Arlington, VA 22206; (703) 237-1133.

Reusch International, 1350 I Street NW, Washington, DC 20005; (202) 408-1200.

Thomas Cook Currency Services, Inc., 1-800-582-4469.

U.S. BANKS OFFERING FOREIGN CURRENCY DEPOSITS

American Security Bank, Attn. Rex Evans, Trading Department, 730 15th Street NW, Washington, DC 20013; (202) 371-0006.

Bank of America, Attn. Foreign Trading Department, 315 Montgomery St., Mezzanine, San Francisco, CA 94104; (415) 622-2414.

Central Fidelity Bank, Investments Department/Foreign Exchange, Attn. Robert Brockmeier, 1021 East Cary Street, Richmond, VA 23219; (804) 697-6776.

Citibank International Personal Banking, MultiMoney Service Center, 666 Fifth Avenue, Seventh Floor, New York, NY 10103; 1-800-755-5654 or (212) 307-8323.

First Union National Bank, One First Union Center, Charlotte, NC 28288; 1-800-736-5636. As for Pat Weaver.

First Wachovia Bank & Trust Company, P.O. Box 3099, Winston-Salem, NC 27102; (919) 770-5000.

Mark Twain Bank, Frontenac Bldg., 1630 South Lindbergh Blvd., St. Louis, MO 63131; 1-800-926-4922 or (314) 997-7444.

Northern Trust Bank, 50 South LaSalle, Chicago, IL 60675; (312) 630-6000.

Security Pacific Asian Bank (Main office), 977 North Broadway, Los Angeles, CA 90012; (213) 680-9000. *Mail-In Service:* Security Pacific Asian Bank, Foreign Currency Exchange, 609 South Grand Ave., Los Angeles, CA 90017; (213) 229-1165.

Union Bank, Attn. Reiko Carnes, Financial Services Officer, 370 California St., San Francisco, CA 94104; (415) 445-0224.

FOREIGN BANKS

ABN-AMRO Bank, P.O. Box 90, 1000AB Amsterdam, Netherlands; Phone: 011-31-20-282-764; Fax: 011-31-20-239-940. Contact Edward Van Tongeren, Senior Vice President.

ABN-AMRO Bank, Switzerland, Talstrasse 41, 8032 Zurich, Switzerland; Phone: 011-411-211-5315; Fax: 011-411-212-1564. Contact Vice President Rene Scholl.

Anker Bank SA (Formerly Banque Indiana and Banque Ankerfina), 50 Avenue de la Gare, P.O. Box 159, CH-1001 Lausanne, Switzerland; Phone: 011-41 (21) 20-4741, Fax: 011-41 (21) 23-9767. Contact Mrs. Francine Misrahi or Mr. Jean Gander.

Bank of Nova Scotia, 44 King St. W, Toronto, Ontario M5H 1H1 Canada; (416) 866-6161. *U.S. Branch:* Bank of Nova Scotia, One Liberty Plaza, New York, NY 10006; (212) 225-5000.

Cambio + Valoren Bank, Utoquai 55, P.O. Box 535, CH-8021 Zurich, Switzerland; Phone: 011-41 (1) 252-2000, Fax: 001-41 (1) 252-2658. Contact Werner W. Schwarz or Jesus Arias.

Credit Suisse (Swiss Credit Bank), Paradeplatz 8, CH-8022 Zurich, Switzerland; Phone: 011-41 (1) 333-1111, Fax: 011-41 (1) 332-5555. *U.S. Branch:* 100 Wall St., New York, NY 10005; (212) 612-8225.

Hong Kong & Shanghai Bank, One Queens Road, Central, Hong Kong; Phone: 011-852-822-1111.

National Westminster Bank, 41 Lothbury, London EC2P 2BP, England; Phone: 011-44-71 (01) 726-1000, Fax: 011-44-71 (01) 588-5728.

Overland Bank (Formerly Foreign Commerce Bank [Focobank]), Bellaria-strasse 82, CH-8038 Zurich, Switzerland; Phone: 011-41 (1) 482-6688, Fax: 011-41 (1) 482-2884. Contact Bruno Brodveck or Jean-Maurice Clerc.

Overland Bank has a representative office in Vancouver, B.C. as well. The address is: *Overland Financial Services,* Ltd., 1450-1176 W. Georgia St., P.O. Box 48326, Vancouver, B.C. V7X 1A1, Canada; 1-800-663-8942 or (604) 682-3626, Fax (604) 682-6643. Contact Mr. Adrian Hartmann.

Royal Bank of Scotland, Offshore Islands Manager, 44 Esplanade, St. Helier, Jersey, Channel Islands; Phone: 011-0534-26322. Write to their head office at 36 St. Andrew Square, Edinburgh EH2 2YB, Scotland, United Kingdom.

Swiss Bank Corporation, Aeschen Vorstadt 1, CH-4002 Basel, Switzerland; Phone: 011-41-61-288-2020. *U.S. Branch:* 4 World Trade Center, New York, NY 10048; (212) 938-3500.

Union Bank of Switzerland, Bahnhofstrasse 45, CH-8021 Zurich, Switzer-land; Phone: 011-41 (01) 234-1111, Fax: 011-41 (01) 236-5111. *U.S. Branch:* 299 Park Ave., New York, NY 10171; (212) 715-3000.

U.S. BRANCHES OF FOREIGN BANKS

Bank International Luxembourg, 540 Madison Ave., New York, NY 10022; (212) 972-6060.

Royal Bank of Scotland, 63 Wall Street, New York, NY 10005; (212) 269-1700.

INTERNATIONAL BANKING CONSULTANTS

Eugene Latham, Apdo Postal 10-7111, Mexico, DF, 11000, Mexico; Phone: 011-52-5-540-07-95.

Otto E. Roethenmund, 230 Park Avenue, Suite 650, New York, NY 10169; (212) 687-9415.

WHERE TO BUY ANNUITIES

ABN-AMRO Bank, P.O. Box 90, 1000AB Amsterdam, Netherlands; Phone: 011-31-20-282-764, Fax: 011-31-20-239-940.

ABN-AMRO Bank Switzerland, Talstrasse 41, 8032 Zurich, Switzerland; Phone: 011-411-211-5315; Fax: 011-411-212-1564. Contact Vice President Rene Scholl.

Annuity and Endowment Specialists, S.A., P.O. Box 170GY, 8033 Zurich, Switzerland.

Assurex, S.A., Postfach 18, 8311 Winterberg ZH, Switzerland.

Globacor Ltd., Jean-Pierre Louvet, 18 Kimbers Drive, Burnham, Green Lane, Bershire, Great Britain SL1 8JE; U.S. Toll-Free 1-800-678-6091 or 011-44-628-660-990.

Independent Advantage Financial and Insurance Services, Inc.(IAF), 330 Washington Blvd., Eighth Floor, Marina Del Rey, CA 90292-5149; 1-800-829-2887 or (213) 821-1660.

Jurg M. Lattman, AG, Swiss Investment Counsellors, Germaniastrasse 55, 8033 Zurich, Switzerland.

BOOKS ON INSURANCE

Life Insurance and Annuities from the Buyer's Point of View ($9), American Institute for Economic Research, Great Barrington, MA 01230.

The Life Insurance Investor, ($27.50) Probus Publishing Company, 1925 N. Clybourn Street, Chicago, IL 60614; (312) 868-1100.

OTHER PUBLICATIONS: INSURANCE

Annuity and Life Insurance Shopper, 98 Hoffman Road, Suite 100, Englishtown, NJ 07726; 1-800-872-6684.

The Donoghue Group, P.O. Box 19535, Seattle, WA 98119; (206) 281-1615. Regularly issues reports on insurances companies, as well as banks.

Insurance Investing, Editor: Doug Fabian, P.O. Box 2090, Huntington Beach, CA 92647; (714) 893-7332.

RETIREMENT RESOURCES

American Association of Retired Persons (AARP), 1909 K Street NW, Washington, DC 20049. They have published a booklet called *Information on Medicare and Health Insurance for Older People* that is available free of charge.

Department of Health and Human Services, Health Care Financing Administration, Baltimore, MD 21207; 1-800-888-1998. Booklets on Medicare: *A Brief Explanation of Medicare, Your Medicare Handbook, Medicare/Medicaid— Which is Which, How to Fill Out a Medicare Claim Form.*

Elderhostel, 80 Boylston Street, Suite 400, Boston, MA 02116; (617) 426-7788.

Health Insurance Association of America, 1025 Connecticut Avenue NW, Washington, DC 20036; (202) 223-7780. Ask for their free *Consumer Guide to Long-Term-Care Insurance* and their list of companies that sell long-term-care insurance.

Merrill Lynch, Pierce, Fenner & Smith, 1-800-637-7455. Publishes the following booklets: *Ensuring an Independent Lifestyle: Retirement Financing Strategies, Making Your Gift Count: Innovative Trends in Charitable Giving, 43 Tax-Saving Ideas for Investors,* and *How to Cut Your Business Tax Bill.*

BOOKS ON TAX SAVING AND RETIREMENT NEEDS

How to Slash Your Mutual Fund Taxes and *Retirement Tax Guide,* by Dr. Robert C. Carlson, P.O. Box 4954, Falls Church, VA 22044.

REAL ESTATE CONSULTANTS

Ameral-Hays; 203 West Sixth Street, P.O. Box 2322, Roswell, NM 88202; (505) 623-2874. Experts on RTC sales.

Allen Cymrot; Cymrot Realty Advisors, Inc., 12120 Edgecliff Place, Los Altos Hills, CA 94022; (415) 949-2236. Allen Cymrot is a nationally recognized advisor to real estate investors and businesses, and author of *Street Smart Real Estate Investing,* published by Dow Jones/Irwin.

John V. Kamin; Consulting Economist with *The Forecaster Moneyletter,* Forecaster Publishing Company, 19623 Ventura Blvd., Tarzana, CA 91356; (818) 345-4421.

SOURCES OF OTHER INFORMATION: REAL ESTATE

American Association of Retired Persons, Fulfillment D12469, 601 E St. NW, Washington, DC 20049. Offers a free 47-page reverse mortgage guide. Ask for the *Home-Made Money: Consumer's Guide to Home Equity Conversion.*

American Society of Home Inspectors (ASHI), 3299 K St. NW 7th Floor, Washington, DC 20007. Send $4 to ASHI for information on choosing a home inspector.

Choice Plan, Delaware Charter Guarantee & Trust Company, 1013 Centre Road, Wilmington, DE 19899; 1-800-441-4303. Accelerated mortgage program.

The Complete Home Buyer and Seller Guide, Communique Marketing, 1528 East 400 South, P.O. Box 178, Pleasant Grove, UT 84062. This condensed real estate guide tells how to buy and sell homes in down markets, how to deal with contractors, and it describes various mortgages (including some very creative methods) for buying real estate, etc. Send $6.95 for a copy.

Making The Most Of Your Money, by Jane Bryant Quinn. Available at most bookstores.

National Center of Home Equity Conversion, Fact Sheet, Suite 300, 12120 E. College Dr., Marshall, MN 56258. Offers a free fact sheet on reverse mortgages. Send a SASE.

Resolution Trust Corporation, 1-800-348-1484. For information on RTC sales, call and ask for their Special Sales Event Calendar that lists current auction, sealed bid, and portfolio sales in your area—both residential and commercial.

Retirement Income on the House, by Ken Scholen ($24.95), available at most bookstores. Excellent book on reverse mortgages.

RECOMMENDED INVESTMENT ADVISORS AND NEWSLETTERS
(ALPHABETIZED BY EDITOR)

Larry Abraham, Editor, *Insider's Report,* P.O. Box 84903, Phoenix, AZ 85071; 1-800-528-0559. A newsletter on political, social and economic events, with an international flavor.

Aden Analysis, P.O. Box 523, Bethel, CT 06801; (203) 798-7967.

Charles Allmon, Editor, *Growth Stock Outlook,* P.O. Box 15381, Chevy Chase, MD 20825; (301) 654-5205. Charles Allmon specializes in small, "non-sexy" companies with a potential for growth.

Asia/Pacific Currency Report, International Business Information, Inc., 700 Walnut St., Cincinnati, OH 45202; (513) 421-5458.

Richard Band, Editor, *Profitable Investing,* Phillips Publishing, Inc., 7811 Montrose Road, Potomac, MD 20854; 1-800-777-5005.

Bank Credit Analyst, BCA Publications Ltd., 3463 Peel Street, Montreal, P.Q. H3A 1W7 Canada; (514) 398-0653.

Bank Stock Analyst, Charles Allmon, Editor, P.O. Box 15381, Chevy Chase, MD 20825; (301) 654-5205.

Bond Fund Survey, Survey Publications Co., P.O. Box 4180, Grand Central Station, New York, NY 10163; (212) 988-2498.

Harry Browne, Editor, *Harry Browne Special Report,* P.O. Box 5586, Austin, TX 78763. A particularly good newsletter on currencies, Swiss banking, and investing in gold and silver.

Capital International Perspective, Capital International S.A., 3 Place des Bergues, CH-1201 Geneva, Switzerland.

Capital Preservation Strategist, Globacor Consultants Ltd, Jean-Pierre Louvet, Editor, P.O. Box 1618, Gainesville, GA 30503; (404) 536-0309.

Robert C. Carlson, C.P.A., Editor, *Tax Avoidance Digest,* 824 East Baltimore Street, Baltimore, MD 21202; 1-800-223-1922, Ext. 418. Robert Carlson writes an excellent newsletter that can provide you hundreds of ways to save on your taxes, including "green flags" that will tell the IRS to let your return through without hassle.

Doug Casey, Editor, *Investing in Crisis,* 824 E. Baltimore Street, Baltimore, MD 21202; 1-800-223-1982. Doug has a very unique way of looking at the world. Well worth reading.

Chicago Economics, The Chicago Corporation, 208 South LaSalle Street, Chicago, IL 60604; (312) 855-6600.

Currency Confidential & Currency Management, International Business Communications, 56 Holborn Viaduct, Bath House, London, EC1A 2EX England.

Davis/Zweig Bond Fund Timer, P.O. Box 360, Bellmore, NY 11710; 1-800-633-2252. A good timing newsletter.

Adrian Day, Editor, *Investment Analyst,* 824 E. Baltimore Street, Baltimore, MD 21202; 1-800-223-1982. Adrian Day comes up with some very interesting special situations that are not big, overbought, mainstream favorites. He writes a very unique and useful letter.

John Dessauer, Editor, *Dessauer's Journal,* Limmat Publications, Inc., P.O. Box 1718, Orleans, MA 02653; (617) 255-1651. An excellent newsletter that reports on foreign currencies and all five major world stock markets.

Bert Dohmen, Editor, *Wellington's Tradeline,* Wellington Financial Corp., 6600 Kalanianaole Hwy., Suite 114C, Honolulu, HI 96825; 1-800-992-9989. Bert Dohmen not only gives advice on international markets, but also manages accounts in foreign currencies.

William E. Donoghue, Editor, *Donoghue's Moneyletter,* 290 Eliot Street, Box 91004, Ashland, MA 01721; 1-800-343-5413 (In MA (508) 429-5930). This is one of the top newsletters following and ranking mutual funds. William E. Donoghue was among the country's first financial experts to advocate and popularize the use of money market funds for the individual investor. He now offers a whole range of services, all of which are geared to mutual funds, money market funds and bank and insurance company safety.

Elliott Ware Currency & Commodity Forecast, James P. Chorek, Peter J.

DeSario and Robert S. Kelley, editors, P.O. Box 1618, Gainesville, GA 30503; 1-800-336-1618 or (404) 536-0309.

Ernst & Young Financial Planning Reporter, William Brennan, Editor, P.O. Box 33337, Washington, DC 20033.

Executive Wealth Advisory, National Institute of Business Management, 1328 Broadway, New York, NY 10001; 1-800-543-2054.

Doug Fabian, Editor, *Telephone Switch Newsletter,* P.O. Box 2538, Huntington Beach, CA 92647; 1-800-950-8765.

Finance Over 50, 661 Calmar Ave., Oakland, CA 94610; 1-800-528-0559.

Norman Fosback, Editor, *Mutual Fund Forecaster,* 3471 N. Federal Highway, Fort Lauderdale, FL 33306; 1-800-327-6720. Norman Fosback provides unique one-year profit projections and risk ratings for over 400 mutual funds.

David Fuller, Editor, *Fullermoney,* Chart Analysis Ltd., 7 Swallow Street, London, United Kingdom WCIE 7AS. Another excellent newsletter that reports on international markets.

G.E.O. Report (The), Larry Abraham, Editor, P.O. Box 84903, Phoenix, AZ 85071; 1-800-528-0559.

Global Investing, 824 E. Baltimore Street, Baltimore, MD 21202; 1-800-433-1528.

Global Market Strategist (The), Dan Ascani, Editor, Supercycle Research Inc., P.O. Box 5309, Gainesville, GA 30505; (404) 967-1332.

Government Bond & Money Market Letter, Newsletter Services, Inc., 1545 New York Ave. NE, Washington, DC 20003; (202) 529-5700.

Income & Safety, Institute for Econometric Research, 3471 N Federal Highway, Fort Lauderdale, FL 33306; 1-800-327-6720.

Insurance Forum, P.O. Box 245, Ellettsville, IN 47429.

Interest Rate Review, Martin Pring, Publisher, International Institute for Economic Research, P.O. Box 329, Washington Depot, CT 06794; (203) 868-7772.

International Advisor (The), P.O. Box 2289, Winter Park, FL 32790; 1-800-333-5697.

International Bond Letter, New Times Publishing, Ltd., 40 Bowling Green Lane, London EC1R ONE, England.

International Currency Report, International Business Information, 700 Walnut St., Cincinnati, OH 45202; (513) 421-5447.

International Fund Monitor, Research International, Inc., P.O. Box 5754, Washington, DC 20016; (202) 363-3097.

International Living, 824 E. Baltimore Street, Baltimore, MD 21202; 1-800-433-1528.

InvesTech Market Analyst, 2472 Birch Glen, Whitefish, MT 59937; 1-800-955-8500.

Investor's Hotline, Joe Bradley, Editor, 10616 Beaver Dam Rd., Hunt Valley, MD 21030; (301) 771-0064.

John Kamin, Editor, *Forecaster Moneyletter (The),* 19623 Ventura Blvd., Tarzana, CA 91356; (818) 345-4421.

Jean-Pierre Louvet, Editor, *Capital Preservation Strategist,* P.O. Box 1618, Gainesville, GA 30503; (404) 536-0309. Jean-Pierre Louvet writes an international investment newsletter that shares the European viewpoint of world economics and investments.

Lynch Municipal Bond Advisory, James F. Lynch, Editor, P.O. Box 1086, Lenox Hill Station, New York, NY 10021; (212) 249-9595.

Ian McAvity, Editor, *Deliberations,* P.O. Box 182, Adelaide Street Station, Toronto, Ontario M5C 2JI, Canada. Ian McAvity covers a lot of overseas markets, offering superb charts and insights in every issue.

James McKeever, Editor, *The McKeever Strategy Letter,* P.O. Box 4130, Medford, OR 97501; 1-800-237-8400. Jim McKeever covers gold, stocks, currencies, and bonds and has posted an enviable investment record.

Paul Merriman, Editor, *Merriman's Fund Exchange,* 1200 Westlake Avenue North, Seattle, WA 98109; 1-800-423-4893. Paul Merriman offers excellent market-timing and no-load mutual fund advice.

Merriman's Fund Exchange, 1200 Westlake Avenue North, Seattle, WA 98109; 1-800-423-4893.

Muni Bond Fund Report, Ralph Norton, Editor, Greystone Media Services., Inc., P.O. Box 2179, Huntington Beach, CA 92647; (617) 721-4511.

John Myers, Editor, *Myers Finance & Energy,* N. 7307 Division, Suite 204, Spokane, WA 99208; (509) 534-7132. John Myers writes a very good, internationally oriented market newsletter.

Mutual Fund Forecaster, 3471 N. Federal Highway, Fort Lauderdale, FL 33306; 1-800-327-6720.

No-Load Fund Investor, The, Sheldon Jacobs, Editor, P.O. Box 283, Hastings-on-Hudson, NY 10706; 1-800-252-2042.

No-Load Fund X, 235 Montgomery Street, Suite 662, San Francisco, CA 94104; (414) 986-7979.

Dr. Gary North, Editor, *Remnant Review,* P.O. Box 7999, Tyler, TX 75711; 1-800-527-8608. Dr. North writes and lectures on the problems of the Social Security system and many other issues.

Bob Prechter, Editor, *Elliott Wave Theorist,* P.O. Box 1618, Gainesville, GA 30503; (404) 536-0309. Elliott Wave International also publishes *Prechters Global Market Perspective,* which covers all major international markets.

Profitable Investing, Richard Band, Editor, 7811 Montrose Road, Potomac, MD 20854; 1-800-777-5505.

Remnant Review, Dr. Gary North, Editor, P.O. Box 7999, Tyler, TX 75711; 1-800-527-8608.

Retirement Letter (the), 7811 Montrose Road, Potomac, MD 20854; 1-800-722-9000.

Dan Rosenthal, Editor, *Silver & Gold Report,* P.O. Box 2923, West Palm Beach, FL 33402; (407) 684-8100. Dan Rosenthal is definitely an original thinker, and always invigorating reading.

Donald Rowe, Editor, *Wall Street Digest,* One Sarasota Tower, Sarasota, FL 34236; (813) 954-5500. One of the largest and most respect newsletters in the country. Donald Rowe writes a fearless and very original newsletter. He does a tremendous amount of research before he writes every letter, and once done, he is not afraid to state his position unequivocally, even if it is one that is not popular at the moment.

Howard Ruff, Editor, *The Ruff Times,* 4457 Willow Road, Pleasanton, CA 94566; 1-800-877-7833. Howard Ruff has a way of making very complicated issues very simple. If you want a newsletter that cuts through the Washington jargon and tells it like it is, you will enjoy his newsletter.

Richard Russell, Editor, *Dow Theory Letters,* P.O. Box 1759, La Jolla, CA 92038; (619) 454-0481. One of the oldest and best newsletters in the business. Richard Russell continues to give very thoughtful observations on the markets, both U.S. and overseas. He is reputed to have an unprecedented 90% renewal rate to his newsletter, which says something about the quality of his advice.

Safe Money Report, (formerly *Money & Markets*), Martin D. Weiss, Editor, Weiss Research, P.O. Box 2923, West Palm Beach, FL 33402; 1-800-289-9222.

Jay Schabacker, Editor, *Jay Schabacker's Mutual Fund Investing,* 7811 Montrose Road, Potomac, MD 20854; 1-800-777-5005. Another good source for investors interested in the latest performance of mutual funds.

Harry Schultz, Editor, *HSL,* P.O. Box 622, CH-1001 Lausanne, Switzerland. One of the oldest newsletters in the world, and certainly the oldest international letter. Harry Schultz packs a tremendous amount of information into his format, which includes his uniquely feisty political commentary, as well as information on all major world markets.

Sector Fund Newsletter, P.O. Box 1210, Escondido, CA 92025; (619) 748-0805.

Mark Skousen, Editor, *Forecasts & Strategies,* Phillips Publishing, 7811 Montrose Road, Potomac, MD 20854; 1-800-722-9000. Mark Skousen doesn't talk much about investing in foreign currencies, but he is good at routing out safe, high-yield funds and other unusual investment situations. He also provides a brief, but incisive, commentary on markets.

James Stack, Editor, InvesTech Market Analyst, 2472 Birch Glen, Whitefish, MT 59937-3349; 1-800-955-8500 or (406) 862-7777. A comprehensive letter on stocks and mutual funds. James Stack uses a unique blend of key technical and monetary indicators that have proven most effective in forecasting the outlook for stocks, inflation and gold.

Strategic Investments, Jim Davidson and Lord William Rees-Mogg, Editors, 824 E. Baltimore Street, Baltimore, MD 21202; 1-800-223-1982.

Swiss Economic Viewpoint, Overland Trust Bank, P.O. Box 5022, 8022 Zurich, Switzerland. (For a complimentary copy call or write to Overland Financial Services, Ltd., 1450-1176 W. Georgia St., P.O. Box 48326, Vancouver, B.C. V7X 1A1, Canada; 1-800-663-8942 or (604) 682-3626.

Taipan, 824 E. Baltimore Street, Baltimore, MD 21202; 1-800-433-1528.

Taurus, Taurus Corporation, P.O. Box 767, Winchester, VA 22601; (703) 667-4827.

Tax Avoidance Digest, Robert C. Carlson, C.P.A., Editor, 824 East Baltimore Street, Baltimore, MD 21202; 1-800-223-1982, Ext. 418.

Telephone Switch Newsletter, Doug Fabian, Editor, P.O. Box 2538, Huntington Beach, CA 92647; 1-800-950-8765.

Timing Device (The), 1020 E. English, Wichita, KS 67211; (316) 685-6034.

Tokyo Financial Letter—Nikkei Bonds & Money, Japan Bond Research Institute, 2-6-1, Nihonbashi-kayabacho, Chuo-ku, Tokyo 103, Japan (published in English).

United Mutual Fund Selector, United Business Service Company, 210 Newbury St., Boston, MA 02116; (617) 267-8855.

Martin D. Weiss, Editor, *Safe Money Report,* (formerly *Money & Markets*), Weiss Research, Inc., P.O. Box 2923, West Palm Beach, FL 33042;

1-800-289-9222. This is a unique publication that monitors the safety of financial institutions and provides you with ways of profiting from the instability.

Wellington's Tradeline, Wellington Financial Corp., 6600 Kalanianaole Hwy., Suite 114C, Honolulu, HI 96825; 1-800-922-9989.

World Market Perspective, Eric Jones, Editor, P.O. Box 2289, Winter Park, FL 32790; 1-800-333-5697.

Richard Young, Editor, *Young's International Gold Report*, Phillips Publishing, 7811 Montrose Road, Potomac, MD 20854; 1-800-722-9000. Richard Young is an excellent gold share analyst, who pours a lot of work into his unique trading strategies and offers some superb international analysis in his monthly newsletter.

MAGAZINES, NEWSPAPERS, OR REFERENCE PUBLICATIONS

Economist, The, P.O. Box 5044, Boulder, CO 80321-0400.

International Financial Statistics gives interest rates and monetary figures for all the countries of the world. Available in most libraries.

Rand McNally Bankers Directory provides a listing of international banks, addresses, phone numbers and officers. The directory is available in most libraries.

Resident Abroad, Marketing Department, Greystoke Place, Fetter Lane, London EC4A 1 ND, England. This is a monthly magazine covering all aspects of living abroad—offshore unit trusts (mutual funds), insurance programs (annuities), individually managed accounts, and items of privacy and lifestyle trends.

Wall Street Journal, The, For subscription information, call 1-800-841-8000.

USEFUL BOOKS AND SPECIAL REPORTS

The 100 Best Stocks to Own in the World, by Gene Walden. (Dearborn Financial Publishing, $24.95.)

Confessions of a Gold Bug, by James U. Blanchard III. (Jefferson Financial, 2400 Jefferson Hwy., Jefferson, LA 70121, $19.95).

Is Your Money Safe? by Dr. Warren G. Heller. (Available in bookstores or from VeriBanc, Inc., Box 461, Wakefield, MA 01880.)

Lies, Myths and Realities, by Mark Skousen. (Business One Irwin, $21.95.)

Your Complete Guide to Bank Safety, by Martin Weiss. (Weiss Research, Inc., P.O. Box 2923, West Palm Beach, FL 33402; 1-800-289-8100.)

Index

Fold this flap in <u>first</u>

BUSINESS REPLY MAIL
FIRST CLASS MAIL   PERMIT NO. 438   NEW ORLEANS, LA

POSTAGE WILL BE PAID BY ADDRESSEE

HIGH YIELD

JEFFERSON FINANCIAL

2400 JEFFERSON HIGHWAY, SIXTH FLOOR

JEFFERSON, LA 70121-9922

Fold this flap over last and seal